THE HISTORIC EMERGENCY 1972 - 2007

My Memoirs Continue

Gary J Jones CBE

To Adam

Best Wishes

Geoff

The History of Emergency Nursing 1972-2007
My Memoirs continue

Published by Gary J Jones CBE

www.facebook.com/gjjonescbe.books

First edition March 2021

© Gary J Jones CBE All rights reserved

No part of this publication may be reproduced, stored in a retrievable system, or transmitted in any form or by any means without the prior written permission of the publisher, nor be otherwise circulated in any form of binding or cover other than that in which it is published and without a similar condition being imposed on the subsequent purchaser

THE HISTORY OF EMERGENCY NURSING 1972 – 2007

My Memoirs Continue

Gary J Jones CBE

"From the labour of yesterday lives the spirit of tomorrow" Su Andi (Performance poet, writer and arts curator)

"To understand the present and anticipate the future one must know enough of the past"
    Lee Kuan Yew (former Prime Minister Singapore)

"The longer you can look back, the farther you can look forward" Winston Churchill

This book is the second in Gary's memoir series and marks 50 years since Gary started nursing as a student nurse in May 1971. It covers the development of emergency nursing 1972-2007, with thirty of those years being what Gary calls 'his time'. Written in the first person, throughout the book Gary's involvement is intertwined with the history of the specialty. The final chapter, provided by a current clinically based emergency nurse of 7 years, demonstrates how changes that were developed during this thirty-five year period are now common place within today's emergency care services.

Part One provides a general overview in chronological order.

Keywords include: History of hospitals; Nursing history; Royal College of Nursing; History of Casualty and Accident & Emergency (A&E) departments; RCN A&E Nursing Forum/Association; Emergency nursing conferences; Developing emergency nursing education; *Emergency Nurse* journal; Modernisation and reform of emergency services; RCN Emergency Care Association.

Part Two focusses on the in-depth account of specific subjects.

Keywords include: Patient attendance in A&E; Hospital bed capacity; Trolley waits; The four-hour target; A&E Challenging the Boundaries: Nursing Models for A&E; Components of Life model; Jones Dependency Tool; Accident prevention; Scope of Professional Practice; Competency development in emergency nursing care; Career pathways in emergency care; Faculty of Emergency Nursing (FEN); Value of initial patient assessment; Triage; Clinical developments in emergency care (including special populations and pre-hospital care).

CONTENT

About the Author	vii
Dedications/Acknowledgments	ix
Foreword	x
Timeline	xii
Introduction	xv

Part One

1. The Early Days	1
2. A&E Nursing – How it all began	9
3. A New Team	24
4. All Change Ahead	32
5. The Pre-Millennium Period	58
6. Into the Millennium	74
7. From Success to Disappointment	86

Part Two

8. Workload	94
9. Professional Development	128
10. The Faculty of Emergency Nursing	166
11. Nursing Assessment & Triage	182

12. Staffing & Skill Mix Including the Jones Dependency Tool	195
13. Clinical Development & Professional Care	209
14. Special Populations	240
15. Pre-Hospital Care	253
Reflection	260
From Picket line to Pandemic - Emergency Nursing in 2020	264
Index	277

References

References are found at the end of each chapter.

Reference to the *newsletter* refers to the RCN A&E Nursing Forum/Association, ECA Association newsletters. (1983 – Summer 2007) RCN Publication

Reference to *Emergency Nurse* refers to the RCN publication *Emergency Nurse* journal (1992 – 2007) RCN Publishing Company

ABOUT THE AUTHOR

Gary Jones CBE was born in Grays, Essex in 1953 and trained as a nurse in the local hospital at Orsett. He is a nurse with over 40 years' experience in emergency care, a Commander of the Order of the British Empire (CBE) for services to Emergency Nursing, Fellow of the Royal College of Nursing, the Florence Nightingale Foundation and Honorary Fellow Faculty of Emergency Nursing. Gary holds a range of nursing qualifications including the Diploma in Nursing, Ophthalmic Nursing Diploma and the City & Guilds 730 Further Education Teaching & Assessing Certificate.

Having established himself in full time Accident & Emergency (A&E) nursing in 1977, and having been awarded the Smith & Nephew Florence Nightingale Scholarship to Canada & the USA in 1980, Gary joined the Royal College of Nursing (RCN) A&E Nursing Forum in 1982. With many years' experience in both clinical and managerial positions Gary has been one of the key developers of emergency nursing within the UK. He has advised at national level on many aspects of emergency care including paramedic training, expert nursing practice and emergency care in the community. Gary is the author of two emergency care books, has edited and contributed to a third and written numerous chapters and articles for other emergency books and journals. The first book in his memoir series, *It's Not All Blood & Guts – My Amazing Life as an A&E Nurse* was published in 2019 and covers the challenges Gary faced in becoming a nurse and follows his cadet and student years as well as his career before and after specialising in A&E nursing. The bulk of the first memoir covers clinical and managerial events during Gary's time in

A&E and also his work with the Red Cross, culminating in being awarded the Voluntary Medical Services Medal, Badge of Honour and Life Membership.

From 1987-1995 Gary was Chair of the RCN A&E Nursing Association and from 1994-1997 the Honorary Consultant Nurse Advisor in Accident & Emergency Nursing to the Chief Nursing Officer at the Department of Health (England). Following his time as Chair of the RCN A&E Nursing Association Gary became an RCN Council member, Vice-Chair of RCN Council and following this term of office, he became the Convener of RCN Fellows.

Apart from his time at Moorfields Eye Hospital, Gary spent his clinical career at Orsett Hospital. Leaving the NHS in 1992, he provided consultancy, expert witness and teaching services and developed a very successful training and development business.

It's Not All Blood and Guts: My Amazing Life as an A&E Nurse is available from Amazon, EBay and Waterstones

DEDICATION

To all the A&E nurse pioneers who moved casualty nursing into the emergency nursing specialty we have today.

To all the A&E nurses who held executive committee, co-opted, local group and special interest group positions. Without the commitment of these nurses it would not have been possible for the specialty to advance in the way it has.

To the RCN nurse advisers who supported the executive committee and the association's members.

ACKNOWLEDGEMENTS

Professor Brian Dolan OBE FFNMRCSI, FRSA, RMN, RGN Director, Health Service 360.
Honorary Professor of Leadership in Healthcare, University of Salford.
Visiting Professor of Nursing, Oxford Institute of Nursing, Midwifery & Allied Health Research (OxINMAHR), Oxford
For reviewing the manuscript and providing the Foreword.

Joanna Sloan, RN, BSc Nursing Sciences (Adult Nursing), NMP, A.N.P. Clinical Sister, Emergency Department, Royal Victoria Hospital, Belfast. For providing the final chapter.

Thank you to
Mary Holmes
Sally McCornack JP RN SEN NMP OHD
Janet Snell Freelance journalist
For reviewing the manuscript and providing valuable feedback.

FOREWORD

'Education', as philosopher and political theorist Michael Oakeshott put it, 'is a conversation between generations' and this book, by renowned and hugely respected emergency nurse leader, Gary Jones CBE, is most certainly both an education and a conversation.

This, the second book of Gary's memoirs, covers the years from the founding of emergency care as a nursing specialty in 1972 to 2007, as well as a series of clinical and professional changes that accord during as he puts it 'his time'. With a ringside seat to the development of the specialty and being both the cheerleader and driver of so many of these changes, he is, quite literally, the only person who could have written this book.

The history of emergency nursing is an extraordinary story and so much of what's taken for granted now, whether it's triage and suturing, to the development of nurse practitioners and the Faculty of Emergency Nursing had to start somewhere. Without the shrewd advocacy, willingness to work with those who were initial resisters and the pragmatism of Gary and so many of his contemporaries, emergency nursing would not be where it is today.

It's also important to understand that Gary has been a mentor, muse, guide and wise counsel to so many of us in emergency care. For his successors as Chair of the Emergency Care Association, such as Prof Robert Crouch OBE and Lynda Holt, to Trauma Nursing Core Course (TNCC) instructors like Gabby Lomas and Jill Windle, to nursing newsletter and journal Editors like Kathie Butcher, Judith Morgan and myself, as well as countless others, Gary's diplomacy, experience and common-sense advice has always been sought and valued. While rightly recognised for his contributions to emergency nursing, culminating in the appointment of CBE by HM The Queen in 2003, it is not for nothing that Gary is sometimes called 'The Godfather of Emergency Nursing' with both respect and great affection!

Part One presents the development of emergency nursing from its infancy to professional adulthood, from new ways of working to standard practices. While the last chapter of Part One ends on a note of disappointment with several members of the Emergency Care Association resigning over our concerns about governance, imposed decisions and a breakdown of relations with the wider RCN – full disclosure, I was Vice-Chair at the time – the ECA continues today and is well represented by great, current leaders – another part of Gary's legacy.

Part Two brings together the history of all the key professional issues of the decades, from initial assessment and triage, to the Faculty of Emergency Nursing and dependency models (both of which he was instrumental in developing) to skill mix and pre-hospital care. Looking back, the pace of change has been breath-taking, and patients and staff alike are safer and better for it.

This is a wonderfully written book which future historians of our profession will be immensely grateful to pore over. As someone whose own journey in emergency nursing began in 1988, Gary Jones helped me and so many others become better clinicians, thinkers and leaders.

It's an honour and privilege to write this Foreword and I hope you love the book as much as I have.

Brian Dolan OBE, FFNMRCSI, FRSA, RMN, RGN.

TIMELINE

1800s ------ Injured/ill patients seen in an outpatient setting

1900s ------ Emergence of GPs and Casualty departments

1960s ------ A&E nurses form a National A&E Nurses Group

1962 ------ The Platt Report – Casualty to A&E

1967 ------ Casualty Surgeons Association (CSA) established

1971 ------ The Bruce Report. A&E Consultants established

1972 ------ The National A&E Nurses Group becomes The RCN A&E Nursing Group

1978 ------ The RCN A&E Nursing Group becomes The RCN A&E Nursing Forum
------ Association of Emergency Medical Technicians established. Start of Paramedic development

1979 ------ First RCN A&E Nursing Forum Annual Conference

1981 ------ Resuscitation Council UK established

1982 ------ RCN A&E/3M Health Care Award established
------ First RCN A&E Nursing Forum/CSA Conference

Timeline

1983 ------First National RCN A&E Nursing Forum Newsletter
 ------Triage starts to develop

1985 ------First International Emergency Nursing Conference

1986 ------First independently run A&E Nursing Conference
 ------Emergency Nurse Practitioners emerge

1989 ------First Pan Pacific Emergency Nurses Conference

1990 ------The RCN A&E Nursing Forum becomes The RCN A&E Nursing Association
 ------Casualty Surgeons Association becomes The British Association for A&E Medicine
 ------The Trauma Nursing Core Course to the UK

1992 ------*Emergency Nurse* Journal launched
 ------RCN A&E Nursing Association Special Interest Groups developed
 ------*The Patient's Charter* published

1993 ------*Emergency Nurse* journal becomes a stand-alone journal
 ------*Accident & Emergency Nursing* journal launched

1994 ------*Challenging the Boundaries* document published

1998 ------Consultant Nurse established
------Pilot studies and setting up of NHS Direct
------Manchester Triage becoming established

2000 ------International Declaration of Co-operation and Friendship signed
------International Collaboration of National Emergency Nursing Organisations launched
------Debate starts regarding changing A&E to ED

2003 ------The Faculty of Emergency Nursing (FEN) launched
------The RCN A&E Nursing Association becomes The RCN Emergency Care Association (ECA)
------Nurse Prescribing for ENPs

2004 ------The British Association for A&E Medicine becomes The British Association for Emergency Medicine (BAEM)

2006 ------The Faculty of Emergency Nursing becomes independent of the RCN
------Joint ECA/FEN Conference

2007 ------Major problems occur between the RCN & ECA
------The early development period comes to an end and a new period begins.

INTRODUCTION

'Outpatients', 'Casualty', 'Accident and Emergency', 'Emergency Department', the name may change but the service continues the same – to provide for those in need of emergency care. Throughout the history of this specialty, despite many attempts, the true definition of 'emergency' has never been achieved. Irrespective of the injury or illness the patient will come for treatment. Multiple life threatening injuries or a sprained ankle, cardiac arrest or a cough and cold, the service is always ready to respond.

From the early days when patients queued outside the Outpatients doors and for just one hour they would be admitted for treatment, to the 24 hour emergency service that is now the norm, the service has developed and changed to meet the continuous demand from an ever growing population with complex needs. Throughout this history emergency nursing has also changed and the 35 year period 1972 – 2007 laid the foundations for the emergency service we have today. It was a time when nurses as well as medical and ambulance staff shifted the boundaries of emergency care. As you read through the book you will come across so many initiatives that today seem as though they have always been there. Imagine emergency care without national resuscitation guidelines, trauma care without trauma training, patient assessment without triage, pre-hospital care without paramedics, minor injury care without nurse practitioners. Imagine nurses not able to cannulate and send bloods for testing, a department without computers, children without specialist emergency care areas within a general A&E department, the list goes on yet all of these and more were developed during that period.

As you read you will discover how time and time again similar or the same themes appear. You will read how ideas that A&E nurses proposed in the early days of this specialty were not always implemented, yet years later those same ideas come to fruition. I have often had colleagues say 'it was ahead of its time.' I am not sure that is helpful when one knows that had some new idea been taken on board at the time improved patient care could have been achieved years earlier.

PART ONE

CHAPTER 1

THE EARLY YEARS

In England, until the time of the dissolution of the monasteries in the middle ages, medicine, nursing and welfare were traditionally in the hands of the church. In fact, in ancient cultures, religion and medicine were linked with temples dedicated to the healer-gods whose function was medical advice, prognosis, and healing.

Although during the reformation monasteries were closed, some buildings such as St Bartholomew's Hospital in London survived and continued to provide hospital care (1546). Between this and the 18th century there was little urge to build hospitals because no more effective care could be given in a hospital than could be given at home by relatives and friends.

Nurses and Nursing (St Bartholomew's Hospital information leaflet 2015) indicates that under the terms of the charter granted to the hospital by Henry VIII in 1546 there was to be one matron and twelve women (sisters) working under the matron to make beds and wash and attend upon the patients. Helpers for the sisters are first mentioned in 1647 and from the 1650s onwards the helpers were often referred to by using the title nurse.

During the 18th century there was a whole range of sometimes conflicting circumstances that led to the establishment of hospitals. With the coming of the industrial revolution, by 1760 great surges of people were entering the industrial towns and crowding and poor housing was leading to injury and disease. There had been an increase in accidents, especially to young people, and amputation of limbs without anaesthetic was common - though great use of opium and wine did help reduce the pain. The first anaesthetic was administered in 1846 for amputation of a leg.

Although capitalism was causing the poor to be disregarded, at the same time a new spirit of philanthropy was developing which led to the initiative for charity hospitals; however these required funding so for the majority of the poor it was the workhouse rather than a charity hospital. Workhouses designed to house the poor and destitute dated back to the Poor Law Act of 1388 and became more popular during the 1600-1800s.

As medicine developed and demand increased from people who could afford to pay for care, by the 19th century many charity hospitals had become voluntary hospitals, receiving funding from public subscriptions and from employers for their employees. By the end of the 19th century, a whole range of institutions had been established including workhouses, charity hospitals, poor law infirmaries, voluntary hospitals, hospitals for fever and isolation and hospitals for the mentally sick.

In my own borough of Thurrock in Essex, Orsett Hospital originated from a workhouse built in 1801 though the history of the hospital site can be traced back to 1669. In 1838, the workhouse was enlarged to accommodate 200 paupers. By 1874, an infirmary was established behind the existing workhouse. Further developments continued throughout the late 1800s and by 1907, the infirmary and workhouse were catering for some 290 people. During the First World War, some of the buildings were converted into a military hospital staffed mainly by Red Cross workers and by 1917, no further 'tramps' (as paupers were also known) were housed; only ill and injured people were admitted to the infirmary and those who qualified were admitted to the workhouse. Throughout the 1920s and 1930s, under the governance of the Board of Guardians, the hospital continued to grow and in 1948 became a hospital within the newly established National Health Service. The South East Essex Hospital Management Committee (that became the South Essex Hospital Management Committee in 1966) began the task of converting the workhouse and infirmary into a modern hospital. Major construction of the new hospital took place in the 1960s with the first phase including A&E opening in 1967 and the main ward block opening in 1968. A further phase which included the last part of the original hospital being demolished occurred during the 1970s resulting in a 500 bed modern hospital.

Nurses

Nurses in the 18th and 19th century resembled domestic workers and were few in number; care was the domain of the doctors. Sheila Hunt (Senior Nurse, A&E, St James's Hospital, Leeds) described nurses of the early 19th century in the September 1985 *A&E newsletter* as being regarded as inferior, disagreeable and a repellent form of domestic service. Charles Dickens's book *Martin Chuzzlewitt* featured the dissolute, sloppy and frequently drunk *Sarah Gamp* who epitomised what most people thought of nurses at the time, though I am sure many, if not most were both caring and 'professional'.

With the emergence of professional nurse training through the work of Florence Nightingale, nursing moved into the profession we have today. Florence Nightingale was born in

1820 and mainly through her work during the Crimean War in 1854/55 at Scutari she became a national heroine. This prominence enabled her to develop a range of health related services such as hygiene, diet, design of hospital wards and nursing. Her first nursing school was established at St Thomas' Hospital London in 1860 and from that emerged many of the early matrons. Further information from the St Bartholomew's leaflet indicates that the School of Nursing at St Bartholomew's was established in 1877 but most training such as application of a bandage or taking a temperature with a thermometer, which was then not considered a suitable routine task for a nurse, was provided by medical staff.

Recognition of the need for a nurse's college and the possibility of registration led to the establishment of the College of Nursing and despite varying views, registration was achieved during the early part of the 1900s.

The College of Nursing was established in 1916 and received the Royal Charter (becoming the Royal College of Nursing) in 1928. As the College of Nursing it was founded on the three functions, which today represent professional, educational, and trade union activities. In fact, because the College was established before the Nurses' Registration Act of 1919, education was a core activity. The Student Nurses' Association was formed in 1926 and male nurses were eventually admitted to the College in 1960 (*A History of the RCN 1916-1990*). The Royal College of Nursing (RCN) is now both a professional body, carrying out work on nursing standards, education and practice, and a trade union. The RCN has five objectives: to promote the science and art of nursing and education and training in the profession of nursing; to promote the advancement of nursing as a profession in all or any of its branches; to promote the professional standing and interests of members; to assist members who by reason of adversity, ill-health or otherwise are in need of assistance of any nature; and to promote through the medium of international agencies and otherwise the foregoing purposes in other countries as well as in the United Kingdom. The RCN celebrated its centenary in 2016.

The Nurses' Registration Act (1919) led to the establishment of the General Nursing Councils (GNCs) of England & Wales, Scotland and Ireland. These were responsible for the standard of training and registration of nurses. In 1983, the GNCs amalgamated to become the United Kingdom Central Council (UKCC) and in 2002 the Nursing and Midwifery Council (NMC) whose function remains the protection of the public through maintaining standards for training and registration of nurses.

Casualty and Accident & Emergency

Within the voluntary hospitals, the outpatients department provided care for casual attenders, often free of charge although the service was nothing like the 24-hour emergency care of today. A report in *The Lancet* 7th May 1932 and published in the *A&E newsletter* (November 1988) describes the routine of the department at St Bartholomew's Hospital London in 1898. '*The patients began to assemble on the steps in Smithfield about 8.30am, but whatever the weather there was no shelter and the doors were kept locked until the last stroke of nine. As one person at a time entered, they were asked what he or she complained of. If attending for the first time they were directed to either a surgeon or physician. Patients returning were directed to their house surgeon or physician. People were allowed to enter until the clock struck ten then the outer doors were closed.*'

Although the word triage was not mentioned in the report, it does clearly state that, *'the doctor made a rapid diagnosis and sorted patients into trivial, teaching and serious. Patients with trivial complaints were handed to the house surgeon who allotted them amongst his dressers; cases useful for teaching were sent to the outpatient room to await the assistant surgeon of the day, and those seriously ill were taken straight to a ward.'* On the medical side, an interesting approach to care was by the resident apothecary who announced to the packed hall *"all those with a cough stand up"* and to them he gave a ticket to collect a bottle of medicine from the dispensary. A similar approach was taken with bellyache.

Records of 1823-1824 from Leeds General Infirmary (a voluntary hospital) and summarised in the September 1985 *A&E newsletter* recorded trauma care of the day. *'A 15 year old male admitted after having his arm twisted in machinery. The Brachial artery gave way and a deluge of blood issued and a pressure bandage and tourniquet applied. He was much reduced by the haemorrhage and wine and brandy gruel were administered to keep up the vital powers.'*

With the emergence of the General Practitioner (GP) in the 19th century (themselves emerging from the surgeon-apothecaries), private care was provided for a fee and the system of everyone being able to go to the outpatients free of charge was felt to be unfair competition. This led to an agreement that a patient should only be seen in the hospital if referred by a GP; however, this could be bypassed in an emergency. The patient in an emergency would be seen as a casual attender in the newly established casualty room. Gradually these rooms developed to become departments that grew in size and activity. From 1948 the casualty department became part of the NHS and although the theory was to encourage people to use their GP more and only attend casualty with injuries or life threatening illness in an emergency, the reality was very different. People continued to use the casualty department for primary care as well as for injuries and illness as there was never an agreement as to the term emergency (a challenge that still exists today).

Little changed until the implementation of recommendations by the Standing Medical Advisory Committee 1962 (The Platt Report). The Platt Report recommended the change of title from 'Casualty' to 'Accident & Emergency' in a deliberate attempt to discourage casual attendees and recommended that the casualty department should change in function. Primary care to casual attendees, it suggested, should be secondary to the provision of a 24-hour A&E service. The major responsibility was to provide care for serious accident and medical and surgical emergencies. The report further recommended that this new service should be appropriately staffed and equipped and a named consultant identified. Although the report was published in 1962, its influence to change the way departments were staffed and functioned was to take much longer. It was even longer for specialist A&E consultants to emerge, as under the Platt Report the designated consultant was to be an orthopaedic consultant (mainly because the medical profession saw casualty as an offshoot of orthopaedics) often managed at arm's length. Following numerous committees and sub-committees of all the Royal Colleges and other interested parties eventually the idea of A&E consultants was supported by the Council of the Royal College of Surgeons of England and the appointment of 32 consultants was given the go-ahead at the end of 1971. This is often called the Bruce Report (Guly 2005).

References

Guly H: (2005) *A History of Accident and Emergency Medicine 1948 – 2004* Palgrave Macmillan.

Nurses and Nursing: (2015) St Bartholomew's Hospital information leaflet. Barts Health NHS Trust

Royal College of Nursing: (2009) *A History of the Royal College of Nursing 1916-90.* Manchester University Press

Standing Medical Advisory Committee: (1962) *Accident & Emergency Services.* London: HMSO (The Platt Report)

CHAPTER 2

A&E NURSING - HOW IT ALL BEGAN 1972-1985

It is difficult to identify when the specialty came about because nurses have always worked in casualty and A&E. In the 1960s however, nurses working in A&E began to identify the need for accident and emergency nursing to be recognised as a specialty. The challenges that faced the early pioneers of A&E nursing were many, including departments being medically dominated and still being run by orthopaedic surgeons. It was not helped by the number of circulars and guidelines that came from the Department of Health and Social Security (DHSS). As far back as 1968 a DHSS circular, HM (68) 82, stated 'the responsibility of sorting patients who present themselves at a hospital into those who need care and those who do not, cannot properly be carried out by other than a registered medical practitioner. It should not be placed on the nursing service.'

A small number of A&E nurses, no more than around 60, came together to create first a national group and then through the Royal College of Nursing (RCN) a formalised group that was established within the College in 1972. The main supporter for this group was Margaret Lee, the nurse advisor at the RCN. This was a great step forward for A&E nurses especially as the specialty was so new. Over the years, the name has changed from RCN A&E Nursing Group to the RCN A&E Nursing Forum, RCN A&E Nursing Association and currently the RCN Emergency Care Association (ECA). These changes in title demonstrate the changing nature of emergency care and the role nurses play in the specialty.

With the founding of the RCN A&E Nursing Group, accident and emergency nurses were able to explore many national issues both internally within A&E departments as well as externally through work with other organisations. By organising the annual conference and establishing local groups under the main national group it was possible to start the process of changing clinical practice across the four countries of the UK. It was also possible to tap into initiatives that individual nurses had developed either from their own practice or from contacts in other countries of the world.

The first Chair of the RCN A&E Nursing Group was Betty Hoy. Betty was nurse manager of the A&E department at the Brook Hospital, Greenwich, London and chaired the group from 1972-1974. During those early years meetings were held throughout England and local groups were established. As there were no nationally recognised A&E courses (some hospitals did offer an A&E certificated course) one of the main functions of the group was the provision of clinical updating and education. In fact, the first major task of this group was to develop a national A&E course under the auspices of the Joint Board of Clinical Nursing Studies. This was successful (course 199 established by 1975) and was the forerunner of today's emergency nursing courses. Established in 1970, the Joint Board of Clinical Nursing Studies (JBCNS) aimed to co-ordinate the post registration training of nurses working in specialised departments of the hospital service. This function is now provided by universities and colleges under the direction of the NMC.

Susan Moore chaired the RCN A&E Nursing Group from 1974-1976 followed by Kate O'Hanlon MBE (1976-May 1983). Kate was the Senior Sister of the A&E department in the Royal Victoria Hospital, Belfast, Northern Ireland and was appointed a Member of the Order of the British Empire (MBE) in 1973 for her nursing leadership and contribution to patient care during the troubles in Northern Ireland. Kate was one of the first emergency nurses to be honoured by the Queen for services to emergency nursing.

The RCN A&E Nursing Group became a forum within the newly established RCN Association of Nursing Practice (ANP) in 1978. At that time the RCN had both a local and regional branch structure and for professional/clinical activities, there were a number of societies. Societies represented well established specialties while the newly established ANP brought together a number of new forums (including A&E). Although each forum had its own committee, these fed into the ANP committee reflecting those of the societies.

During Kate's period as Chair, the forum continually ran meetings that provided clinical updating to A&E nurses and all the activists continued to push forward A&E nursing as a specialty. The first RCN A&E Nursing Forum Conference was held in 1979 at the University of East Anglia. Topics at that first meeting included violence in A&E departments, the extending role of the accident and emergency nurse and seat belt legislation, which the forum supported. In 1980, work continued for seat belt legislation and this was successful.

The Rutherford study (October 1984 and reported in the *A&E newsletter* January 1985) showed that since the wearing of seatbelts became compulsory in 1983, there had been reduced numbers of deaths and serious injuries with a 64% drop in facial injuries, 45% drop in concussion and other brain injuries, 46% drop in skull fractures and a 71% drop in chest injuries. These figures obtained from four hospitals in Northern Ireland and eleven hospitals in the rest of the UK demonstrate how social change can have a positive effect on workload as well as resulting in reduced injury to the individual.

The second annual conference in 1980 debated a range of issues from closure of A&E departments to collecting prescription charges out of pharmacy hours. There was joint working with the Casualty Surgeons Association (now the Royal College of Emergency Medicine) and the first joint Casualty Surgeons and RCN A&E Nursing Forum Conference held in Dublin in 1982.

1982 was the year that the RCN A&E/3M Health Care Award was established. The award, sponsored each year until 2000 enabled A&E nurses to travel and research A&E practices outside of their own departments. Many recipients of the award published their work and contributed to the development of accident and emergency nursing. I myself was a successful recipient in 1985 and was able to research waiting times and the potential for reducing them by direct nursing intervention. It also meant I could review current extended and advanced life support procedures practised by nurses in A&E, current nurse education within A&E and the requirements for training to enable the nurse to contribute to an improvement in the service.

In January 1983, the first national *A&E newsletter* was published. Published is probably an overstatement, as it comprised three double-sided A4 photocopied sheets of paper stapled together. The editor was Margaret King (Treasurer of the forum), and she indicated that the newsletter was the vehicle to distribute news across the forum (social media, mobile phones and e-mail were not available in 1983).

In that first edition it was reported that seven local groups had been established under the umbrella of the forum - Central Southern, South East Thames, North West Thames, South West, Wessex, North West and Northern Ireland. The structure of the groups was flexible and decisions taken locally. The local group Chair or Secretary could submit items to the national honorary officers for consideration. The *A&E newsletter* indicated several groups had held evening meetings and some had held study days. Local groups were self-financing and most received generous support from manufactures and local representatives.

Margaret Lee the RCN professional officer sent best wishes and wrote that before the courses run by the Joint Board of Clinical Nursing Studies (JBCNS), the forums' main function was running meetings, which provided clinical updating to A&E nurses. She also observed the more active role the forum was taking in the politics of A&E.

A major aim of the *A&E newsletter* was to provide a vehicle for news and views. The first edition included a request for members to send in any experience of ambulance personnel training in the A&E departments. It also requested information on nurses undertaking clerical duties. An update on work by the joint medical/nursing group on staffing levels and information regarding a project on computerised A&E records was reported.

The annual conference in May 1983 was held at the University of York. This was my first attendance at a national conference and the Wednesday afternoon was a free period. I recall sitting in my small university room, the rain lashing down outside, questioning why I was there? Fortunately, this feeling was soon dispelled the next day as many of the clinical papers were of great interest, and when things became very heated over the election procedure I realised how committed those who attended were. The residential block, restaurant and conference venue were all separate buildings and this meant walking from one to the other. Had it been nice May weather it would have been fine but throughout those three days it poured with rain and was very cold. Following that meeting it was decided hotels were to become the venues for the future.

Jill Milnthorpe chaired the forum from May 1983 – September 1985. Jill was nurse manager in the A&E department Milton Keynes. Work continued to develop the forum and the specialty with much work being undertaken to improve the education and development of A&E nurses. Local groups were growing with 11 established by the end of 1983. Topics discussed at conference and study days included solvent abuse, ambulance paramedic training, staffing levels, the role of nursing auxiliaries and clerical duties undertaken by nurses. As a Forum within the ANP officers attended the RCN Representative Body (RRB) meeting (now RCN Congress). Due to the concern regarding solvent abuse in the young the Forum submitted an item for the 1984 agenda. It was a discussion item highlighting the problem of solvent abuse and promoting preventative policies, especially amongst children and young adults. This, following on from the support for seatbelt legislation demonstrated how the forum members supported accident prevention and health promotion.

During the 1983 National Conference the probability of an international A&E conference, sponsored by *Nursing Mirror* (a well-known nursing journal at that time) was discussed and agreed by delegates. It would be held in September 1985. A request was made for members who had contacts in other countries to make themselves known. As I had recently studied in Canada and the USA I put myself forward. With the honorary officers (Jill Milnthorpe, Kate O'Hanlon, Fiona Gordon and Margaret Berry) plus other members Bob Wright (Leeds), Elizabeth Mclkerney (Northern Ireland), and Peter Blythin (Stoke on Trent) we formed the planning group. The first meeting was held on 12th May 1983.

       *   *   *   *

Following a very positive response from members to the first *A&E newsletter*, the second edition was published in June1983. Ethel Buckles had become the Editor. It comprised four photocopied double-sided sheets of paper. The newsletter reported there were 465 registered forum members and a request was made for information on – paramedics, computers, telemetry, triage, the extended role of the nurse, altering role of the A&E nurse, education of the public in resuscitation and views on A&E staff dispensing the morning after pill. It was also reported that three further local groups had been established, Home Counties (North), Inner London and Scotland. Ethel pointed out in her editorial that the development of emergency medicine throughout the 1970s had resulted in an explosion of scientific and technological advances and therefore there was an increasing need for nurses to meet together, exchange ideas and information. The growth of the local groups was a valuable aid to improving communication and the newsletter was another link in what was happening nationally.

The second edition also reported that the joint medical/nursing journal, *The British Journal of Accident & Emergency Medicine,* had engaged Margaret King as the nursing editor and with a journal committee it was hoped to encourage nurses to submit articles, case reviews and letters. Further information and encouragement to publish was reported in the third *A&E newsletter.*

During 1983/4, the third, fourth and fifth editions of the *A&E newsletter* continued along similar lines including: the ongoing debate of GP patients attending A&E, difficulties with bed provision and work on health and safety issues. Information on clinical advancements, sharing news items from drug addiction to super-glue remover and the establishment of two more local groups in Yorkshire and Liverpool were also reported. These editions also started the trend that continued throughout all further *A&E newsletters*, that of advertising and reporting on successful locally run study days and conferences.

The government's concern regarding drugs including heroin, aerosol abuse and glue-sniffing were all highlighted in the fourth edition of the *A&E newsletter* (January 1984) and it included the new measures being introduced to combat glue sniffing through restricted sale of solvents to young people. Reports of further action to combat solvent abuse were reported in the May 1984 *A&E newsletter* including a regional co-ordinated approach by professionals working in the NHS and the formation of a nurses special interest group for drug, alcohol and solvent abuse within the RCN. Clearly the Forum's action at RRB was showing results.

During the 1984 A&E annual conference held in Edinburgh, a presentation from Yvonne McEwen, a nurse disaster specialist from Scotland, rallied all delegates to become more autonomous, to stop being the handmaidens of doctors and to prove that A&E nurses could provide excellent care to the patient. Following this speech, a number of A&E nurses (including me) gathered in the bar and started to discuss how right Yvonne was. Several of us decided to take on her challenge. Elections for the RCN A&E Nursing Forum honorary officers were to take place in 1985 so Peter Blythin (Stoke on Trent), Ethel Buckles (Preston), Bob Wright (Leeds), Fiona Gordon (London) and I decided to stand.

The first edition of the new style *A&E newsletter* was published in January 1985. No longer printed on stapled RCN Association of Nursing Practice A4 paper, it became a published newsletter under the RCN A&E Nursing Forum's heading. It included a report on a very successful three day conference in Wessex during October 1984 including an extract from the opening address given by Dora Frost MBE SRN, RCN Chaplin & activist. In the address Miss Frost commented on the issue of patients who attend A&E who should be at the GP as well as her concern regarding lengthy waiting times. She indicated that the health service was being starved of resources, being subjected to needless upheaval and poor pay for staff. Miss Frost voiced her concern over the recently established Griffiths Inquiry into reorganisation of the NHS (The Griffiths Inquiry led to general management being introduced into the NHS during 1985/86). The back page contained an excellent description of a mobile accident call out by Aileen Parsons, one of the staff nurses who worked with me at Orsett Hospital.

Peter Blythin, a member of the editorial board, wrote that the *A&E newsletter* in the new style would allow it to incorporate learned articles and academic comment as well as news, views and chat. He indicated that the publication gave the opportunity to establish the newsletter as the definitive British publication for the specialty. That was certainly the case and articles on clinical issues such as tetanus, local anaesthetic, bite wounds, use of glue in wound closure (then quite a new concept) and hepatitis B were just some of the many excellent articles published in those early years, including in the April 1987 edition a two page spread on emergency childbirth in A&E.

The editorial from the September 1984 *Paramedic UK* written by Yvonne McEwen was reproduced in the *A&E newsletter*. The editorial highlighted the development of ambulance personnel in immediate aid and opened the debate on who does what in emergency care and territorial and professional jealousy. It highlighted that many doctors did not want nurses to advance and many nurses did not want ambulance personnel to advance. Yvonne quite rightly emphasised that we were all in the position of saving life and limb and that required total team commitment. There was no room in this field of medicine, she wrote, for people doing their own thing.

Launched as *Paramedic UK* in 1983/4 the journal of the Association of Emergency Medical Technicians (AEMT) became *Emergency Care* in 1987. Articles covered a whole range of subjects that were relevant to the developing role of the Paramedic. These included clinical articles as well as articles on disaster planning, equipment and guidelines and the AEMT national training programme and examinations.

The approach to working together was also reflected in a new publication *Care of the Critically Ill*. Published by Critical Care Publications Limited in 1984/5, this journal included a range of important topics across the whole field of critical care including disaster care, trauma care and the challenge of the serious road traffic accident.

The second edition of the new look *A&E newsletter* (May 1985) contained a number of members' letters offering views on a whole range of issues. This was the start of a regular letters page. With the regular diary dates column the newsletter was now well established as the key communication tool between the honorary officers of the forum and the members. The editor requested further information on some of the current issues regarding changing roles within A&E nursing, the impact on A&E following the introduction of general management and the demise of the chief nursing officer at local level. There was also a request to provide updated information on 'trolley waits' due to hospital beds being full.

Having become a member of the editorial board in January 1985, one of my early guest editorials in this second edition was on the published guidelines from the RCN and Department of Health on the nursing care to patients suffering from acquired immunodeficiency syndrome (AIDS). It was a condition new to the UK and there was much concern about the care of such patients and the risks to health care staff. In the editorial I pointed out that the guidelines helped once the diagnosis was confirmed but in A&E we had to take precautions on the assumption the person was suffering from AIDS (chapter 13).

*   *   *   *

By 1985 the international conference planning group had identified a number of key subjects, speakers had been invited and the programme was taking shape. One request the planning committee made was to invite the Queen Mother to open the conference, however hopes were dashed when the RCN General Secretary's PA refused to allow the invite, pointing out we were only a forum! A special bumper edition of the *A&E newsletter* was published to coincide with the conference. Funded by the medical company Smith & Nephew, this began a long association with the forum (until 2000) as sponsors of the newsletter.

The special bumper edition of the *A&E newsletter* (International Conference September 1985) included information on emergency nursing in the USA, the history of the RCN A&E Nursing Forum by Ethel Buckles and the development of A&E over the last 200 years by Sheila Hunt (St James Hospital, Leeds). Bob Wright (Leeds) wrote an article on psychiatric emergencies and Jill Milnthorpe (Milton Keynes) wrote an article on commissioning an A&E department. Kate O'Hanlon MBE (Belfast) wrote the first part of a three part article on the continuing civil disorder in Northern Ireland. A competition was launched, the prize being a Land/Range Rover river road and jungle track adventure.

Also reported was the first meeting of the Essex local group held in March 1985. It attracted 29 nurses from the hospitals in the County. The nurses present elected me Chair of the group, a position I held until 1995. Study evenings were held every two months and an annual study day held at Orsett Hospital. Successful study days had been held jointly between the RCN Basildon & Thurrock Branch and the Essex Branch of the Association of Emergency Medical

Technicians (AEMT) since 1983. For a local study day the response was incredible, papers were mainly clinical with speakers coming from across the UK and nurses attending from far and wide. In 1986 we had a first-hand account of the Grand Hotel Bomb, Brighton (the Conservative Party bomb) by Sister Valerie Relton and in 1988 the Northern Ireland troubles by Kate O'Hanlon MBE, Senior Sister, The Royal Victoria Hospital, Belfast.

Following the publication of the *Paramedic UK* editorial in September 1984 (reproduced in the January 1985 *A&E newsletter*), the letters page of the September 1985 *A&E newsletter* included one from Eileen Jones (no relation) from Middlesex pointing out the disparity between the way ambulance paramedics were moving forward with clinical skills while the nurses role was being reduced. This linked nicely into the report in the same newsletter of the national study day that had been held at the RCN HQ in April 1985. The study day had focussed on the anomalies that existed since the introduction of the extended role of the nurse guidelines primarily in the areas of clinical practice and the need for national standards for emergency nursing practice across the UK (chapter 9).

On Monday 23rd September 1985 at 9.30am Cate Campbell, Editor of *Nursing Mirror* welcomed delegates to the international conference. The President and General Secretary of the RCN and the President of the Emergency Department Nurses Association of the USA followed her with their opening remarks. Sheila Quinn President of the RCN said that she was proud of the specialist nurses gathered together under the umbrella of the RCN. She noted that A&E nurses in the UK were amongst the first of the specialist nurses to become organised and were joined together as a group before the A&E doctors started their Association. The President sent greetings to emergency nurses worldwide; nurses whom she felt were at the heart of the hospital services. The five days, including a product exhibition, covered every aspect of emergency nursing including main hall presentations, workshops and visits for the international guests to London A&E departments. Subjects ranged from crisis intervention, disasters, trauma, paediatrics and violence. Over 600 delegates attended from 28 countries. *Nursing Mirror* reported over the following three weeks on many of the excellent papers presented. The RCN A&E Nursing Forum was well and truly established and very much on the national and international stage.

Summary

Over the past 15 years the early pioneers had moved A&E nursing from an informal group to both a formal group and then a forum within the Royal College of Nursing. They had established strong links with the Casualty Surgeons Association and held a joint conference with them. They had participated at the RCN Representative meetings and had developed the first ever A&E course (under the auspice of the Joint Board of Clinical Nursing Studies). Despite all of that work they had also compiled and published the *A&E newsletter*, were joint editors of the *British Journal of A&E Medicine*, helped achieve seat belt legislation and organised the first ever international emergency nursing conference. All of the up and coming A&E nurses (including me) had a lot to live up to.

References

Care of the Critically Ill. (1984/5) Critical Care Publications Limited

DHSS: (1968) Accident & Emergency Services. Circular HM (68) 82. London: HMSO

Emergency Care: (1987) The Journal of the Association of Emergency Medical Technicians (AEMT). Blackwell Scientific Publications

Nursing Mirror: September 25 1985 vol 161 no 13: October 9 1985 vol 161 no 15: October 16 1985 vol 161 no 16.

Paramedic UK: (1983/84) The Journal of the Association of Emergency Medical Technicians (AEMT). Published by AEMT.

The British Journal of Accident & Emergency Medicine (1983). Now published as *Emergency Medicine* Journal. A BMJ publication

CHAPTER 3

A NEW TEAM
SEPTEMBER 1985 – NOVEMBER 1987

On the last day of the international conference, the RCN A&E Nursing Forum held the annual AGM. At that meeting, the results of the committee elections were announced. Peter Blythin had been elected Chair, Ethel Buckles Secretary, Fiona Gordon Treasurer and me as Public Relations Officer (PRO). The January 1986 *A&E newsletter* reported on the election results and published a photo of the new officers standing with the RCN assistant professional officer and a number of local group link members.

As a group, and with the help of the RCN assistant professional officer, we were determined to advance A&E nursing and the forum, to continue the excellent work of our predecessors and build on their success. Our objectives included a significant growth in membership and the establishment of more local groups. A major part of our work was to develop the role of the A&E nurse through increased educational and enhanced courses.

As PRO I was elected by the committee to represent the RCN A&E Nursing Forum on the RCN Association of Nursing Practice (ANP). I was also to attend as a voting member at the RCN Representative Body (RRB) meeting, held in Blackpool in April 1986. Peter, Ethel and Fiona also attended as it was our aim to achieve a much higher profile for A&E nursing within the wider nursing family. Attendance at what is now RCN Congress continues today through the RCN Emergency Care Association (ECA) members.

The first decision we made was to cancel draft plans to hold the A&E national conference in Guernsey in 1986. It was going to be far too expensive for the majority of our members. Peter and Ethel also felt that if we organised the conference ourselves rather than through the RCN we could keep costs to a minimum. Ethel and Peter started looking for conference venues around the Manchester area and negotiated an excellent deal with the Cottons Hotel in Knutsford. My job as PRO was to write to companies linked with A&E and persuade them to come and exhibit at the conference and, of course, to pay for the privilege.

The new look conference was promoted in the July 1986 *A&E newsletter* along with the conclusion of Kate O'Hanlon's articles on the civil unrest in Northern Ireland and the results of the Land Rover competition winner and experience on the track. The guest editorial by Bob Wright from A&E, Leeds General Infirmary was devoted to the pay freeze on special duty payments. Other information in that edition included the recently published RCN A&E Nursing Forum guidelines on health and safety (formulated by the previous Chair Jill Milnthorpe) and the results from a survey of needle stick injuries.

The October 1986 *A&E newsletter* was a special conference issue highlighting the first ever A&E conference run entirely by the forum members. Ethel described the title of the conference, 'Cornucopia' – the horn of plenty as representing how A&E nurses embrace everything – a hotpot made up of the basic ingredients but still full of surprises. She gave examples of how A&E staff knew the current social trends long before government statistics because they saw the issues every day. This edition also covered the topics of A&E courses, violence, the elderly and diving emergencies. There was also an important reminder to all A&E nurses that they should not be involved in collecting prescription charges or making up packages of drugs from stock or department containers, such as I used to do at night back in 1975 when dispensing drugs from bottles into envelopes was the norm.

The price per delegate for the three days conference plus accommodation, all meals and social events was £86.95 per person. We had to fill the conference as we were looking at a £30,000 bill from the hotel. Fortunately, when the time came we had a good number of exhibitors and the delegate packages were sold out. The conference was a resounding success.

The conference was run over a three-day period Friday 24th October – Sunday 26th October 1986. Looking back on the programme many of the papers reflected the time including 'the myths of A&E nursing practice', 'paramedics – time to get involved', 'nurse triage' and 'an appraisal of national board courses for A&E nurses.' As well as the excellent clinical presentations, we also held a number of clinical workshops that enabled the nurses to acquire new skills such as the use of wound glue and skin staples. I ran an endotracheal intubation workshop; something most nurses at that time would not have practised themselves. Both the Friday and Saturday nights had sponsored social events enabling all delegates to have dinner and a good dance. In those days obtaining sponsorship from major health-related companies was far easier than today.

In September, before our annual conference, the BBC programme *Casualty* had been transmitted for the first time. A photo of Peter Salt, Charge Nurse A&E, Bristol Royal Infirmary and nurse advisor to the programme, and Derek Thompson who played Charlie Fairhead, the charge nurse modelled on Peter's position, appeared on the back page of the October 1986 *A&E newsletter* with a description of the new Saturday night hospital soap. The first few episodes depicted a small group of night staff in a large urban A&E unit. Not only did the title irritate many A&E nurses as the name casualty was dropped in 1962 in favour of 'Accident & Emergency', but the initial episodes did not reflect good A&E nursing. Ethel, the forum Secretary, had written to the programme's producer Geraint Morris and let him know what we thought. She also indicated that if he wanted to meet real A&E nurses he should come to the conference. To our surprise, he agreed and said he would bring his writers and the show's nurse advisor.

Grasping the opportunity to influence the increasingly popular series we organised a special slot in the conference programme. Peter Salt indicated this was his first insight into working with television. He explained that he was low down the pecking order of who decided what, and although he knew many of the practices shown on the programme were not accurate, he was told that was OK because it was 'drama'. He welcomed the conference session as it gave him greater leverage when on set with the actors and crew.

Geraint, the producer, was also pleased and promised that the programme would better reflect A&E today and the role nurses played. He went further and invited the forum honorary officers to the BBC studios at White City in

London to go on set, watch the filming and work with the team to ensure the programme improved.

It was a fascinating experience and we took full advantage of having our photographs taken at all the key locations around the department. We met many of the cast and spoke openly about how we believed the programme could be better. At that stage, the BBC did not have long-term plans for the show so the set had to be erected in a studio each week for filming and then dismantled. Although the scenery was very flimsy and had no ceilings, and some walls were missing (so that cameras could film the action) as we walked around it was easy to believe we were in a real A&E department.

We visited again over the next couple of years, and *Casualty* was given a more permanent home in Bristol. The producer and writers had also decided to change from just depicting night duty to the whole 24-hour period with incidents and action during the day shift as well as at night. The production team sought advice from Peter Salt as to how Charlie could be a senior nurse manager of the department, with 24-hour responsibility, yet still be clinically involved with patients. Peter suggested they came to see me at Orsett to discuss my nursing officer role as this was exactly what they were looking for. Writers came to visit and when the new series was broadcast, there was Charlie reflecting my role as a clinical nurse manager with 24hr responsibility. The success of *Casualty* continued well into the 1990s and is still on our TV screens in 2021. In the autumn 1995 edition of *Emergency Nurse*, Peter Salt adviser to the programme gave a unique view of his role. He described the process from the first script to the finished product. He mentioned some of the comments he got from other A&E nurses/managers such as,

'I was horrified to see the staff nurse's nose stud' to 'In my time as a sister, I never heard a nurse swear on duty.'

Due to the success of the 1986 A&E conference we decided to go one better for 1987 so the new venue was a much larger hotel in Cheshire, the Lord Daresbury Hotel near Warrington. This became the venue for the national conference until 2008. The hotel could accommodate over 500 delegates in the main hall and if required the manager was willing to allow bedrooms to accommodate three people rather than the normal maximum of two. The conference was held on 13th-15th November 1987 and we had some tremendous clinical papers and great social events. On the Sunday morning, with 500 plus nurses in the hall, you could have heard a pin drop as Jan Lammens, Assistant Director of Nursing, A.Z. St Jan Hospital, Brugge described how by using a heart lung bypass machine they successfully achieved total blood warming of a hypothermic female victim of the Zeebrugge Ferry Disaster.

A morning event that became a conference feature for many years was champagne and croissants in the swimming pool and jacuzzi; this was sponsored by 3M Health Care. It was surprising that despite a late Friday night of partying many delegates were up at 7am for this event. Unfortunately with the arrival of 1990 and money being restricted, the morning event that year changed to hot chocolate and doughnuts and attendance numbers fell. From then the morning event was no more.

During the two year period 1985-1987 one challenge for the committee was to increase the membership. A request to the RCN for recruitment posters was rejected (we were told only the ANP could have posters not forums) so with sponsorship from a company we had our own printed and distributed. This initiative was a huge success and a massive increase in members (1,500) occurred bringing the membership of the forum to 3,000 (*A&E newsletter* November 1987). As summarised in the January 1987 *A&E newsletter*, further local groups had been established and by November 1987 16 local A&E groups were spread across the UK. As PRO I would often be asked to represent the forum at the launch of a new local group and it was not unheard of for me to travel several hundred miles to be present and welcome the new members.

Other successes included a number of forum working parties that started work on establishing guidelines on handling aggression, how to establish triage, the nursing process and standards of care. As Ethel put it, we were now being recognised as a specialty rather than Jacks of all trades and master of none.

As a committee we were determined to develop A&E nursing education and the emerging emergency nurse practitioner role. A number of A&E nurses helped with curriculum designs. Other important developments during this period included a greater awareness of the needs of the suddenly bereaved and the need to improve the care of children in A&E. Bob Wright (Leeds) and Lisa Hadfield (London) became well-known names in developing better care for the suddenly bereaved with Lisa becoming the 1986 Nursing Standard Nurse of the Year. Triage was becoming far more established and the development of the Emergency Nurse Practitioner (ENP) was taking place. As a committee and following a number of meetings and a study day we were able to produce guidelines on the ENP (chapter 9).

The Thatcher years of government had brought reforms to many industries and services and in 1983 it was the turn of the NHS (NHS Management enquiry (1983) The Griffiths Report). The Griffiths Report into the management structure in the NHS was implemented and general management replaced 'consensus' management. District Health Authorities appointed unit general managers and by 1987 the results of the change were beginning to show. Ethel's editorial in the April 1987 edition of the *A&E newsletter* highlighted the fact that the clinical nurse had less of a voice in the midst of all the changes. She pointed out that unrealistic expectations by managers to improve standards with fewer resources and fewer staff, despite the increased workload was taking its toll. These changes went further in the 1990s with the introduction of hospital trusts and the purchaser/provider system of heath care.

Summary

This two year period set the scene for how the A&E Nursing Forum was going to develop in the future. Taking charge and organising our own annual conference had been a resounding success. The number of local groups and membership of the forum had increased dramatically and preparation for improved education and development of A&E nurses was well established. It also heralded in the new ways the NHS and nursing was going and this would require a whole new approach if nursing was to survive.

References

Griffiths ER (1983) NHS Management Inquiry: Griffiths Report on NHS. London: HMSO

CHAPTER 4
ALL CHANGE AHEAD
NOVEMBER 1987 – APRIL 1995

During the November 1987 breakfast AGM I was elected Chair of the forum, a role I was honoured to maintain until 1995. Throughout the eight years of my tenure, I was privileged to work with some amazing emergency nurses and advisers at the RCN. During the last two years of Peter Blythin's Chairmanship we had made great strides in developing our objectives. A review of our 1987 achievements was published in the May 1988 *A&E newsletter* and included:

- meetings with the DHSS regarding the structural layout and equipping of any new A&E departments
- a joint study day with the BAEM (A&E medical staff)
- congress attendance as voting members
- establishment of six further local groups
- attendance by members at DHSS meetings on a variety of A&E issues
- setting up and development of a number of working parties:
    - Future education for A&E nurses
    - Standards of care for A&E departments
    - Development of Nurse Practitioners
    - Development of Triage
- further development of the annual A&E conference

Although the RCN A&E Nursing Forum was key to the development of A&E services, so too were many advisory documents that over the years had been published by organisations or from the Department of Health. These seemed to grow in number as the A&E specialty became more established. Many highlighted areas that most A&E nurses were aware of and that were already being addressed. However such documents were able to be used by the RCN A&E Nursing Forum as well as the wider RCN to support our efforts for change.

One such document published in 1988 *Managing A&E – a guide to good practice* reviewed a number of issues based on the patient's experience and comments made by patients. It included reasons for patients coming to A&E rather than visiting the GP. It covered staffing including the recognition of the increase in A&E consultants as opposed to orthopaedic consultants heading up A&E departments. The booklet questioned if there was now a need for 24 hour clerical staff as many departments did not have clerical staff at night and other support staff such as porters. It recognised triage was being introduced into most A&E departments but it was not universally accepted. The guide gave support to the development of emergency nurse practitioners (ENPs). There was recognition of the problems with admissions and waiting times and the booklet suggested maximum waiting times should be established. Communication within the hospital and the A&E departments' environment were emphasised as in need of improvement. Typical issues raised by patients and highlighted in the booklet included car parking problems leading to frustration and uncomfortable waiting room chairs.

* * * *

Participating at RCN Congress (previously called RRB) was very important as it not only gave us an opportunity to get A&E issues directly to RCN Council, it also enabled us to participate with others on the national stage for nursing. In 1988, while attending Congress in Brighton, I was interviewed by one of the *Nursing Standard* journalists with regard to the developments that were occurring in A&E, 'It's no accident' (July 2 1988). Using the analogy of the Phoenix rising from the ashes, I explained how A&E had risen from the casualty units of the past and moved from their Cinderella image into a true specialty. It was also at this Congress that I proposed the motion on behalf of the RCN A&E Nursing Forum for random breath testing of car drivers. We produced figures that showed that around 7,700 car passengers a year were involved in accidents related to alcohol with 1,200 involving pedestrians. The majority of speakers supported the resolution with one speaker telling of her 21-year-old son who was killed while a passenger in a car with a drunk driver. The resolution was carried.

In 1989, we proposed and supported the continuation of Nursing Development Units and spoke out against those being closed and others that were under threat. Jane Salvage, Director of the Nursing Development Project at the King's Fund, outlined the importance of such units and the resolution was passed with resounding success. Our intervention in this important area of nursing was reported in the *Nursing Standard Congress Daily*. At the 1990 Congress it was my job to present the resolution which focussed on our concern that hospitals had closed beds and this was leading to long waits and long stays for patients in A&E. The resolution also flagged up the problems with early patient discharge, lack of community services and many patients returning to A&E sicker than when they had left the hospital.

*   *   *   *

In our quest to produce quality assurance criteria for A&E departments, in 1989 we negotiated a liaison with Leeds Polytechnic Department of Health and Community Studies to produce 'Monitor' for A&E. Using money raised from our annual conferences we paid for a research nurse from North Staffordshire hospital to work under the direction of Professor Leonard Goldstone. 'Monitor' was a quality assurance tool that enabled A&E managers to ensure the standards and quality of care met agreed criteria. Speaking at the *Nursing 91* A&E Conference in Bournemouth in April that year, Professor Goldstone explained that the 'Monitor' quality audit programme commenced in 1977 and had resulted in 14 audits of nursing. 'Monitor' had been researched by using literature, working parties and trials. A&E 'Monitor' audited patient care, nursing management, the special cases of children, minor injured patients, the A&E's facilities and department policies. The final document was published in 1990.

Bob Wright, Charge Nurse from Leeds UK with Marg Nuttall and Marg Walker from Australia, all senior A&E nurses, organised the first Pan Pacific Emergency Nurses Conference in Hong Kong. Although not arranged as part of the RCN A&E Nursing Association the committee were happy to support the conference as it reaffirmed our commitment to international links. Many UK nurses took the opportunity to visit Hong Kong and to present papers. I myself presented two papers, one on the subject of hydrofluoric acid burns and the second on pre-hospital care in the UK. The conference ran from 10-13th October 1989. This event following on from the international conference held in London in 1985 brought more A&E nurses together across the globe and many new contacts were made. A further Pan Pacific Emergency Nurses Conference was held in Singapore in 1992.

Continuing the international theme, for the first time two representative of the United States Emergency Nurses Association (ENA) Estelle McPhail, President and Susan Buddasi – Sheehey, Secretary, spoke at the annual A&E conference in 1989. This was the beginning of a continuous working relationship between the two organisations and each year representatives of the two organisations attended each of the respective conferences. At the same conference Christine Hancock RCN General Secretary reflected the progress A&E nurses had made. In her address to the conference she said, 'A&E nurses are a mixture of high tech and high touch who have to get it right first time and fast.'

In the January 1990 edition of the *A&E newsletter* I wrote a lengthy editorial reflecting back on the success of the forum since 1985. At that time there were seven local groups, now there were twenty-three. Chairs of local groups came to regular meetings with the honorary officers. I reflected on the success of the conferences since we had started organising them ourselves as well as highlighting the publications produced including - introducing triage, nurse practitioners, care of children in A&E and the 'Monitor' quality audit criteria for A&E. The newsletter also reported that Kate O'Hanlon MBE had been awarded the Cross of Merit from the Sovereign & Military Order of St John of Jerusalem Rhodes & Malta for her services to the public.

In the March 1990 edition of *Nursing Standard* 'A&E Nursing: today and the future' I highlighted our success and detailed that as the forum was to become an association from April 1990, we had a range of objectives and immediate tasks. While explaining these in the article they had also been published in the October 1989 *A&E newsletter*.

Main objectives:
- to promote A&E nursing as a specialty in its own right
- to develop the role of the A&E nurse
- to provide post basic education in the field of A&E nursing
- to promote the use of triage and the development of the nurse practitioner in A&E nursing
- to ensure A&E nursing could meet the implications of the government White Paper and Project 2000
- to engage in the discussions on the future of trauma care in the UK including the development of trauma training for nurses

Immediate tasks:
- publishing the guidelines on the development of a training curriculum for the nurse practitioner
- publishing the guidelines on the care of children in A&E
- formulating the standards of care for A&E
- establishing a mechanism whereby ethical issues relating to emergency nursing practice could be assessed

On 1st April 1990, the RCN A&E Nursing Forum became an association within the RCN. At last we had the same status as all other groups. We no longer were a small part of a larger group. Our move to an association came about due to a restructuring of the professional entities within the college and the result of the RCN A&E Nursing Forum officers for many years arguing for such a change in status. The current committee members were entitled to start their tenure again, so for me, that meant another four years as Chair. Becoming an association enabled us to work directly with RCN Council and other departments within the College. We were also able to expand our committee to seven members (four elected and three co-opted) ensuring a UK wide approach.

Purely by coincidence, the following month the Casualty Surgeons Association changed its name to the British Association for Accident & Emergency Medicine (BAEM) and as Ethel said in her July editorial report, 'perhaps it is a case of "great minds think alike" and we are all tuned into the same wavelength at last.'

Following a great deal of negotiation with ENA by the Vice-Chair of our RCN A&E Nursing Association, Ethel Buckles, in October 1990 eight A&E nurses were invited to undertake the Trauma Nursing Core Course (TNCC) in Chicago USA. Funded by the RCN A&E Nursing Association this was the process by which the Emergency Nurses Association (ENA) of the United States of America introduced the TNCC course to the UK (chapter 13).

Since we had started running the annual conference numbers continued to rise. With over 500 delegates attending and a full programme plus social events, it was the highlight of the

A&E calendar and it had become an 'annual must' for hundreds of emergency nurses. In 1991 a change to the structure of the conference enabled members during an afternoon assembly to put forward resolutions and matters for discussion that would then be taken forward by the RCN A&E Nursing Association's committee (similar format to RCN congress). This event proved popular for a number of years.

October 1990 saw the last editorial of the *A&E newsletter* written by Ethel Buckles. After editing the newsletter since its second edition back in 1983 Ethel had decided a new editor was required to take the newsletter forward. In 1991, Kathie Butcher, Senior Nurse, A&E, Addenbrook's Hospital, Cambridge took that task on.

On 27th December 1991 the A&E nursing world was shattered by the sudden and untimely death of Ethel Buckles. Ethel, the Senior A&E Sister at Preston and Vice-Chair of the RCN A&E Nursing Association, had been one of those early pioneers back in 1972 and was the main force behind the conference being held at the Daresbury hotel and TNCC coming over from the USA. I dedicated the whole of the front page of the 1992 spring edition of the *A&E newsletter* to a tribute to Ethel. This was appropriate as the newsletter had been in Ethel's own words 'her baby'. She had taken it from a few photocopied sheets back in 1983 to the almost journal like production it was in 1992. Ethel's life was celebrated with the first Ethel Buckles Memorial Lecture in November 1992. Baroness Caroline Cox who as a nurse and was the Deputy Speaker in the House of Lords at that time gave the lecture.

I was heavily involved in the production of the document *Accident & Emergency Services – A Guide to Good Practice (1992)*. In fact, this was the first piece of work I undertook as a self-employed nurse consultant. Developed by a multidisciplinary group in North East Thames Region, comprising A&E nurse managers and representatives from medicine, police, church, and architects it was structured under key headings. Two documents were produced; one for providers and a smaller guide for purchasers. The summary from the main document gives an indication of the content. It includes some statistics of the A&E services in the region at the time and some key recommendations including:

- all departments urgently required effective management information systems (computers were not commonplace at that time and most records were hand written).
- referrals from GPs should not be received in A&E (something that was commonplace in the early 1990s, as assessment units had not been developed).
- Primary Care should be improved to deter inappropriate use of A&E
- development of triage and nurse practitioners should be encouraged.
- there should be 24-hour support from other hospital departments, social workers and community staff (this was very sporadic in those days).
- trauma teams should be established (not common at that time) and staffing and skill mix should be improved.

One recommendation from the work that has spanned the whole of the UK is the white H on a red background indicating that the hospital has an A&E department. Kate Harmond, then Nursing Officer at the NHS Regional Health Authority came up with the idea of the current white H with blue background remaining for non-A&E hospitals and the red background with white H for hospitals with A&Es. The recommendation was discussed with the Department of Health and Department for Transport and now signs are seen universally across the UK.

Another key recommendation was the nurse staffing of A&E departments. A number of recommendations under this heading were put forward including using patient dependency as part of the staffing and skill mix review. An appendix to this recommendation was included and from this work, in 1993 the RCN A&E Nursing Association produced a skill mix guide for A&E nurse managers, which was the basis of staffing and skill mix for many years (*Skill Mix in Accident and Emergency Nursing: A Framework for Managers*).

Like all other entities within the RCN we were often invited to events that enabled us to promote our specialty. As Chair I regularly attended the annual Nursing Standard awards dinner and other events such as a reception held by the Corporation of London at the Guildhall in recognition of the European Road Safety conference. As part of the RCN 75th anniversary celebrations in 1990 I was invited to a government reception at Lancaster House in London and to the Service, in the presence of HRH Princess Margaret, of Thanksgiving and Rededication at Westminster Abbey. In July 1992 I represented the RCN A&E Nursing Association at one of the Queen's summer garden parties at Buckingham

Palace. Other invites included appearing on BBC and ITV news and participating in programmes that focussed on A&E attendances particularly relating to elderly patients and violence in A&E.

*   *   *   *

Despite the success of the *A&E newsletter* under the editorship of Margaret King, Ethel Buckles and Kathie Butcher members had always looked to the day when A&E would achieve its own journal. In 1992/3, like buses, two came along within a year of each other.

Emergency Nurse the journal of the RCN A&E Nursing Association was first published on 25th March 1992. A supplement in the *Nursing Standard* journal, the managing editor was Norah Casey, Editor *Nursing Standard*, consultant editor was Ernie Botley, Lecturer Practitioner, A&E, John Radcliffe Hospital, Oxford and a board of advisers was made up of A&E nurses and Rosie Wilkinson, RCN Nurse Adviser. Ernie's opening editorial looked at change and the challenges to emergency care. Hospitals, he said, now as NHS Trusts had to comply with local and government enforced targets and tightly controlled budgets while at the same time ensuring standards of care and providing a quality driven service. He highlighted how nurses would be scrutinised by purchasers and patients armed with the recently introduced *The Patient's Charter*.

The Patient's Charter (1992) was how the *Citizen's Charter* (introduced in 1991 to ensure public services were responsive to the citizens they served) was to be put into practice in the NHS. A number of rights and expectations (standards) were published, some generic and some specific to key areas of the NHS. For A&E the charter had two specifics - If you go to an A&E department you can expect to be seen immediately and have your need for treatment assessed. From April 1996, if admitted to hospital through A&E, you can expect to be given a bed as soon as possible and certainly within two hours. The one generic was – you can expect a qualified nurse to be responsible for your nursing care. You will be told their name. Numerous developments came from this charter and they are highlighted in Part Two.

News of particular interest in the first edition of *Emergency Nurse* included the RCN A&E Nursing Association setting up a database of information so nurses could share research findings, ideas and expertise. The journal would act as a contact point for A&E nurses and as a means of encouraging publication. Although the *A&E newsletter* had included clinical articles, letters from members and a journal scan there was now the opportunity to expand on all of this.

The Second edition of *Emergency Nurse* was published in November 1992. Some changes to the editorial board occurred with the managing editor now Brian Dolan, Clinical Consultant at Nursing Standard, consultant editor Kathie Butcher (Kathie also continued to edit the *A&E newsletter*) and I joined the editorial board.

Articles of note included: 'The future of A&E' – Rosie Wilkinson, RCN Nurse Adviser presented an overview of current activity and influences on our practice including *The Health of the Nation* document, *The Patient's Charter*, the reduction in junior doctors' hours, GPs as fund holders and trauma centres.

There was an article on value for money (National Audit office reports – see below) and an article on disaster planning that described the international disaster and emergency training centre in Sweden. Originally a 1944 hospital built underground as a war time shelter, it had been developed into the international training centre.

NHS A&E departments in England (National Audit Office 1992)
The National Audit Office concluded that the A&Es visited were well run. However, they required stronger representation in hospital management, more flexible and capable computerised management information systems, measures to improve management of the department's rising workload, constantly better use of nurses skills, monitoring adequacy and timeliness of support from other specialties and services. On planning, there needed to be concerted action to ensure that departments are not overloaded with patients who might be better treated elsewhere. On severe injuries there was a need for early and continuing improvements for care of all severely injured patients. This appeared to support the 1988 Royal College of Surgeons report to improve care of patients with severe injuries (*The Management of Patients with Major Injuries*).

NHS A&E departments in Scotland (National Audit Office 1992)
Although similar recommendations were made the overall thrust was the way A&E departments were distributed, especially the vast difference between large units and smaller facilities in rural hospitals. The Scottish Government needed to review the service they wish to provide over the next 10 years.

Following the success of the first two supplements of *Emergency Nurse* and coupled with the negotiations I had held with suture material company Davis & Geck to obtain sponsorship, in spring 1993, Vol 1 No 1 of the relaunched *Emergency Nurse* as a stand-alone journal was published. Brian Dolan continued as Editor, Kathie Butcher as Consultant Editor and I became the Public Relations Consultant. There was also a small editorial board of four.

Brian's editorial in this new stand-alone journal indicated that A&E was seen as a specialty both within and outside of the emergency department's doors and *Emergency Nurse*, relaunched in the 21st anniversary year of the RCN A&E Nursing Association, was a time for celebration of a very special specialty.

Kathie indicated that the new journal would be sent to every A&E department and to all association members. This continued for a year and then the journal became subscription based, though because of the sponsorship the cost to the individual was minimal. Being a 32 page journal, it gave the editorial board the opportunity to accept more comprehensive clinical articles. It also provided more space for diary events, adverts, journal scans and members letters. The *A&E newsletter* would continue but focus on news relevant to the RCN A&E Nursing Association rather than publishing clinical articles.

One of the first articles in the new journal was written by Una Bell, Clinical Services Manager, A&E King's Health Care, London. It demonstrated how A&E nurses continued to look beyond the injured or ill and considered the wider social issues that impact on A&E activity. 'Homelessness: the A&E response' highlighted the increasing numbers of homeless people on the streets of our major cities. She broke the homeless into five categories giving an explanation of each – people in temporary accommodation, squatters, hostel dwellers, sleeping out and the hidden homeless (the ones that get forgotten because they occupy a sofa in a friend's house or those moved back to parents). She presented statistics based on 1991 figures under the various headings, for example, under sleeping out on the street 2,703 in England & Wales of whom 1,275 were in London. Giving some possible causes Una included the changes in the social welfare benefits system in 1988 and the shift from hospital based psychiatric care to the community. She linked the plight of the homeless with the need for staff in A&E to be aware and fully assess for conditions such as malnutrition, dermatological conditions, digestive tract problems and psychiatric issues.

Being the first edition and in our RCN A&E Nursing Association's 21st year, I wrote a historical article demonstrating that A&E nursing was going through a quiet revolution and offered a vision for the future. The article reported that from 1972 -1993 RCN A&E Nursing Association membership had grown to 3,000; we had three special interest groups (emergency nurse practitioner; children and young people; education and research) and a trauma nursing committee. Triage, ENPs, primary nursing, standard setting, health promotion, bereavement counselling and improved trauma care were some of the innovations that had been developed. My vision for the future was for A&E to be identified as a service to the community and not solely as a department in the hospital. There should be fast track systems for minor injuries/GP patients provided in both settings by GPs and ENPs. These staff should rotate between the community and A&E. The fundamental difference was for the emergency services in both the community and hospital to be managed as a comprehensive service under one management structure and the need for senior nurse management to be maintained.

For the autumn 1993 *Emergency Nurse* I wrote an article on oxygen administration (chapter 13). This was the first of a new continuing education series that enabled the reader to fill out an answer sheet to gain continuing education points through the RCN Nursing Institute of Advanced Nursing Education. These articles written by a range of A&E nursing experts continued in each edition (with some modification) until September 2000. This edition also highlighted the story of the way emergency nurses from the John Radcliffe Hospital, Oxford and other nurses from across the UK had responded to the civil war in Bosnia. Operation Irma involved a team of nurses airlifting sick and injured casualties from the war zone.

From the first publication in 1993 *Emergency Nurse* continued to be a success and covered all aspects of emergency nursing from ethical and legal issues to, as Brian Dolan once said, 'the dread most A&E nurses had when the new intake of SHO's arrived on the 1st February and 1st August every year'. In 2012 the journal celebrated 20 years of publication. For that edition, I reflected in an article how the journal had reported on the most important developments in the profession and the Editor Claire Picton picked up on this theme - 'had the journal not been published, there would have been no record of the changes that have taken place and events that have occurred in emergency care during the past two decades.'

Accident & Emergency Nursing was the second A&E journal, launched in January 1993. Published by Churchill-Livingstone, Bob Wright, (A&E Charge Nurse and Bereavement Nurse Specialist, Leeds General Hospital) was the Editor. This international journal was aimed primarily at a UK audience with the intention of becoming much more global. Many of the early articles were research based with the aim of it becoming a learned journal for emergency nurses (which it achieved). Articles covered a range of subjects including clinical, professional practice and management. While being independent of the RCN the journal complemented the RCN A&E Nursing Association's journal *Emergency Nurse*. Initially I was one of the editorial board members but due to my position as Chair of the RCN A&E Nursing Association and editorial board member of *Emergency Nurse,* senior staff at RCN publishing, and staff within the RCN nursing department felt that there could be a conflict of interest if I remained on the board of what they perceived as a rival journal. Although disagreeing I resigned and focussed on *Emergency Nurse*.

Not intended to compete with the two journals, in 1995 3M Health Care published the *3M A&E Focus magazine*. This magazine ran for several years and was distributed free to A&E departments, minor injury units and to individuals who returned a registration card. It was a clinical magazine providing short but comprehensive care tips to nurses.

*   *   *   *

The RCN A&E conference of 1993 enabled members to celebrate 21 years since the RCN A&E Nursing Group had been established. The Gala dinner on the Saturday evening was a great success and followed a year of celebrations including in March 11 link members from the local groups attending a network meeting with the RCN A&E Nursing Association officers and staff from the RCN. During the celebratory lunch an anniversary cake was cut and enjoyed by all present.

Throughout the 1990s hospital beds had continued to be reduced, A&E departments closed, yet community services were not keeping up with demand. As the next four years progressed the real impact of the business approach to the NHS was taking its toll (chapter 8).

Despite the business approach to the NHS, the *Citizen's Charter* and *The Patient's Charter* still focussed minds on quality of care. In December 1994, a *Citizen's Charter booklet* aimed at allowing the patient's point of view to be heard was published by the NHS Executive and focussed on Accident & Emergency departments. The booklet identified the role and characteristics of an A&E department and identified seven areas that the public valued when using A&E departments ranging from welcoming reception to compassion following bereavement. It also identified three challenges for funding bodies (purchasers) of these services.

It was not only national documents that influenced A&E development during the 1990s, local work also played a key role as I identified earlier from the North East Thames Region in 1992. In 1995, a significant publication from the Anglia and Oxford Emergency Health Care Project (*Emergency Care Handbook*) covered a spectrum of emergency health care services including self-care, informal and social care, primary health care teams, scene of the incident care, hospital care and non-elective admissions. Although focussed on the Anglia and Oxford region, like the work from North East Thames, many of the recommendations could be implemented on a UK wide basis.

During my period as Chair there was great change within the NHS due to general management and hospitals and community services becoming NHS trusts. Finance dominated the agenda and co-operation between hospitals started to become competition. As Robert Crouch reported in *Emergency Nurse* (winter1994), 'It is interesting that the American health system is being politically steered towards a model of 'socialised medicine' in a time when our health care system is being nudged towards theirs.'

Fortunately, the RCN A&E Nursing Association maintained the ability for nurses to share practice development outside of this competition mentality but concern was running high within the nursing profession that the government planned to deskill the NHS. With the introduction of extensive National Vocational Qualification (NVQ) training of the Health Care Assistant (HCA), unless nurses could clearly articulate the uniqueness of nursing, and in our case A&E nursing, we could lose ground towards a more diluted workforce. Following extensive work *Accident & Emergency - Challenging the Boundaries (*RCN 1994*)* was published. Probably for the first time, this demonstrated what emergency nursing was all about (chapter 9).

Despite this document, concern was still present regarding the doing and craft of A&E nursing as the editorial for *Emergency Nurse* (Summer 1995) demonstrated. Editor, Brian Dolan voiced his concern that A&E nurses for so long had been absorbed in the doing rather than what the specialty was, he felt the craft of nursing was being devalued as the work of nurses was reduced to a series of tasks. He argued that if nursing practice was central to the development of our specialty, then it was critical to actively seek to define the values and our *raison d'etre*. A&E nurses he said, 'needed to take the lead in defining their future: who A&E nurses need to be, what A&E nurses need to know, and what A&E nurses need to do. If not, a loss of professional self-determination may manifest itself in a willingness of others to set the agenda for change – with or without our co-operation.'

When in 1995 the Audit Commission asked health authorities, trusts and professional bodies what topics would benefit from a review of their economy, efficiency and effectiveness, A&E came near the top of the list. Increase in A&E attendances, emergency referrals and difficulty in staffing had added to the high profile. The full report *By Accident or Design – improving emergency care in acute hospitals* gave a general indication of the function of A&E and listed patients as falling into 6 main categories (chapter 8). *The Patient's Charter* relating to immediate assessment was highlighted, however the report indicated that the promptness of initial assessment was not necessarily related to how soon treatment commenced or was completed.

The report looked at doctors and nursing numbers in some detail. It advocated expansion of triage to initiating tests and x-rays. An important sentence was, 'It is important to ensure that more attention is now paid to *how well* patient assessment is carried out rather than just *how fast* it is done.' This led to a recommendation to review *The Patient's Charter* standard (chapter 11).

By Accident or Design covered recommendations for care for children, frail older people, mental health and the bereaved, as well as recommending improved links with GP/primary care. It recommended a variety of services including minor injury units, nurse led telephone triage, 24-hour GP surgeries, open access X-ray departments and specialist out-patient departments. It highlighted that only 30% of departments use nurse practitioners despite evidence that they can improve care and reduce waiting times.

It recognised A&E on its own could do little to reduce 'trolley waits' and recommended a whole system approach with a senior manager responsible for promoting and co-ordinating initiatives.

On major injury the report referred to the 1988 Royal College of Surgeons report on the management of patients with major injuries and how this had stimulated major changes in the treatment of serious injury in Britain, many of which were still being implemented. It showed that some departments/hospitals did not have dedicated trauma teams and indicated trauma centres were still up for debate and the results of the North Staffordshire Trauma Centre initiative was to be published in early 1996.

Looking to the future, the report did not advocate concentrating A&E resources to fewer sites, indicating that it would not reduce the ratio of attendances to staff numbers unless the total number of patients also fell due to the closures. It also linked creating larger A&E departments with the challenges for the hospital of coping with more admissions. Its conclusion was that to maintain expertise, further work was needed to establish the most appropriate size of A&E departments (number of attenders) and this may mean some smaller units closing.

In *Emergency Nurse* (Spring 1996) an article by Ian Jones, senior manager, health studies directorate at the Audit Commission explained how the review had been carried out and highlighted the reason the report led on the issue of waiting times. Ian indicated that while waiting times was not the most important aspect of quality of care it was an issue that most patients wanted to see improved.

The Clinical Standards Advisory Group was set up in 1991 under the NHS & Community Care Act 1990 as an independent source of expert advice to UK Health Ministers and to the NHS on standards of clinical care for, and access to and availability of, services to NHS patients. The group's members came from a range of Royal Colleges and co-opted experts. Their report *Urgent & Emergency Admissions to Hospital (1995)* contained a number of recommendations to improve urgent clinical care within the 24 hour period after arrival in hospital. The recommendations covered a range of issues from setting national standards and guidelines for emergency services, contracting arrangements, admission management (bed ownership, admission wards, observation wards, emergency operating theatres, bed managers, staffing, support services, discharge planning) through to hospital layout and design including single site rather than split or multiple sites. The report also recommended improvements in 24 hour GP provision and substantive arrangements to be developed by psychiatrists for psychiatric patients in A&E departments.

*   *   *   *

Many of the recommendations from both national and local documents formed part of our RCN A&E Nursing Association's agenda and members played active roles by attending meetings at the RCN and Department of Health.

Other recommendations led to the RCN A&E Nursing Association setting up specific working groups to produce guidance documents for nurses in A&E such as the ones published on the implementation of the nurse practitioner. As already reported the RCN A&E Nursing Association addressed trauma by introducing trauma training for emergency nurses through the TNCC courses. At the same time other emergency nurses, independent of the RCN A&E Nursing Association, worked with A&E consultants to set up the advanced trauma nursing course (ATNC). With the two courses available throughout the UK many nurses were now able to provide improved trauma nursing care (chapter 13).

The concerns surrounding bereavement care (highlighted in the *Citizen's Charter booklet 1994* and the report *By Accident or Design 1995)* were addressed by the RCN A&E Nursing Association with the setting up of a joint working party between the RCN A&E Nursing Association and the British Association for Emergency Medicine (BAEM). Statistics obtained estimated that 2-3 per 1,000 new attendances involved relatives bereaved following a patient dying in A&E or certified dead on arrival. A range of recommendations linked with the phrase, 'Everybody's death should matter to someone' was published in 1995 (*Bereavement care in A&E departments*). Recommendations included linking a named nurse to the relatives, through to the type of relative's room required. It covered taking photographs of the loved one, through to care of property. It focussed on religious issues, training of staff and staff support as well as documentation and audit. The document also supported relatives witnessing resuscitation (chapter 13).

Accident prevention, highlighted in the *Health of the Nation handbook (1993)* was another key objective for the RCN A&E Nursing Association. As far back as the early days of the forum, accident prevention through seat belt legislation had been achieved. The RCN A&E Nursing Association's special interest group for paediatrics were at the forefront for the use of cycle helmets and through our resolutions at RCN congress and using the journal *Emergency Nurse* many of the initiatives for preventing accidents and injury were linked with our RCN A&E Nursing Association.

Summary

As I came towards the end of my eight years as Chair I was pleased with the way the RCN A&E Nursing Association and A&E in more general terms had developed. The number of initiatives that had been achieved and the way the series of government papers had linked with the work the association had put in place bode well for the future. With two A&E journals, the quality assurance tool 'Monitor', guidelines on a range of activities from triage to developing nurse practitioners and the document *Challenging the Boundaries* clearly stating for the first time what A&E nursing was really about, it was now up to the next group of enthusiasts to take the work forward. However, as will be seen I continued to be very active within the RCN A&E Nursing Association and in the development of emergency care.

References

3M Health Care: (1995) *A&E Focus magazine*. 3M Health Care Ltd Publication

Accident & Emergency Nursing – An International Journal (1993) Churchill Livingstone

Audit Commission England/Wales: (1996) *By Accident or Design – improving emergency care in acute hospitals.* London: HMSO

Anglia and Oxford Emergency Health Care Project: (1995) *Emergency Care Handbook*: NHS Publication

Clinical Standards Advisory Group: (1995): *(Urgent & Emergency Admissions to Hospital.* London: HMSO

Department of Health: (1991/94) *The Citizen's Charter* London: HMSO

Department of Health: (1992) *The Patient's Charter* London: HMSO

Department of Health: (1992) *The Health of the Nation: a strategy for health in England.* London: HMSO

Department of Health: (1993): *The Health of the Nation: Key Area Handbook – Accidents.* London: HMSO

Dutton J, Grylls L, Goldstone L. Accident and Emergency Nursing Monitor: An Audit of the Quality of Nursing Care in Hospital Accident and Emergency Departments (Quality Assurance Nursing Monitors) Gale Centre Publications

Institute of Health Services Management & Association of Community Health Councils for England & Wales: (1988) *Managing A&E - A Guide to Good Practice.* IHSM Portland Place London

Jones G (1988) *It's No Accident.* Nursing Standard, week ending July 2 1988. 46

Jones G (1990) *A&E Nursing -today and the future.* Nursing Standard: March 28/volume 4/Number 27/1990. 51-52

National Audit Office: (1992) *NHS A&E Departments in England.* London: HMSO

National Audit Office: (1992) *NHS A&E Departments in Scotland.* London: HMSO

North East Thames Regional Health Authority: (1992) *Accident & Emergency Services – A Guide to Good Practice.* NETRHA publication.

Nursing Standard Congress Daily Issue 5 April 7 1989

NHS Executive: (December 1994) *Accident & Emergency Departments Citizen's Charter booklet.* London: HMSO

Royal College of Surgeons: (1988) *Report on the Management of Patients with Major Injuries.* London, Royal College of Surgeons

Royal College of Nursing: (1993) *Skill Mix in Accident and Emergency Nursing: A Framework for Managers.* RCN Publication

Royal College of Nursing: (1994) *Accident & Emergency - Challenging the Boundaries* RCN Publication

Royal College of Nursing & British Association for Accident and Emergency Medicine: (1995) *Bereavement Care in A&E Departments.* RCN Publication

CHAPTER 5

THE PRE-MILLENNIUM PERIOD APRIL 1995 – SEPTEMBER 1999

Following my eight year tenure as Chair of the RCN A&E Nursing Association, the membership elected Robert Crouch to Chair for the following two years and then in 1997 Karen Castille took the Chair until September 1999. I moved on to become the RCN Council member for what was then the North East Thames Region. The April 1995 *A&E newsletter* editorial was very complimentary about my achievements over the past eight years and in May of that year I was awarded Fellowship of the Florence Nightingale Foundation for services to emergency nursing.

Since *Emergency Nurse* had been launched, the *A&E newsletter* had changed considerably with the editions in 1995 providing more news from the RCN A&E Nursing Association (especially from the special interest groups), diary dates and journal scans.

In the January 1996 *A&E newsletter* Robert took the opportunity to summarise all the achievements the RCN A&E Nursing Association had made over the past decade and reassert the key aims of the Association which were to:

- promote the art and science of A&E nursing
- represent views of members to government and appropriate bodies and ensure A&E voices were heard
- support the Trauma Nursing Committee, the three special interest groups and the 20 plus local groups

- promote the journal *Emergency Nurse* and support the Association's newsletter

Other news included a number of short reports from papers presented at the 1995 A&E conference. Major changes had been made to the annual conference including the establishment of an organising and scientific committee and the introduction of concurrent as well as plenary sessions. Although many people played a part in continuing to make the conference such a success, Gabby Lomas, as Chair of the organising committee has to be thanked for doing such sterling work. The report of the Ethel Buckles Memorial Lecture given by Norah Casey, Editor of Nursing Standard, challenged A&E nurses to stop fighting the losing battle of year on year increases in A&E attendances and to build partnerships with other health professionals which met the needs of the consumers and used the full range of expertise in nursing. Her summary was, 'Take control of your environment before it takes control of you.'

The editorial by Kathie Butcher in the July 1996 edition of the *A&E newsletter* highlighted the annual league tables for *The Patient's Charter* achievement. Kathie argued that while showing improvement the league tables had done little to improve the overall standard of care given. She gave an example from standard 5 (initial assessment) where some staff were eyeballing patients on arrival only to achieve the standard, but patients still had to wait for assessment (chapter 11).

As in previous years yet more documents and guidance letters from organisations and government were produced to help take forward A&E services, including *Developing*

Emergency Services in the Community – NHS Executive 1996. This report followed the Chief Medical Officer's (CMO) review of all aspects of emergency care outside of hospital and how it could be developed further. Members of the RCN A&E Nursing Association including Robert Crouch, Simon Davies, Rosie Wilkinson (RCN Nurse Adviser) and I were members of the working group. The conclusion from the work included a need for a co-ordinated approach 24 hours a day, an increased education of people to recognise emergencies and how to deal with them as well as knowing when professional help was required. One recommendation was a need to research the viability of other models of access to emergency care including a free telephone helpline. In 1998, this recommendation led to three pilot sites and following their success the setting up of NHS Direct, the 24 hour emergency advice telephone helpline. Although controversial at the time NHS Direct went on to become a vital service for patient advice and by 2002 the whole country was able to access the service. On Boxing Day 2001 NHS Direct received 24,000 calls across the 22 call centres in England. The top five symptoms included vomiting, fever, coughs, diarrhoea, rashes. Unfortunately, by 2006 a review of the cost of NHS Direct led to a move to change the service which resulted in the establishment of NHS 111 in 2014 with the loss of nearly 600 jobs and the closure of 12 call centres.

Included in the conclusion of the CMO's report were recommendations to map emergency services in the community, develop more first aid training by employers, schools and other organisations and further develop minor injury units. The main thrust of the report was getting all community emergency services (including mental health) to operate in a more co-ordinated and partnership way.

Robert Crouch presented a very detailed report to the members at the AGM in November 1996 outlining the work that had been undertaken by the RCN A&E Nursing Association during 1995/6. The report was subsequently published in the April 1997 *A&E newsletter*. Some of the key points included:

- the change to the structure of the professional committees in the RCN meant the term steering committee would be the norm for all forums/associations and apart from the Chair no other titles would be used. It was felt previous titles such as Vice-Chair, Treasurer and Secretary were outdated and not relevant to the way the RCN now worked.

- an update on the development of the Faculty of Emergency Nursing. This major piece of work had started in 1995 and was supported by RCN Council (chapter 10).

- at the 1996 RCN Congress the A&E Nursing Association had presented a matter for discussion urging Congress to discuss the implications for nursing due to the reduction of junior doctors' hours and the consequences for patient care.

- a report by Robert on the continued move to a national triage scale and how work between the RCN/BAEM and the Manchester Triage Group (MTG) was linking together and the MTG work was under consideration for national adoption (chapter 11).

- the work with the Chief Medical Officer on emergency care in the community and the launch of the faculty of pre-hospital care were all reported.

- in 1996 the RCN A&E Nursing Association had held a one-day conference on mental health issues in A&E where both A&E nurses and mental health specialists were able to debate and discuss many of the issues that were faced on a daily basis. Work from the day would enable the development of a position statement by the Association on mental health issues in A&E.

- position statements on a number of other key issues were in production and included:
  - The role of the Health Care Assistant in A&E
  - Triage
  - Care of children in A&E
  - Care of the elderly in A&E

Although nurse staffing in A&E had always been an issue in some departments, during the 1990s more departments were finding recruitment difficult. Although it is not easy to pinpoint any one factor, 'trolley waits' and increased workload certainly had an influence over who wanted to work in A&E. 'Trolley waits', as they had become known, continued to increase and more departments had to cope with patients waiting several hours or even days for a hospital bed. Because of the concern regarding these waits the RCN had surveyed the situation in 1994 and again in 1996. Finding the situation had not changed led to further meetings with political parties and the Department of Health to discuss these issues, highlight concerns and move to develop a plan to prevent the situation occurring the following year (chapter 8).

To help with recruitment, *Nursing Opportunities in Emergency Care* was issued by the Department of Health in 1997. This was one in a series of booklets offering a brief introduction to nursing in specialist areas within the NHS. It described the role of an emergency nurse indicating the unpredictability to be expected and the clinical knowledge required. 'If you enjoy variety and absence of routine – if juggling priorities and making decisions is a responsibility you feel comfortable with – emergency care nursing offers the stimulus of working with all kinds of people, with all kinds of needs.' The booklet bullet pointed the role of an emergency nurse identifying both lifesaving and minor injury care. It picked up the definition of what an emergency nurse is from the RCN A&E Nursing Associations *Challenging the Boundaries* (1994).

Having been appointed as the Honorary Consultant Nurse Advisor in Accident & Emergency Nursing to the Chief Nursing Officer, Yvonne Moores, at the Department of Health between 1994-1997, I was commissioned to undertake a Scoping exercise in January 1997. The report *Accident & Emergency – A Scoping report* was produced over a short period and reflected the current position and some of the issues affecting A&E and A&E nurses in England in 1997 (G Jones March 1997). Information was obtained from 26 A&E departments, three NHS regional offices and from informal discussions with a number of senior A&E nurses.

Main points from the summary showed:

- there were 227 major A&E departments in England and Wales
- many departments acted as a GP referral unit
- new attendances continued to rise, with a rapid increase in the number of medical, surgical and elderly patients
- all departments reported an increase in patient dependency especially in the medical and elderly patients
- increased activity was not linked with additional funding
- a number of departments were seeing an increase in primary care patients which appeared to be linked with the changes in GP call out arrangements
- only six out of the twenty six nurse managers considered their current nursing establishment to be reasonable. Twenty considered it to be under established
- a number of quality initiatives were in place as well as initiatives to support Health of the Nation targets
- despite complying with audit targets, nearly all departments either had no information technology or poor systems were in place
- all departments were complying with *The Patient's Charter* standards though outcomes varied
- all complained about 'trolley waits' due to lack of bed availability in the hospital, though some did report good bed management systems
- violence to staff was an increasing concern

- five areas of clinical practice were surveyed including trauma care, bereavement care, children, elderly and mental health. In all five, improvements had been achieved but more was required

Key recommendations included:

- a need for a national nursing establishment and skill mix framework based on patient dependency and patient activity
- NHS Executive guidelines on emergency bed management to be developed
- An ENB approved paediatric A&E module to be available to RGNs
- A study of elderly care in A&E departments and the production of principles of good practice
- A study of mental health care in A&E departments and the production of principles of good practice
- a study of the named nurse standard in A&E and the development of guidelines for implementation

*   *   *   *

Following Robert Crouch, Karen Castille, as Chair, steered the RCN A&E Nursing Association towards the millennium and further changes that were going to impact on A&E. In her first *A&E newsletter* report (Autumn 1997) Karen used the title 'Old chestnuts, new brooms.' Her emphasis was that although a new team was taking the Association forward many of the tasks ahead were extremely familiar including, skill mix, 'trolley waits', violence and aggression and meeting *The Patient's Charter* standards.

Other information included the annual presence of the committee at RCN Congress and two of the many important issues that had been discussed – the presence of relatives in the resuscitation room and the rationalisation of community and hospital services. The latter was of concern to A&E as it normally meant the threat of A&E department closures. A new editor had taken over the *A&E newsletter*. Lynn C Sbaih dedicated the Autumn edition to Kathie Butcher, the previous editor, and thanked her for all her hard work. Lynn encouraged nurses to contribute to the newsletter.

In the same newsletter I took the opportunity of explaining RCN Council to the membership and how it contributed to A&E nursing and how members could become more involved. Linking with local branches, regional co-ordinating committees, local A&E groups and attending RCN Congress were just some ways of members influencing the RCN and Council to A&E issues. I pointed out that the membership was the college and like shareholders of a company each RCN member in a sense, collectively owned the RCN, it was their organisation.

Although the membership was aware of the development of the Faculty of Emergency Nursing it was in this newsletter that for the first time Robert Crouch and I put the complete proposal to the membership. We explained what a faculty was, what it could achieve and how we intended taking the development forward. We encouraged members to give us their views and indicated that we would keep members updated through both *Emergency Nurse* and the *A&E newsletter* (chapter 10).

Another important article in the Autumn newsletter was the setting up of benchmarking in A&E. Benchmarking in the NHS was established in 1993 and this article demonstrated how the North West A&E Benchmarking group was taking it forward. The purpose of the group was to use benchmarking as a way of networking between A&Es so that good practice could be identified and compared. For me this reflected how A&E nurses have always moved quality of care forward and was a natural follow on from the RCN A&E Nursing Forum's 'Monitor' work and the networking group of A&E nurse managers in North East Thames during the 1980s.

Due to reader interest and the request for more editions of *Emergency Nurse,* in 1997 the journal went from 4 editions per year to 10 editions per year and from 32 pages to 40 pages. New features included the RCN A&E Nursing Association's report page and clinical articles becoming more in-depth and an increased length to 3,000 words.

* * * *

Following the 1997 landslide election victory for the Labour party, the June 1997 *Emergency Nurse* reported that the new Secretary of State for Health was Frank Dobson and he had spoken at RCN Congress in May. Mr Dobson said he believed in the treasured principles of fairness, quality and equality in health care and promised to remove the internal market and the paper chase which it created. He indicated that local commissioning would replace GP fundholding, that nurse prescribing would be implemented nationally, he would scrap local pay bargaining and take a fresh look at nurses pay. For me this signalled the NHS returning to being a service not a business; however, that was not to be as

Frank Dobson was eventually moved on and the business ethos continued. Despite this, New Labour was committed to strengthening the NHS and to helping resolve many of the A&E challenges both with money and enabling nurses in A&E to fully utilise their skills.

The RCN A&E Nursing Association celebrated its silver anniversary during 1997. In Brian Dolan's editorial in *Emergency Nurse* (October 1997) he reflected on some of the Association's achievements during its 25 years including seat belt legislation, managing 'trolley waits', the TNCC trauma course and the establishment of the three emergency nurse special interest groups of education and research, children in A&E, and the emergency nurse practitioner group.

At the annual conference the silver anniversary was celebrated with a great deal of nostalgia including my presentation of our 25-year history and the regular Friday night fancy dress dinner, that year based on a 1970's theme. It was also the 10th anniversary of our conference held at the Lord Daresbury Hotel. The staff of the hotel enjoyed our conferences so much they would hold a lottery to decide who would work that weekend as so many wanted to join us. Whatever theme we used for the Friday dinner the staff would dress up so they felt a part of the evening. Saturday night was always a formal black tie event.

At the 1997 annual *Nursing Standard* awards, the special recognition award was presented to Julie Watson and Margaret Marshall, staff nurses at Stirling A&E, Scotland for their professionalism displayed during the Dunblane primary school incident.

As the RCN A&E Nursing Association entered 1998 the spring *A&E newsletter* covered some current activities including the setting up of a working party to define the role of the A&E nurse in pre-hospital care and the training needs required. There was an article on the reform of the registration body (UKCC) and an article on how nurses could work in EU countries.

Emergency nursing was again recognised in 1998 with Una Bell, Director of A&E Services at Whipps Cross Hospital, London being awarded an RCN/*Nursing Standard* Lifetime Achievement Award. Presented by the Prime Minister Tony Blair, Una demonstrated the commitment of emergency nurses. Being one of the early pioneers of the national A&E Nurses Group as well as chairing the local London group, throughout her career Una had always reflected the diversity of emergency nursing. At the same event Tony Blair announced the establishment of the Consultant Nurse.

Several changes to the *A&E newsletter* took place in the winter of 1998. A new editor Jill Stringer took over from Lynn Sbaih but funding by the RCN to the Association was not keeping pace with membership numbers (now 10,136) and the cost of postage. Therefore the newsletter was reduced to two a year. Fortunately Smith &Nephew continued to support the costs of printing/design. The winter 1998 edition highlighted presentations from the November 1997 conference, reported on the emergency nursing research conference, updates on current association work and an interesting article on skin staples as an alternative to sutures.

The shift between the professions within emergency care was becoming much more apparent in the 1990s and despite as far back as 1984 when Yvonne McEwen wrote in *Paramedic UK* regarding territorial issues, at the 1998 A&E conference territorial shifts were again highlighted. Director of Nursing Developments at the King's Fund, Barbara Vaughan, spoke of territorial shifts in clinical practice and how junior doctors were frightened of the erosion of their role and the change of power relationship between themselves and nurses. She said, 'Stop worrying about turf, territories and boundaries and develop new approaches to breaking down traditional boundaries between medicine and nursing.'

Continuing New Labour's commitment to improving A&Es in England, in 1998, the 50th year of the NHS, £30 million was earmarked for A&E modernisation in 50 departments - a quarter of all A&Es in England. At the same time the NHS celebrated 50 years (1948 -1998) and on Wednesday 1st July 1998 the Chief Nursing Officer Yvonne Moores hosted a reception at the British Telecom tower. Fifty nurses both past and present were invited to attend; I was privileged to be one of them.

Demonstrating the flexibility of A&E nurses to respond to any situation, Sarah Caine, Staff Nurse at St Mary's Hospital, Paddington, came into her own during the 1999 Paddington rail crash. Sarah demonstrated how adaptable A&E nurses are by using her initiative when faced with a supermarket full of injured commuters. She used post-it notes as triage labels.

Developing the role of nurses was a key part of the government's strategy and *Making a difference strengthening nursing (NHS 1999)* aimed to strengthen the nurse's role and recognise the value of nurses, midwives and health visitors. In the foreword Frank Dobson said that all that the government was doing added up to a clear statement by the government of the value it placed on the contribution nurses, midwives and health visitors made to all our lives. *Making a difference* indicated that nurses, midwives and health visitors were crucial to the government's plans to modernise the NHS and to improve the public's health. The plan contained detail of how more nurses were to be recruited, strengthening education and training, developing a modern career framework (including pay modernisation and consultant nurse posts), improving working lives, enhancing the quality of care, strengthening leadership, modernisation of professional self-regulation, working in new ways (extending roles) and modernising including more nurse-led primary care services.

Making a difference linked nicely with my *Nursing Standard* careers article 'Accident and Emergency Nursing'(April 21 1999) where I summarised the developments taking place in A&E nursing and encouraged nurses to make a career in the specialty.

*   *   *   *

In preparation for the millennium, the RCN A&E Nursing Association published its action plan including further development of clinical care and a range of other issues that would impact on the service. The Association would continue the work on:

- the nurses role in pre-hospital care
- trauma care
- care of older people
- the health of young people

- skill mix
- the Faculty of Emergency Nursing
- health promotion/accident prevention
- Emergency Nurse Practitioners
- the future of A&E nursing
- communication and support to members
- violence and aggression
- european links

At the same time as the RCN A&E Nursing Association was planning for the millennium so too was the RCN Council. The proposal was a national structure that linked forum activists and branch activists closer together, the integrated membership framework.

Summary

This period reflected the major changes that occurred within the NHS, the change in government and the continuing closure of hospital beds and A&E departments leading to the unprecedented increase in 'trolley waits'. The annual conference had a facelift reflecting the increased popularity and demand for more choice in the programme. The need to divide the work of the conference between a scientific committee and the organising committee led to a dynamic conference that stood the test of time. The introduction of NHS Direct and the continued development of a number of RCN A&E Nursing Association initiatives prepared the A&E service for the new millennium.

References

Department of Health: (1992) *The Patient's Charter*. London: HMSO

Department of Health: (1997) *Nursing Opportunities in Emergency Care*. London: HMSO

Department of Health: (1999) *Making A Difference - strengthening the nursing, midwifery and health visiting contribution to health and healthcare*. London: HMSO

Jones G. (1997) *Accident & Emergency – A Scoping report* (Report to the Chief Nursing Officer Department of Health)

Jones G (1999) *Accident & Emergency Nursing*. Nursing Standard April 21/vol13/no31/1999 (59)

NHS Executive: (1996) *Developing Emergency Services in the Community*. London: HMSO

Paramedic UK: (1983/84) The Journal of the Association of Emergency Medical Technicians (AEMT). Published by AEMT.

Royal College of Nursing: (1994) *Accident & Emergency - Challenging the Boundaries*. RCN Publication

CHAPTER 6
INTO THE MILLENNIUM
SEPTEMBER 1999 – NOVEMBER 2004

Lynda Holt took over as the Chair from Karen Castille in September 1999, becoming the ninth Chair of the RCN A&E Nursing Forum/Association. The membership of the Association was over 11,000. Under a new RCN system, although election of individuals to the steering committee was in the hands of the membership, the election of Chair was made by the committee members. In her address to the membership at the November 1999 conference and in her follow up article in *Emergency Nurse* (December 1999/January 2000) and the spring 2000 edition of the *A&E newsletter*, Lynda highlighted how nurses were trying to maintain a quality service in the face of 'trolley waits', experienced emergency nurses leaving in droves and increased abuse and violence. She indicated how day to day nurses troubleshoot their way through the shift but recognised these were all considered to be 'old chestnuts' but were now linked with citizen power. Lynda emphasised, 'no one else was going to put it right for us; we must shake off the despondency and disempowerment and start to believe in ourselves.' She encouraged delegates to take responsibility, value their contribution and unlock the potential of emergency nursing. For me that speech and article was a reminder of the 1984 challenge in Edinburgh that inspired me to become involved with the forum at national level.

Yet again in 2000 changes to the RCN structure meant the steering group was now renamed the policy and practice group. This came about because of the move to link forums/associations into what was termed 'fields of practice'. As Vice-Chair of RCN Council I chaired the National Forums Committee. At one meeting a year earlier I had suggested linking forums/associations with council members so they had a direct link into policy without having to go through other channels. This led to the children's advisor suggesting all the children's groups could work together, link with one council member and the term 'field of practice' was born. Although this worked well for such groupings, for others it was impractical but as often occurred in the RCN, the staff wanted to link other forums and associations together into 'fields of practice' which was something I opposed because of the diversity of the forums. Despite much opposition from the forums/associations that had little similarity they were brought together as 'fields of practice' and for a period of about two years this structure remained. By 2002 the name policy and practice group reverted to steering committee and the term 'field of practice' was no longer used.

Jill Stringer relinquished the editorship of the *A&E newsletter* due to moving to one of the new posts created at NHS Direct and Judith Morgan became the new editor in spring 2000. Judith thanked Jill for her contribution and continued her editorial on reporting the success of the November 1999 conference that for one year only had been held in Blackpool. From feedback and letters in the *A&E newsletter*, delegates appeared to appreciate the more informal approach the conference had taken on, especially the fringe meetings between the delegates and the steering committee members. The newsletter continued to report on a number of issues including the role of the health care assistant (previously the auxiliary), staffing and skill mix, violence and aggression and increased workload.

In the summer of 2000 the RCN A&E Nursing Association celebrated the millennium by organising the second international conference for emergency nursing. *Emergency Nursing 2000 and Beyond* was held in Edinburgh, Scotland in August and two major events within the conference moved emergency nurses across the world closer together. The first was the signing of the 'International Declaration of Co-operation and Friendship'. Signed by over 200 emergency nurses representing nineteen countries, the wording affirmed the shared principles, in a spirit of partnership and mutual respect:

> To promote the value of emergency nursing worldwide, to the family of nursing, fellow health workers and the communities we serve
>
> To promote the science and art of emergency nursing worldwide
>
> To promote co-operation and friendship among emergency nurses worldwide
>
> And to do this through every channel available, including local, national and international nursing organisations, traditional and new forms of communication and decision-making bodies everywhere.

Linked with the declaration we were privileged to have attending the conference Mireille Kingmar, International Council of Nurses (ICN) Nursing and Health Policy Consultant. One of Mireille's remits was emergency care. Following a discussion we were offered the opportunity of a web page on the ICN website. Officially recorded as the

'International Collaboration of National Emergency Nursing Organisations', the declaration was published on the site and each organisation added information enabling the tool to maintain international links without the bureaucracy of a formal organisation.

Following the conference I travelled to the ENA conference in Chicago in September and again emergency nurses signed the declaration. This was followed up with a visit in June 2001 to the International Council of Nurses (ICN) conference in Copenhagen. I spoke on the subject and then chaired an inaugural meeting with representatives from the UK, Cyprus, Denmark, Greece, Italy, Jamaica, Taiwan, Seychelles, South Africa, Sweden and the USA to formally launch the emergency nursing ICN webpage.

*   *   *   *

Although the bed reduction, increased workload and 'trolley waits' had escalated during the whole of the 1990s the situation came to a head during the new millennium. The RCN A&E Nursing Association worked closely with the Community Health Councils and the RCN Council regarding pressures in A&E. The RCN formed an emergency pressure group to address the continuing challenge of emergency workload and Lynda Holt was involved in top-level meetings both at the RCN and government level over A&E 'trolley waits'. Despite all previous work the pressure in all A&E units was relentless (chapter 8).

As more A&E units were being closed or amalgamated other initiatives were emerging such as the hybrid emergency care model in North West London. Opened in early 1999 following the closure of an A&E department, the model was designed to fill a gap between minor injury units and the A&E department. Staffing was a mix of staff grade doctors

ENPs and other nurses. Reported in *Emergency Nurse* (February 2001) the conclusion was that the model seemed a viable proposition for the provision of services.

In June 1999, Her Majesty the Queen formally opened the Scottish Parliament which took over responsibility for the NHS in Scotland. The achievements in the first year as reported in the winter 2000 *A&E newsletter* included an acute services strategy, creation of the Nursing and Midwifery Practice Development Unit, development of the Scottish version of NHS Direct, a range of developments in education and training and an occupational health strategy.

In early 2000, the Prime Minister Tony Blair promised a revolution in A&E care including giving appropriate trained nurses greater powers to order x-rays, blood tests and other diagnostic procedures, to interpret the results, give medication and discharge patients. Through the modernising A&E initiatives the plan was to empower triage nurses so patients received a streamlined service – either whole treatment from the triage nurse, be side-tracked to a more appropriate part of the system or referred directly to other services. Dr Mike Lambert, A&E Consultant who led the programme with the input from three emergency nurses (Karen Castille, Andrew Kent and David MacPhee) suggested the present system delivered largely by junior doctors should be replaced by experienced, autonomous staff, such as nurse practitioners, community psychiatric nurses and paramedics. These developments it was hoped would reduce the waiting times especially for the less acute patients.

In July 2001, the idea of improved links between all parts of emergency care was highlighted by the health minister, indicating a need for a strategy to integrate all the different parts of emergency care - A&E, GP out of hours service, minor injury units, walk-in centres and NHS Direct. This of course was not the first time this idea had been suggested. Back in September 1998, Robert Crouch in his guest editorial in *Emergency Nurse* suggested the development of an integrated emergency care system and I had suggested a similar approach in 1993 (*Emergency Nurse* spring 1993).

As well as the number of initiatives the government had launched, they also continued to inject money into the service. A cash injection of £2bn per year for the next four years was announced and in addition modernisation fund monies were made available to improve A&E departments throughout England. This money was an additional £35 million for further modernisation of A&E departments on top of the money provided under the modernisation programme in England which started in 1998. This meant that £150 million was invested. The money led to new assessment and observation wards, improved resuscitation facilities, specific areas for children, better links between A&E and primary care and faster access to diagnostic facilitates.

The NHS Plan (DOH 2000) and *Reforming Emergency Care* (DOH 2001) both highlighted a traditional system of service provision that was inadequate, lacking in national standards, in drastic need of modernisation and unable to cope with the demands placed upon it. A massive plan of investment outlined in each document identified a vision of patient-centred care that was free of many of the old fashioned barriers and demarcations between staff groups. A need for improved access, new systems and processes and new ways of working was identified together with a demand for less waiting and more appropriate trained staff.

Reforming Emergency Care was developed by a working party comprising representatives from most of the Royal Colleges including the RCN to which the A&E Nursing Association was a key contributor. The objective of the reform was to develop a fast, responsive and effective emergency care service for patients. The major impacts were envisaged as being:

- ending long waits in A&E for admission to hospital
- improving ambulance responses to life threatening emergencies
- providing a wider range of services appropriate to patients' needs
- ending widespread bed blocking in the NHS
- minimising the number of cases where patients have their operations cancelled on the day of surgery

Lynda Holt commented in the spring 2002 *A&E newsletter* that one of the most important elements of *Reforming Emergency Care* was that it talked about competency rather than the professional background as the key driver for delivering patient-centred, quality care. Lynda considered the principle behind the document sound and it offered emergency nursing profound opportunities. As she said, 'We must grab them because we have been asking for them long enough.'

During 2002 a series of guidelines and monitoring initiatives were released ensuring that the government reforms were taking place and that waiting times were being adhered to. In April 2002 a news item in *Emergency Nurse* reported that the Department of Health had issued guidelines to all A&E

departments that patients must be 'streamed' into minor, major and resus by the end of the year. In reality, this had always happened however when one area became busy other areas slowed or stopped (usually the minors). The intention was to ensure all three streams continued to function. Two more streams were to be established by 2004, these were self-care and primary care. It was also reported that protocols to allow triage nurses where possible to refer directly to inpatient specialties would be established.

By May 2002 the Department of Health was reported to be 'cracking down' on waiting times. It was reported that it was 'no longer acceptable for patients to wait very long periods.' There was also concern around a lack of active bed management in some hospitals and there was to be closer collaboration between health and social care.

Despite this, at the 2002 RCN Congress concern was raised about the worsening in patient care as pressures on the NHS continue to increase. It was reported in *Emergency Nurse* in June that a lack of adequate long-term care provision and inappropriate primary care use had led to extra workload for A&E nurses.

The October 2002 *Emergency Nurse* reported that the 1st anniversary of *Reforming Emergency Care* showed figures suggesting that some improvement had occurred with fewer patients waiting more than four hours. Streaming to ENPs was reducing minor injury waiting and ambulance staff were treating more patients in their own homes.

The NHS Modernisation Agency launched a nationwide emergency service collaborative across 30 sites in November 2002. It aimed to cut waiting times and improve patient experiences with each site awarded £115,000 to take a whole systems look at how to improve the services. There were also workshops developed to enable a faster service which was named 'see and treat'. By February 2003 *Emergency Nurse* reported that a further 69 departments were to join the national emergency services collaborative, bringing the total to 99.

In my November 2002 *Emergency Nurse* board's eye view I reflected on the 30th anniversary of the RCN A&E Nursing Association and pointed out that very little in the *Reforming Emergency Care* document was new but what it did was to lay out what has worked well in hospital and community settings so that others could benefit from good practice. Of course this was not the end of the story.

*   *   *   *

Although there was a long way to go to solve many of the A&E issues, by 2003 England was doing far better than Wales as Kevin Randall and Jamie Jones of the Emergency Nursing Forum of Wales (established in October 2001) pointed out in an article in the spring 2003 *A&E newsletter*. The article indicated the NHS plan for Wales lacked measurable objectives for emergency care. NHS trusts in Wales did not receive a 'pot of gold' to redevelop their A&E departments. Walk-in centres were developed in England, not in Wales and ENPs, while thriving in England, were a rare breed in Wales as were consultant nurse posts in emergency care. One light however, was the Welsh Assembly announcing a review of emergency services. This led to the establishment of the Welsh Emergency Care Access Collaborative to support the delivery of emergency care services across Wales. The goal was to radically improve patient and carer experiences in emergency access by reducing treatment delays and waiting times while supporting staff through the improvement of systems and processes (chapter 8).

In 2003 the RCN A&E Nursing Association changed its name to the RCN Emergency Care Association (ECA) and the *A&E newsletter* was renamed *Emergency Care Association newsletter*. The special interest groups and local groups followed suit. These changes reflected far better the diversity of emergency nursing that was now available to the public as well as reflecting the key specialty developments under the wider heading of emergency nursing. The name change also reflected the association's support for A&E departments to be renamed emergency departments.

This change from Accident & Emergency to Emergency was also linked with a growing debate over the word 'Accident'. Many in trauma care argued that very few injuries were truly accidents as many could have been predicted. The person who stands below a cliff where a notice clearly states 'falling rocks' can hardly say that when hit by a rock it was an accident. The same applies to many road crash incidents, hence the change from road traffic accident (RTA) to road traffic crash (RTC).

In 2004 The British Association for Accident & Emergency Medicine followed suit, becoming the British Association for Emergency Medicine (BAEM).

To further support emergency care staff to achieve the modernisation programme in England, in April 2004 *Emergency Nurse* reported the appointment of Jane Cummings as the Department of Health's national project lead for emergency care. She said, 'I probably didn't think that emergency care would be at the point it is today, although I always felt very strongly that its time would come.' Her job was to direct and support the development and improvement of emergency care services and bring together the people and resources working across the health department and the NHS Modernisation Agency. In 2005 this post was taken up by Lis Nixon.

Over the next 12 months further developments of emergency care networks were planned that encompassed health and social services across local and strategic community and acute care settings. Health Secretary John Reid indicated that a proper, clear, comprehensive system of care and an end to the borders between the old empires of primary secondary and social services must occur.

*   *   *   *

Awards/honours were endowed to emergency care members during this five year period reflecting the commitment shown to emergency nursing, to the association and to the advancement of emergency care. Fellowship of the RCN was awarded to Robert Crouch in 1999 and I followed with my Fellowship in 2002. In 2001 Gabby Lomas was awarded the RCN Award of Merit for services to members of the RCN. This was in recognition of her work provided through TNCC and her role organising the annual A&E conference. In 2003 I was appointed Commander of the Order of the British Empire (CBE) for services to emergency nursing and Robert Crouch as an Officer of the Order of the British Empire (OBE). Also in 2003, Pat Moir, Sister, A&E, Royal Aberdeen Children's Hospital was appointed a Member of the Order of the British Empire (MBE) for services to emergency nursing. Elizabeth Yates, Nurse Manager at Preston A&E Lancashire was awarded the *Nursing Standard* Millennium Medical Nursing Award for her work with victims of domestic violence. Nick Castle, Consultant Nurse,

Frimley Park Hospital, Surrey was a winner in the *Nursing Standard* awards (2004) for his work on shared learning between A&E and the ambulance service in the UK and South Africa. Also in 2004, Karen Castille was appointed an OBE for services to nursing.

Summary

This five year period was the worst time for A&E waiting and 'trolley waits'. At the same time, it was the period when A&E nurses and in particular representatives of the RCN A&E Nursing Association had the opportunity to influence the way these issues could be addressed. As the reader will see in the forthcoming chapters, the changes that were embryonic at this time were the catalyst to the successful delivery of a much improved service and the almost total eradication of 'trolley waits'. On the international stage it was the time when A&E nurses had and took the opportunity to join together in the declaration of co-operation and friendship and through the ICN website had the means of staying in contact across the globe.

References

Department of Health: (2000) *The NHS Plan- a plan for investment, a plan for reform.* London: HMSO

Department of Health: (2001) *Reforming Emergency Care.* London: HMSO

CHAPTER 7

FROM SUCCESS TO DISAPPOINTMENT NOVEMBER 2004 – SEPTEMBER 2007

Grant Williams became Chair of the ECA during the 2004 conference and continued the excellent work that had been established over many years. In his first Chair's *ECA newsletter* report (spring 2005), he welcomed the new committee members and thanked Lynda for her leadership and enthusiasm over the past six years. Administrative errors during the election of the steering group members earlier in the year resulted in the committee that Grant now led being nine-strong. The sub groups of the RCN Emergency Care Association continued to flourish with the minor injury network having over 200 members and the paediatric group renamed and with a new committee.

The editor of what was now the *ECA newsletter* Judith Morgan, headed her editorial '2005 is filled with exciting opportunities'. Listing those opportunities she included the Faculty of Emergency Nursing moving from the project and founding status to becoming a reality, the international conference that was planned for November 2005 and planned conferences in Northern Ireland, Wales and a multi-professional paediatric conference in London

In the report of Grant's election in *Emergency Nurse* (December 2004), he indicated that he wanted to bring a fresh focus to developments in UK emergency nursing outside England. He was also keen to make the ECA more 'membership led' and for the steering committee to be more 'transparent and accessible'. Grant pointed out that he was the first Chair from Wales in the organisation's 32-year history.

The March 2005 edition of *Emergency Nurse* was the last to be edited by Brian Dolan. Brian had taken the journal from its very early days as an insert in *Nursing Standard* through to one of the most successful emergency nursing journals in the UK. In his last editorial he looked back at how the journal had developed to become the top selling subscription-only journal of its kind in the world. The new editor from the April edition was Claire Picton. Claire mapped out her ideas for the future. On reflection I should have stepped down from the editorial board at this time but continued for a further year until being asked to 'stand aside' so making room for new talent!

Following the July 2005 London terrorist attacks, Grant reported in his autumn 2005 Chair's report that he had received an overwhelming number of messages of support and goodwill from colleagues at home and across the globe to all the staff who had provided care during and following the atrocity.

The *Healthcare Commission review of A&E services* published in August 2005 urged the recruitment of emergency staff to become more focussed on specific activities. The review showed that there had been a 'substantial increase' in staffing levels since 2000 with records suggesting a 20% rise in the number of nurses, a 27% rise in doctors and 37% rise in consultants working in A&E departments in England. However, the Commission said there was no association between relative increases in staff and improvement in time patients spent in A&E. The commission report stated that when funding was made available for extra staff, it should be used to fulfil a specific purpose. The review called for more use of nurse practitioners and nurses trained to treat children.

In September 2005 *Emergency Nurse* reported that the Department of Health was funding 100 places on a unique leadership programme for consultant nurses, senior nurses and modern matrons in emergency care. The purpose was aimed at improving unscheduled care, to sustain the 4-hour target, ensure that patients remained at the heart of modernisation and increase staff satisfaction. Unfortunately by November 2006 a report in *Emergency Nurse* suggested that the second wave funding was in question across England due to NHS Trusts struggling with multi-million pound deficits.

The ECA Conference in November 2005 celebrated international partnerships that had lasted 20 years. Since the first ever international conference held in London in 1985, emergency nurses from across the globe had continued links. As emergency nurses from across the globe gathered together at the De Vere Carden Park Hotel in Cheshire, they rededicated the international declaration of co-operation and friendship that was first signed at the second international conference in 2000. The conference also celebrated 15 years since TNCC had come to the UK.

Due to the RCN Council voting in February 2006 to adopt a new 'professional development framework', doubts were raised in the March *Emergency Nurse* regarding the future viability of the ECA and Faculty of Emergency Nursing (FEN). Originally proposed in late 2004, under the plan the College's 76 forums, including the ECA, would be replaced with eight divisions. This caused uproar amongst all the professional entities in the RCN and led to the Faculty of Emergency Nursing leaving the RCN and becoming an independent body (chapter 10). Discussions across all forums/associations continued throughout 2006.

Also reported in the March edition of *Emergency Nurse* was the success of Grant Williams being elected to represent Wales as a member of the Nursing and Midwifery Council (NMC). Responding to the congratulations Grant indicated he would continue his term of office as Chair of the ECA until November.

In 2006 for the first time, and unfortunately the only time, the membership celebrated the first joint conference of the RCN Emergency Care Association and the Faculty of Emergency Nursing. Held as the national conference in November of that year it had been hoped that this joint approach to the conference would become the norm. However, due to the proposed changes to the RCN professional entities and other factors highlighted below and in chapter 10, this was never to be. During an updated report on FEN given by Jill Windle, Chair of FEN, she took the opportunity to present me with the first Honorary Fellowship of the Faculty of Emergency Nursing. I was honoured to receive this recognition of my work and was speechless when 500 A&E nurses gave me a standing ovation.

*   *   *   *

On the closing day of the 2006 conference Kevin Randall became the 11th Chair of the RCN A&E/Emergency Care Association. Unfortunately this was the last conference on the scale that had been the norm since 1986. Despite 20 years of successful independently run conferences and the ability of the Association to use any profits to enhance the service of emergency care, change of RCN financial guidelines and internal audits meant that the ECA was no longer allowed to run the conference independently. This, with the RCN proposed changes to the ECA structure, was yet another blow to the members.

Not long into 2007, internal issues within the ECA committee came to the fore and this meant they were unable to put forward a united front to ensure the conference remained in the hands of the ECA and to reject the proposed changes to the forum structure.

It is difficult for me to give a clear account of the reasons behind the internal issues, however it is safe to say that with the possible changes to the ECA within the RCN structure, the loss of the ability to continue to organise the annual conference and a range of internal issues between individual committee and staff members, it was not surprising that *Emergency Nurse* (June 2007) reported the RCN was discussing the future of the ECA following the resignation of the chair, vice-chair, one committee member and the *ECA newsletter* editor. It was very disappointing for so many members and for me personally as I could see an Association that had developed so well over the last 35 years losing much that had been achieved and it was going to take a lot to return it to its former glory. Rather than celebrating 35 years of emergency nursing the ECA was in meltdown.

Following widespread criticism of the planned changes to the professional entities, by September 2007 the controversial plans had been shelved. Ironically, had these proposals never been agreed in the first place the Faculty of Emergency Nursing may not have dissociated from the RCN and perhaps the individuals running the ECA could have found a way forward. Over my many years with the RCN, in my opinion one of its major downfalls has been the almost continual re-structuring of the specialist entities and always taking a top down approach. It never works.

The ECA was not the only body that had major challenges ahead; some A&E nurses felt the NHS was possibly heading into a crisis. The board's eye view by Julian Newell (*Emergency Nurse* April 2007) looked at cuts and efficiency savings. While agreeing there were ways to make efficiency savings, his concern was the move by some trusts to demote or make nurses redundant, including senior staff posts being disestablished. Julian pointed out that even Health Secretary Patricia Hewitt seemed to agree with this move as she was reported by the BBC to have said, 'The NHS is on track to break even by the end of March 2007' but that 'jobs would be cut.' Further cuts were also reported in the May 2007 *Emergency Nurse* board's eye view and this time it was funding cuts to training and education with trusts achieving solvency by slashing training budgets.

In 2007 the Department of Health set up an advisory team to help configure emergency services. Ten members made up the team yet only one was a nurse. Reporting in the May 2007 *Emergency Nurse*, the ECA indicated that they were very disappointed with the team make up. Despite this intervention and a 'healthy exchange of views', *Emergency Nurse* (December 2007) reported on the interim report *Our NHS Our Future*. Published in October by Health Minister Sir Ara Darzi it set out a vision of a health service that was fair, personalised, effective and safe. For emergency care it opened up the possibility of growth in urgent care centres and minor injury units. Due to the proposed 'super emergency centres' for the provision of trauma, stroke and cardiac care, a move to radically reconfigure emergency departments was suggested. The report continued to support further development of the paramedic service, community nurses and GP out-of-hours services.

Summary

This period started off so well with the continuation of the excellent work that had gone before but ended with the ECA in meltdown. Ironically the emergency care service had almost settled from many years of 'trolley waits' and the opportunities were there to once again focus on the future development of emergency nursing. Unfortunately the unique conferences of the past have never returned and the opportunities that so many A&E nurses had to join together on an annual basis have been lost. The Faculty of Emergency Nursing is still active as an independent organisation but has never achieved the full aims and objectives of the original pioneers.

To end Part One on a positive note although outside of the dates covered in this book, the ECA has survived the turmoil of 2007 and committee members still represent emergency nurses and continue to develop emergency care. A prime example of this is the development of the Baseline Emergency Staffing Tool (chapter 12).

The RCN ECA webpage shows the Association has 8,561 members (January 2021) and a clear strategy:

- lobbying on issues affecting emergency care nurses in a variety of arenas locally, nationally and internationally.

- maintaining a visible presence in National Emergency Care strategy meetings, including meeting with the key political parties in all four nations.

- formally responding to consultations and representing emergency care views in the media.

- ensuring that the RCN understand issues which are important to the emergency care fraternity.

- promoting professional development through affiliation with the RCNi publication *Emergency Nurse*.

References

Department of Health: (2007) *Our NHS Our Future*. London: HMSO

Healthcare Commission: (2005) *Review of A&E services*. London: HMSO

PART TWO
CHAPTER 8
WORKLOAD

Since the first casualty unit was established in the 19th century, workload and staffing have always been a challenge and year on year the number of people attending for care continues to increase. As far back as the days before casualty, in 1678, staff of St Bartholomew's Hospital London thought 8 injured/ill patients a week was burdensome and in 1696 that had increased to 50 patients per week (Guly 2005).

It was often difficult to obtain accurate attendance figures in the early days of A&E mainly due to a lack of computerised records; the first two trials of micro-computers in A&E for record keeping were in early 1983 (*A&E newsletter* January 1983) and even in 1989 82% of 115 A&E departments surveyed did not have computer systems. The difficulty also arose because of the way individual patients were listed. In those early days some departments included patients referred from a GP, in others that was not the case. Not all departments recorded new patients separately from re-attenders, arguing that it was the total number of patients that created the workload. While I agree that total numbers are essential it is important to differentiate the number of new attenders from re-attenders. However, what we do see from the examples below is that year on year A&E attendances increased and the reasons were complex.

A report initiated in September 1976 by the RCN Association of Nursing Practice and reported in the March 1977 *Nursing Standard* showed that social changes during the past 25 years had a striking effect on both the quantity and the quality of demand for nursing care. It highlighted the sharp increase in the number of vulnerable people, more people living alone and fewer being personally cared for by relatives thus creating more demand for medical and social services. Changed morbidity patterns showed that as infectious diseases declined these were replaced by the effects of degenerative changes. The report showed the increase in casualties from road accidents was up from 216,000 in 1959 to 325,000 in 1974. Concern was also raised regarding the effect the increased workload was having on nurses and in particular indicating that accident and emergency departments were most at risk. It was reported that A&E staff were working overtime and missing meals in order to minimise the risk to patients.

The *A&E newsletter* (January 1986) reported attendance figures produced by the Department of Health and Social Security (England) in 1984. These showed new attendances up 2.6% to 10.2 million and total attendances up 1.2% to 13.8 million. The National Audit Office reports (1992 England & Scotland) showed new patient attendance had increased in England to 11.2 million in 1990/91 and in Scotland for the same period 1.2 million new patients. For England, a lack of GP and community services especially at night, weekends and bank holidays were suggested as some of the reasons for the increase.

The Audit Commission report *By Accident or Design* in 1996 reported that there were 15 million visits to A&E departments in England & Wales each year covering 227 major A&E departments, treating on average between 70-200 patients a day and costing about £600 million each year. The report gave a general indication of the function of A&E and listed patients as falling into 6 main categories - multiple injuries (less than 0.5%), others for immediate care (average 12%), GP referred (17%), follow up patients to A&E clinics

(12%), return to specialist outpatient (9%), patients discharged after examination/treatment (60%). The report indicated that new attendances had risen by a third over the past 15 years, an average of 2% a year since 1981. It also listed a host of reasons patients attend A&E, with most for lacerations and least for burns. The report indicated that the increased workload was due to medical and surgical emergencies and gave a number of reasons from clinical to social. The Commission also considered two thirds of A&E departments to be too small to be fully effective and that some should close.

The RCN children in A&E special interest group reported in the October 1998 *Emergency Nurse* that in 1997 25-30% of A&E workload was from the 0-16 years old

The Department of Health figures reported in *Emergency Nurse* (November 2000) showed total A&E attendance in England had increased by 2.4% to 14.6 million.

Apart from annual figures, it is also useful to look at special events as these often show a massive increase, albeit for a shorter period. Five examples taken from the Department of Health millennium night summary (*Emergency Nurse* February 2000) show that in London 2,300 ambulance calls were taken in the first 6 hours of the New Year (42% up on the same period in 1999). St Thomas' Hospital, London saw over 200 patients after midnight, many of which were alcohol related. In the Trent region, A&E attendances were up by 20% and ambulance calls up 25%. In the Eastern region, hospitals saw a 50% increase in attendances and in Greater Manchester the ambulance service had its busiest night ever and took just under 1,200 calls in the 12 hours either side of midnight.

In 2003, *Freedom to practice: dispelling the myths,* a joint RCN & Department of Health booklet, while providing a resource to nurses and others to clarify what they were allowed and able to do within their codes of practice, also provided some interesting statistics. It indicated that in a typical day 1 million people contacted a GP, 11,500 required urgent transport to hospital by ambulance and 33,000 people attended an emergency department. One in 4 patients attending the emergency department were children and 1 in 10 was over 75yrs. Around 16% of patients needed admission and over 24% of those were over 75 years.

Based on these statistics, the report highlighted a number of basic principles, the first of which was all services must be designed from the point of view of the patient. It emphasised the investment in walk-in centres to support the 24/48 hour primary care access target and the 4-hour Emergency department target.

The report emphasised that all hospitals, primary care, social care and ambulance services were part of the Emergency Services Collaborative, a national programme designed to help reduce waiting times in Emergency Departments and improve the experience of patients and carers.

*   *   *   *

No single factor can explain the continued increase in attendance figures; rather it is a complex multifactorial event. One obvious factor is an increased population and movement of people due to new housing and job location; however, it is also about an ageing population, how individuals interpret an emergency and use the A&E services, various social trends of society and how these impacted on the department and the reduction in the number of A&E departments since the mid-1980s.

The ageing population.
As the 1990s progressed, one factor leading to the increased workload in most emergency departments was the ageing population. The increase in acute on chronic conditions, plus far more people living to an older age, had a dramatic influence on the way emergency departments functioned. Once linked to orthopaedic departments due to A&E being seen as an off shoot of orthopaedics, now many departments were being linked to medicine and care of the elderly units.

How individuals interpret an emergency and use the A&E services.
This has been one of the most long running debates between the public and health professionals since the beginning of health care, and certainly continues today. As reported in Part One this topic began with the emergence of the GP in the 19th century, continued with the establishment of the NHS in 1948, again was emphasised in the change of name from casualty to A&E in the 1960s and from A&E to emergency departments in the early 2000s.

As far back as October 1986, the *A&E newsletter* reported on two initiatives to persuade patients to attend their GP and not the A&E department. One was a campaign in Brent & Harrow, London where it was suggested that an estimated 30% of all patients were not emergencies. By using leaflets and posters it stressed that A&E was for serious accidents and life-threatening emergencies. The second was what was termed an innovative scheme for a GP unit to be located in the London Hospital, Whitechapel where studies showed that 60% of patients should have attended their GP.

A King's Fund survey in 1991/2 involving 855 A&E primary care attenders and 744 patients visiting a GP in Camberwell, London showed a range of reasons why individuals use A&E and this was mainly due to their symptoms rather than dissatisfaction with the GP. Trauma and minor injuries were mainly seen as A&E attendance while respiratory problems were seen as GP related (*Emergency Nurse* March 1992).

Further work at King's College Hospital, London in 1993 identified the primary care and A&E needs of the patient. King's was already providing a primary care service through GPs located within the department. *New Challenges in A&E: Developing the Primary Care Role of A&E Nurses* describes the results of a one-year project in 1992/3 which aimed to develop a new system of patient-centred triage as part of a high quality, responsive A&E service. New triage decision pathways were developed that helped the triage nurse categorise the patient into A&E or primary care and each with a timed to doctor scale. A training programme was developed to help the nurse make the correct decision and the philosophy was that primary care was as important as A&E.

An article by Robert Crouch, 'Inappropriate attender' in the first *Emergency Nurse* (March 1992) looked at how the public's perception of A&E is often at odds with the nurses' view. As he pointed out, the patient attends for help or advice because the service is available 24 hours per day, 365 days per year. He concluded that despite the workload and frustration, A&E should maintain an open door policy. Despite Robert's request many A&E staff still continued to regard many patients as 'inappropriate'. The *A&E newsletter* (June 1993) reported on an article published in the *Nursing Times* journal suggesting that providers of A&E services regarded approximately 40-50% of patients attending A&E as more appropriate attenders at GP surgeries.

The autumn 2002 *A&E newsletter* contained an article by consultant nurse Robert Sowney on providing non-judgemental care. He argued that non-judgemental care is based on the notion that health care professionals will not apportion blame or a degree of patient responsibility for the cause of a health need or problem. It implies that the professional will recognise a patient's weakness or failure without actually judging them. He pointed out that work by Sanders (2000) revealed that nurses considered non-urgent and inappropriate work trivial, time-consuming and unrewarding. Nurses tended to show frustration, irritation and less sympathy and were less motivated to help this category of patient.

Fast forward to March 2006 and the debate continued with the *Emergency Nurse* Editor Claire Picton reviewing why patients attend A&E rather than many of the community services available. The conclusion she drew was because they have choice and in her view there was two reasons: 1) Patients have, or believe they have, little choice but to go to A&E because they find making appointments with GPs too difficult or appointments are too far in the future. 2) Patients believe that they will receive a better, easier and quicker service if they present to A&E.

Probably the most significant comment made on the subject was from the Editor of *Emergency Nurse* (Brian Dolan) in his February 1999 editorial, 'There is no such thing as inappropriate attenders, only services that are inappropriate for their needs.'

Social trends of society and how these impacted on the department. Both healthy and not so healthy recreational activities all had an influence on the numbers of patients attending A&E. Healthy activities included marathon runners, sporting activities, and diving incidents. The not so healthy included an increase in drug misuse including glue sniffing, opiates, alcohol and other mind changing substances including the increased abuse of inhalers by adolescents (May 1984 *A&E newsletter*). In the January 1984 *A&E newsletter* it was reported that an article in the journal *Pulse* drew attention to a new problem identified by the Home Secretary, that of 'body packing'. The report indicated that due to the increased success of catching criminals where heroin was being brought into the country in conventional means, it was now being brought in as 'body packing' (heroin swallowed in impermeable material) and cocaine being wrapped in aluminium foil and latex tubing. These inevitably had a risk of perforating and the drug leaking out into the individual's stomach/bowel and then to the blood. I recall one such person admitted to our hospital because of this happening.

Measures that were being put in place to address the drug misuse problems included restrictive sales, investigation into large quantity purchase especially by teenagers and a regional authority assessment of the problems. The same newsletter (January 1984) indicated that despite a decline in suicide rates between 1965 and 1975, considered in part due to the change from coal gas to natural gas and in the reduction in prescriptions for barbiturates, there was now an increase. The increase was due to the use of car exhaust fumes (increased by 75%), the person physically setting themselves on fire, using firearms and explosives. The more common methods of suicide were also on the increase including hanging, drowning and jumping. Criminal activity in the local area also increased or changed the workload such as seen in blunt versus penetrating trauma with increased knife crime being an example. A rise in the number of patients attending A&E with alcohol related conditions was also reported in the May 2006 *Emergency Nurse*.

Reduction in the number of A&E departments since the mid-1980s. While often supported by clinical staff on clinical grounds, any closure of a department has a knock on effect on those left open. In Essex alone, three A&E departments were closed in the 1990s. In March 1994 A&E consultant Dr Keith Little from Edinburgh, Scotland and I (as Chair of the RCN A&E Nursing Association) were interviewed for the magazine *Candis* on the effects of 'rationalisation' on A&E services or as the article put it 'efficiency' directives within the NHS. While both of us agreed with the principle of centralising emergency services when a better service can be achieved, both of us were also critical of the way it is often conducted. Dr Little pointed out that in the 'centralisation' process in Edinburgh not enough provision was made in the form of increased staffing levels. I indicated that 'centralisation' or 'rationalisations' are still only euphemisms for closure of services.

With the reduction in A&E departments and centralisation often leading to larger departments but within the same size hospital, the ability of the hospital to cope with the increased workload can be a challenge. As the Audit Commission identified in their review (2001), while waits to be assessed and treated were under the control of A&E, admissions were affected by waits for test results, absence of other doctors or lack of beds - exactly my experience in 1991/2 at Basildon when Orsett A&E was closed. The Audit Commission also recognised that delays for admission can hold up assessment and treatment due to waiting patients taking up cubicles. They found smaller departments were more efficient across the board in waiting times than larger departments. Despite these findings, an article in the May 2006 *Emergency Nurse* described the proposal from members of the health and social care think-tank to cut emergency departments (*Strengthening Local Services: The future of the acute hospital*). This proposal was supported by the President of the Royal College of Surgeons, indicating that departments should be halved from the current 200 to 100. This was followed up by a report in the October 2006 *Emergency Nurse* that a possible 60 departments were to close in England.

*   *   *   *

Another factor that influenced workload was the way individual departments were used to assess patients seen by the GP and then referred to a specialty within the hospital. As reported in the third edition of the *A&E newsletter* (December 1983) the Editor Ethel Buckles said, 'Quite often these very ill people have to wait for hours; we then discover that we have run out of beds in that specialty'. She went on to say, 'The department rapidly becomes blocked by admissions and we have great difficulty in finding the space and the staff to accommodate the accident patient.' This was the first reference in the *A&E newsletter* to admission/bed issues but was certainly not going to be the last. More recently due to changes brought forward in the 1990s and 2000s most hospitals have medical/surgical assessment units where GP referred patients attend.

Although bed availability had always been a challenge in some hospitals, it started to become commonplace in almost all hospitals from the mid-1980s onwards due to bed reductions across the whole of the NHS. By 1995, NHS beds had been cut to 212,000 from the previous 335,000 in 1984 (*Emergency Nurse* November 2000) and the so called 'trolley waits' were becoming the norm. A&E departments started to look more like a hospital ward. There is no doubt that 'trolley waits' created an unprecedented workload that fundamentally changed the normal workings of most A&E departments in the UK. Even at Orsett Hospital in the late 1980s, where the problems were far less than in other hospitals in the region, I recall being asked if some patients could stay in the fracture clinic overnight. My answer was no. I had seen too much of this during my tour of Canada & USA in 1980 and was determined not to see it in our department.

The January 1994 *A&E newsletter* requested information on 'trolley waits' as many members were reporting increased pressure across the UK, particularly so in England. Despite many voices suggesting that bed reduction was not a cause of trolley waits but rather it was the number of patients in hospital that should be cared for in the community, the reality was patients in A&E could not get to a ward. The editorial of the August 1995 *A&E newsletter* graphically summed up the situation, reporting that A&E staff had been saddened to hear of another patient dying while waiting in a corridor to be admitted to a ward. The editor asked 'How many more incidents like this has there got to be before the problem is addressed.'

The answer came with the publication of *The Patient's Charter & You 1995*. It indicated that from April 1st 1996, a patient admitted to hospital through an A&E department should expect to be given a bed as soon as possible and certainly within two hours. In my *Emergency Nurse* article of Spring 1996, while I welcomed the change from the previous standard of three to four hours, I pointed out that while this sounded good, the reality was the clock did not start until the decision to admit had been made so the longer that decision was delayed the shorter the audit time. There was significant distortion between the spirit of the Charter standard and the reality of complying. I recommended going to one overall standard from arrival to admission based on clinical time frames and audit including quality as well as quantitative measures.

Due to the concern regarding bed waits the RCN surveyed the situation both in 1994 and again in 1996 (*Emergency Nurse* April 1997). Finding the situation had not changed led to further meetings with political parties and the Department of Health in a move to prevent the situation occurring the following year. On June 2nd 1997 a summit of key policy makers (RCN, BMA, NHS confederation, Age concern, Department of Health) was held at the RCN (*Emergency Nurse* July/August 1997). From the summit three messages became clear:

- there was a siege mentality affecting the service at large and not just A&E

- there had been a lack of ownership of the problem, with a tendency to diffuse responsibility and centralise blame – usually on A&E departments (that was the experience for most A&E managers at the time including my own experience at Basildon Hospital in the early 1990s)

- the implementation of many process issues – using bed managers, telephone advice lines and so on – would ease the tensions within the system

The final paragraph of the report summed up the situation – 'If we don't act now to avoid a bed crisis, we could be in for a long hot winter in the NHS, and A&E once again will be generating most of the heat.' The RCN A&E Nursing Association was very active in helping A&Es and producing guidelines for good practice. Much emphasis was placed on pressure sore prevention and a whole range of recommendations were published including the use of risk calculators and the need for correct equipment to aid in the prevention.

Despite all these meetings the crisis continued and at St Helier Hospital in Surrey, nurses requested the RCN to allow them to take industrial action due to a whole raft of issues including lost meal breaks, not getting off duty on time, increased patient numbers and after five years of formal complaints no action had been forthcoming. Following the RCN Council meeting, where I was a member of council, it was agreed that industrial action could be taken. Immediately the trust management moved quickly and developed a 14-point action plan preventing the need for industrial action.

By November 1997 *Emergency Nurse* reported on two new reports, 'New Standards' that had set out a voluntary code of practice for A&E departments. They included all non-urgent patients should wait no longer than 4 hours and patients for admission should not wait more than 12 hours. All hospitals should provide 24 hour bed management services. Despite this the February 1998 edition of *Emergency Nurse* indicated that bed shortages was now recognised as a year round problem and three quarters of hospitals had bed managers and half said they were having to open more beds.

Emergency Nurse (March 1998) reported that the Association of Community Health Councils had initiated a 'Casualty

Watch' survey which showed waiting continued to increase. The survey carried out during an afternoon in February 1998 involved over 200 A&E departments covering 100 community health councils. It showed in some departments patients waited a day and a half for treatment. At the same time The Royal Liverpool Hospital A&E had suffered for over a year with staff having to deal with up to 30 patients in corridors. The problem was now intolerable.

The debate continued at the RCN A&E Nursing Association conference in November 1999 with calls for the issue to be accepted as a NHS Trust issue rather than an A&E issue. That GP referrals should not be seen in A&E as described earlier. There was also a call for hospitals to have bed management not bed allocation - specialties having an allocated number of beds despite others requiring more.

Although the bed reduction, increased workload and 'trolley waits' had escalated during the whole of the 1990s the situation came to a head during the new millennium. Despite all previous work the pressure in all A&E units was relentless. The RCN A&E Nursing Association worked closely with the Community Health Councils and the RCN Council regarding pressures in A&E. The RCN formed an emergency pressure group to address the continuing challenge of emergency workload and Lynda Holt (Chair of the RCN A&E Nursing Association) was involved in top-level meetings both at the RCN and government level. Even the National Institute for Clinical Excellence (NICE) issued a report on risk assessment and prevention strategies for pressure area care due to the increased risk in the elderly linked with longer 'trolley waits' and lack of bed availability.

In March 2000, the editorial in *Emergency Nurse* again focussed on the annual snapshot 'Casualty Watch' survey of 'trolley waits' undertaken by the Association of Community Health Councils in England & Wales. It reported that the way one hospital made sure they would not be named and shamed was to have beds in A&E so patients waiting admission were not on a trolley and therefore waits would not be recorded! The same editorial reported that despite all of the problems with 'trolley waits' hospital beds had declined even further to just 147,000 in 2000 (previously 335,000 in 1984 to 212,000 in 1995). The editorial said changing demographics, increased acuity and growing numbers of emergency admissions suggest we were desperately in need of more, not fewer beds.

The RCN snapshot survey of emergency pressures (*Emergency Nurse* April 2000) showed most hospitals by then had bed managers, fast tracking systems and rapid response teams. About half of the 109 hospitals that responded (out of 263 surveyed and the total number of A&Es 313) had an admission ward or unit. Other information showed less than one in four had separate paediatric facilities in A&E and staffing levels varied considerably both in terms of numbers and grade mix. Over half of respondents described the workload as constantly busy.

Combining the 2000 'Casualty Watch' with the RCN snapshot created a powerful image of A&E units full to overflowing, with nurses and other staff unable to provide even essential care. In a vicious circle, due to nurses being too busy trying to provide ongoing care for patients waiting for beds they were unable to manage the less urgent cases - almost the same words used by Ethel Buckles in her *A&E newsletter* editorial of 1983.

Although everyone was now focussed on improving the situation, it was still necessary in the winter of 2000/2001 for the RCN to launch a 24hour action line to help members tackle winter pressures plus provide an emergency pressures action card/pack.

To help with the on-going crisis, in the November 2000 edition of *Emergency Nurse* the editorial reported that retired nurses were being lured back with lucrative incentives in an attempt to avert a threatened crisis that winter. The editorial continued by pointing out that summer never really arrived as pressures continued throughout the year. This theme continued in the October 2001 edition where the editorial focussed on the number of incidents leading to nurses being blamed for systematic problems facing the NHS. In his editorial Brian Dolan believed that despite some of the hysteria surrounding A&E departments, he had a heartfelt belief that emergency nursing would come out of the dark hours stronger and even more patient centred than ever before.

The National Patient Access Team (NPAT), part of the Department of Health's initiative to reduce waits, drew up guidance on 'trolley waits' in the spring of 2001 (*Emergency Nurse* May 2001). The guidelines focussed on clinical and managerial leadership, matching capacity with demand and tailoring staffing levels and skill mix to requirements, including using staff to their full potential and empowering bed managers. The report indicated that by April 2004 no one should wait more than 4 hours in A&E. Through *Reforming Emergency Care* for the first time the issues of long 'trolley waits' and backlogs were not seen as an A&E problem. A whole system approach, both primary and secondary care, was demanded.

Although up to this point the focus had been on time to admit and bed availability, the government were now keen to remove the fragmented time frames such as the time to initial assessment (chapter 11), time to see a doctor or other health professional and time to admit. Instead a single time from arrival to admission or discharge was to be implemented - I had recommended this in my *Emergency Nurse* article of spring 1996. The clock was now to start from the patient's arrival and stop when the patient left the department on admission, transfer or discharge. The set target for 2002 was that 75% of patients must be processed through the system within four hours and by 1st April 2003, the percentage of patients seen/treated and admitted or discharged in four hours was to rise to 90%. These targets kept increasing year on year to first 95% then reaching 98% in the winter of 2004. For the first time organisations had to address the bed availability and other issues that prevented patients leaving A&E within four hours. They also had to address the issue of other patients waiting for assessment and treatment through streaming (chapters 6 and 11). The four hour target had arrived.

By July/August 2002 *Emergency Nurse* reported that the last ever 'Casualty Watch' survey had been published (England) and in the September edition an article by Brian Dolan demonstrated how things could be improved. He linked his suggestions to the paper *Reforming Emergency Care*. Some of the suggestions from the article included:

- executive management to be fully involved
- up to date IT systems required

- closer liaison with community and social services/improved services in community to free up hospital beds
- bed managers/site managers 24 hrs
- better system of beds becoming free/discharge systems improved/discharge lounge
- increased consultant ward rounds
- expert review of emergency department staffing
- community psychiatric nurses employed in A&E plus other support staff such as physiotherapists
- liaise with ambulance service with regard to waiting times
- implement care pathways
- clinical decision-making units
- use of nursing expertise
- improved services to ensure the elderly can be discharged from A&E such as a quick response for home alterations (carpenter services available)

The last suggestion could well have been linked with the report of findings in the *British Medical Journal* (February 1992) showing that during a six month study at Charing Cross Hospital, London 55 out of 66 patients over 75 years were safely discharged within 2 hours when a senior nurse had made a nursing and social assessment prior to discharge. However when senior nurse assessment was not available only 25 of 57 patients with similar injuries could be discharged.

In the autumn of 2002 Professor Sir George Alberti was appointed National Clinical Director for Emergency Access in England ('emergency tsar'). A former president of the Royal College of Physicians, his remit included advising on the implementation of *Reforming Emergency Care,* improving the patient experience, acting as a link between policy makers and clinicians across the NHS and helping trusts with particular difficulties in providing emergency care. Everything now was focussed on improving the care of patients in a timely manner.

Trust managers having had to comply with the target of 75% were, according to the president of the BAEM, going into panic mode to achieve the 90% target. Managers were offering bonuses and engaging extra agency staff. Unfortunately despite this mandate not all trusts played the game as the editorial in the October 2002 edition of *Emergency Nurse* pointed out. The editorial showed how waiting times were being manipulated by re-designating areas of A&E as observation areas thus not recording these patients as 'trolley waits'. Fortunately within a few months tighter waiting time definitions had come into effect to stop the abuse of using areas in A&E or other unsuitable areas as 'wards' to reduce waiting time figures (February 2003 *Emergency Nurse*). Although outside the dates of this book, the Healthcare Commission report into care at Mid Staffordshire NHS Foundation Trust in 2009 found patients for admission were put in a ward near A&E without nursing care so the four-hour waiting time target could be met. My article in *Nursing Standard,* 'Targeted for blame' (April 2009) questioned why the four-hour A&E waiting target had been made a scapegoat for poor care. I wonder if some managers will ever learn!

By June 2003 it was reported in *Emergency Nurse* that there were calls from some medical quarters for a list of conditions to be exempt from the target. Also Lynda Holt (Chair of the RCN A&E Nursing Association) pointed out in the July/August 2003 *Emergency Nurse* that targets were causing staff to be scared and to fear their job depended on achieving the target. 'Priorities and clinical decision making are being taken away from those with clinical ability' she said. Lynda was not critical of targets but there was a need to refocus, a 'call to arms on what we know and what we can do. It is a challenge to stay clear of the target hype. To focus on what we can fix, and not waste our energy on what we can't.'

By August 2003 with the four hour target firmly established, for the first time since the mid-1990s waiting times were beginning to be reduced. The editorial by Brian Dolan in *Emergency Nurse* (July/August 2003) indicated that, 'Four years ago only one in four patients in England escaped the emergency department in less than four hours but now it was about nine out of ten.' Brian asked how this had happened? He answered – 'It's because we got our collective act together and, with some pushing and shoving, we made it happen.' He went on, 'And here's the rub; many of the changes in emergency care have happened because nurses are liberated to make these things happen.'

Despite some concerns around targets, overall the staff and patients were pleased with the progress and this was certainly the view of Rhian Wood, Clinical Practice lead, A&E St Thomas' Hospital, London in her article, 'Modernising emergency care' (*Emergency Nurse* October 2003). 'We are now several years into the modernisation plans for delivering emergency care' she said. 'Over the last few years we have developed streaming and see and treat, and witnessed managers running down corridors with patients in wheelchairs to avoid breaching waiting times. In addition, we have all developed our data collection and statistical manipulation skills to a standard only previously reached by the spin doctors at Number 10. The modernisation plans were introduced following the largest consultation exercise ever undertaken by a government, in which members of the public and health service staff had the opportunity to mail, email and phone in their views on what they wanted from the NHS. The overwhelming response was that access to emergency care should be easier and waiting times should be less. Can you remember looking in despair at the minors queue as it continued to grow? The waiting room was a no go zone because you feared for your safety as the crowd grew increasingly agitated. Patients lined the corridors, while managers explained they didn't count as 'trolley waits' because they were on beds. Patients were two to a cubicle and no one seemed to care. Now we have GPs, ENPs with extended parameters, and senior emergency department doctors fighting over fewer and fewer patients. Diagnostic tests are performed quicker, senior staff in A&E have the right to admit and the phrase 'the patient is about to breach' now has the same effect on ward staff as Open Sesame had for Ali Baba; the whole hospital takes ownership of waiting time targets. Only time will tell if these changes are sustainable but, as emergency nurses, we need to seize this opportunity to get the best for our patients and ourselves.'

Although great improvements had been achieved, due to the ongoing legitimate concerns raised during 2002/3 regarding clinical care and clinical decision making, in November 2003 Jonathan Asbridge, Chief Nurse at Barts and the London NHS Trust, was appointed the national patient champion for

A&E. In his March 2004 *Emergency Nurse* article he explained his role was to focus minds on patient care across the whole hospital and not just on A&E. At the same time in response to some of the concerns around clinical need verses target time, the Health Secretary John Read said, 'There are certain exceptional cases where it is better for the patient to remain in A&E for longer than the four-hour target. Targets are a means to an end. They are about putting patients first. If the target gets in the way of clinical requirements then it must be refined.'

One of the key factors for bed availability had always been the discharge of patients already in a hospital bed. This was especially so with patients requiring social care outside of hospital. According to the Department of Health plans reported in the February 2004 *Emergency Nurse*, the health service expected to see an end to widespread so-called 'bed blocking' by April of that year. Social services were to face fines if they hindered hospital discharge by failing to assess patients or provide the necessary services. It was reported that over the previous year improvements had been made and most hospitals had seen a reduction in delayed discharge.

Despite a dramatic increase in patient numbers, especially those with chronic diseases, reports of success continued throughout 2004 though some departments were not able to achieve the 95% target. The spring 2004 *ECA newsletter* reported progress was well on its way with the editorial reporting tremendous change since the four hour target had been implemented. Departments were back to what they should be doing, was the comment.

Concern was highlighted in the March 2004 *Emergency Nurse* regarding a report suggesting that the government proposed to replace targets with a number of standards. However the

Health Secretary pointed out that departments were still expected to reach the four-hour target by the end of the year, taking clinical exceptions into account. The April 2004 *Emergency Nurse* reported that winter 2003/4 had been far better than previously. It noted that with the extra investment and new ways of working, winter pressures were managed more efficiently. The range of new ways of working demonstrated how collaboration with other specialties was helping reduce waiting times. An article in the July 2004 *Emergency Nurse* 'Collaborative working' explained how extending the scope of practice for physiotherapists in A&E enabled many patients with limb injuries to be seen, investigated and treated more efficiently.

The increased target of 98% that came into force in the winter of 2004 led the BAEM in 2005, supported by leading nurses, to lobby for a return to 95%. This was based on the concern of risks to patient care and bullying of staff, as hospital managers attempted to meet the four hour target.

By September 2005 a review of achievements over the last 4 years by Health Minister Lord Warner showed huge improvements in emergency care. NHS staff had transformed the service and 98% of patients were being seen and treated in the 4 hour standard. The new ways of working including see and treat, streaming and staff development programmes had all led to this improvement. At Basildon & Thurrock, Basildon A&E had introduced a rapid assessment patient treatment service (RAPT). Gerard Cronin, Emergency Care Matron of A&E, along with J Wright, also from Basildon presented this new way of working at the 2005 A&E Conference. Explaining the system of a team comprising senior clinician, senior nurse and emergency support worker, they went on to describe the process of a rapid (15 minutes maximum) nursing/medical assessment of patients in the 'majors' stream and the benefits derived.

By May 2006 the Department of Health closed the intervention arm of its emergency care team. Intensive support teams that had helped NHS Trusts across the country to meet the four-hour target were considered to be no longer required; however, the quarterly meetings of the emergency care team would continue under the Chair of the 'emergency tsar' Sir George Alberti.

Articles and news reports of further changes and performance against the targets continued throughout 2006 including in the February *Emergency Nurse* where it was reported that the Department of Health document *Our Health, Our Care, Our Say: A new direction for community services* described a fundamental shift in focus that would provide integrated health and social care services in local communities and services closer to people's homes. It meant more walk-in centres and minor injury units.

There was also the report in the journal scan section of the 2006 *Emergency Nurse* that a paper published in the *Emergency Medicine Journal* had shown that the biggest influence on improved performance was the number of measures taken rather than any specific measure. The authors concluded that reduced waiting times in emergency departments may depend more on the amount of effort spent than on single changes, and predictably that the measures most likely to help required additional resources.

Despite all the improvements there was still concern in 2007 when according to Gerard Cronin, Emergency Care Matron at Basildon hospital, Essex (*Emergency Nurse* July 2007). 'While the priority for emergency nurses was the quality of the patient journey' he said 'management staff took a different approach focussing on measurable, quantifiable and statistical results.'

*   *   *   *

Although England had improved the waiting time, other countries in the UK were still struggling. By 2005, despite the setting up of the Welsh Emergency Care Access Collaboration in 2003, Wales was holding crisis summits to address the same issues that had plagued England for so long. A major paper was presented to the Welsh Assembly officials by the RCN Wales describing the emergency service as a whole system dysfunction. They submitted a list of 28 recommendations; however, by 2006 in the opinion of the RCN Wales, the assembly had failed to note the 28 recommendations made by the college the previous year. The July 2006 *Emergency Nurse* reported that the Welsh Assembly had launched a national strategy for developing emergency care that included a common form of assessment and direction to the most appropriate service and developing urgent care centres at both hospital and community trust sites. However, not everyone was convinced that walk-in centres were the answer. In the June 2007 *Emergency Nurse,* emergency care experts called on the Welsh government to shelve proposals for introducing the centres claiming that such services would not reduce pressure on A&E departments. Others disagreed.

Scotland launched its 'Unscheduled care collaborative programme' to ensure that by 2007 virtually no one would wait in an emergency department more than 4 hours. Although Scotland had not experienced the waits like England, over the last year things had gone downhill. In the opinion of Barbara Neades, an RCN ECA member, this was due to several things including new consultant doctors, GP contracts, change of junior doctors' hours, failure of NHS24 (Scotland's NHS Direct) to recruit and retain staff and slow uptake of nurse practitioners and nurse prescribers The programme underpinned the need for a whole system approach.

In Northern Ireland increased 'trolley waits' and other issues, especially care of minor injury/illness, led to a plan to establish standardised criteria to monitor waits. It was to take a whole system approach looking at the use of beds, community services and reducing attendance in A&E by improving emergency care in the community (*Emergency Nurse* October 2006). There was also the Focused Assessment Systematic Treatment (FAST) initiative that was implemented in an attempt to transform the culture of emergency care and ensure a more positive patient experience. Focussed on the minor injury/illness patient it involved the right person intervening at the right time to ensure the right patient received the right treatment. It meant the nurses working in teams with medical and allied health professionals initiating investigations, prescribing treatments and if appropriate discharging patients. Three competency levels allowed nurses to intervene in requesting investigations as well as prescribing treatment and discharging patients.

*   *   *   *

The impact of violence and aggression on workload
When I visited Canada and the USA in 1980 I saw how the impact of violence towards others spilled over into the emergency department. This was far worse than anything I had witnessed in my own department at that time. The cause of the violence was often attributed to drugs but in other cases it was the frustration of the system that caused sudden

outbursts. The October 1986 *A&E newsletter* contained many reports of violence in A&E including figures from a study in the A&E Edinburgh Royal Infirmary which showed that in 1984 the main culprits were aged 16-25, most occurred within the first hour from arrival and alcohol and drugs were a factor in 70% of incidents. Other violent incidents included use of CS gas in civil disturbance and verbal abuse.

Responding to the increase in violence and aggression, in 1986 the RCN A&E Nursing Forum produced *Guidelines for Dealing with Aggression in A&E departments*. Published as an RCN leaflet it covered some of the causes of aggression, factors that increased the risk and how the nurse should respond. It also included how to conduct the post aggressive episode. The leaflet contained information on how to access the NHS injury benefits regulations and the criminal injuries compensation scheme. Although not an answer to preventing violence, in 1984 the Criminal Injuries Compensation Board was set up giving a mechanism for staff to seek some form of redress (currently the *Criminal Injuries Compensation Scheme 2012*).

As the system tried to cope with the increased workload there was an increase in violence and abuse to staff. Kathie Butcher, Editor of the *A&E newsletter*, indicated her concern in the September 1993 edition, pointing out that staff in A&E were frequently exposed to the unsocial behaviour and aggressive outbursts of patients and visitors. She recognised that pain, fear, anxiety and uncertainty often underpinned this aggressive behaviour but as she pointed out, staff had a right to work in a safe environment.

Accident & Emergency – A Scoping report (G Jones March 1997) revealed further reasons for violence and aggression including stress related to car parking issues, poor signposting, inadequate access to the A&E department and lack of wheelchairs. The departments involved in the report had undertaken a whole series of measures including staff training on handling aggression, control and restraint training, security cameras and improving the environment such as removing barriers between the patient and reception staff and reviewing the layout and décor of the department.

Una Bell, Clinical Director, A&E, Whipps Cross Hospital, London was known throughout the A&E profession to have knowledge and skills in tackling violence in A&E, however she herself became a victim when held hostage in her office by a woman who tied her up and threatened to set her alight. Fortunately due to Una's ability to deal with such a crisis and the staff's quick thinking, the incident was concluded without any physical injury. Ironically the judge gave a 2 year suspended sentence and as Una pointed out in *Emergency Nurse* (December/January 1998 edition) this gives out the wrong message to NHS staff and suggested that all the words of Health Secretary Frank Dodson about cracking down on assaults and violence to NHS staff was little more than lip service.

Unfortunately the increased trend of violence and aggression to staff continued to rise and in *Emergency Nurse* (May 1998) an article on violence in A&E by Robert Sowney, one of the RCN A&E Nursing Association steering group members, suggested that the Friday/Saturday night syndrome had been replaced by the daily/nightly syndrome. Drug use, increased waiting times, longer 'trolley waits' and alcohol were just some of the triggers. In the same edition an article on stress and burnout indicated that most problems can be traced to resource issues including lengthy waiting times and patient aggression.

Emergency Nurse (June 1998) reported on the outcome from the violence conference held by the RCN. It reported that 33% of nurses were victims of violence and verbal abuse and it was the third most common cause of stress in the workplace. Research by the Health & Safety Executive indicated that one in three nurses were victims of violence while on duty compared with one in four police officers. As Brian Dolan said in his June editorial - nursing is officially the most dangerous occupation in the UK.

Despite as far back as 1979 when the RCN A&E Nursing Forum discussed violence to staff and ways of preventing such attacks, 20 years later the RCN A&E Nursing Association was still trying to tackle the issue. At RCN Congress in March 1999 the A&E Nursing Association proposed the motion that a policy of 'zero tolerance' should be adopted towards violent patients, their relatives or friends. Lynda Holt, Chair of the RCN A&E Nursing Association argued that patients who injure a nurse should expect to be prosecuted, and that accepting abuse in the workplace must be changed. 96% of voting members supported the resolution.

In the October 1999 *Emergency Nurse,* violence was still high on the agenda with a news article reporting that three nurses and a health care assistant had been attacked at West Middlesex Hospital. This incident following previous concerns led to 50 staff picketing the main entrance and demanding 24-hour security in the A&E department, extra panic buttons and anti-violence training.

The fringe meeting on violence held at the A&E conference in November 1999 highlighted how opinions differed as to what constituted violence and aggressive behaviour. Speakers held very differing views as to levels of acceptable verbal abuse especially in relation to the patient's condition or disability. A number of key themes emerged including the need for a national strategy for reducing violence, increased staff training and a review of the effectiveness of security staff.

In the early 2000s government ministers gave the go-ahead to ban violent or abusive patients under the zero tolerance scheme, however many staff were concerned it was unworkable as there were a whole raft of issues that emerged around its implementation.

Such was the problem of violence in some departments, staff were even being awarded police bravery awards such as those presented to Michael Paynter, Charge Nurse and David Lowe, Paramedic for confronting a man terrorising staff at Bristol Royal Infirmary. Also in 2000 Lee Orgill, staff nurse, Kings Mill A&E, Nottinghamshire received a police bravery award for tackling a violent patient who had seriously injured a nurse colleague.

The National Audit office report published in March 2003, *A safer place to work: protecting NHS hospital and ambulance staff from violence and aggression* showed that four out of five A&E managers were unhappy with security arrangements at work and overall 80% of NHS Trust A&E department managers believed the level and coverage of violence and aggression training their staff received was inadequate. The report continued to show that there were averages of 130 violent or aggressive incidents a day in the NHS, an increase of 13% over the past two years.

Set up in 2003, the NHS Security Management Services was designed to help police and the Crown Prosecution Service ensure that legal action was taken against people who attacked NHS staff and to ensure that assailants were not simply 'let off' with cautions. The service advised that every nurse likely to encounter violent patients would have 3 days training over the next 4 years. The service also secured private prosecutions when police did not view prosecution as being in the public interest. In 2005, the National Institute for Clinical Excellence (NICE) published guidance on managing disturbed or violent behaviour in emergency departments.

In the September 2005 *Emergency Nurse*, Ken Madine and Ben Smith, both from the Victim Support Workforce, outlined employers' responsibility when staff were victims of violence. They pointed out that one in four NHS staff were abused or harassed by patients in 2004. Alcohol, drugs and high levels of tension were largely responsible.

Despite a number of efforts to reduce violence, the March 2006 *Emergency Nurse* reported that RCN figures from a survey 'working well' showed a shocking 79% of A&E nurses had reported being victims of violence in the previous 12 months and 95% reported verbal abuse.

Probably the most depressing aspect of this whole subject was the report in the February 2007 *Emergency Nurse* when magistrates awarded an A&E sister £75 in compensation after an assault by a drunken patient. The sister suffered a number of injuries and said, 'The punishment hardly fits the crime. The message being sent out is that you can just go out and wallop a nurse and it will cost you less than 100 quid.'

Although outside the dates of this book it is important to highlight the *Assaults on Emergency Workers (Offences) Act 2018*. This act covers a person employed for the purposes of providing, or engaged to provide (i) NHS health services, or (ii) services in the support of the provision of NHS health services, and whose general activities in doing so involve face to face interaction with individuals receiving the services or with other members of the public. The main outcome of the act is longer prison sentences for common assault and battery.

References

Audit Commission England/Wales: (1996) *By Accident or Design – improving emergency care in acute hospitals*. London: HMSO

Audit Commission: (2001) *Accident & Emergency - Review of National findings*. London: HMSO

Audit Commission report
http://www.nhshistory.net/midstaffs.pdf

Assaults on Emergency Workers (Offences) Act 2018. Gov UK

British Medical Journal: (February 1992) Published by BMJ UK

Candis: (March 1994) *A Matter of Life & Death*. Vol 9 issue 3. Candis Club publication

Criminal Injuries Compensation Scheme: (2012) Ministry of Justice. London: HMSO

Department of Health: (1995) *The Patient's Charter & You.* London: HMSO

Department of Health: (2001) *Reforming Emergency Care* London: HMSO

Department of Health National Leadership Network: (March 2002) *Strengthening Local Services: The future of the acute hospital.* www.nationalleadershipnetwork.org

Department of Health: (2003) *Freedom to Practice: dispelling the myths.* London: HMSO

Department of Health (2006) *Our Health, Our Care, Our Say: A New Direction for Community Services.* London: HMSO

Guly. H: (2005) *A History of Accident and Emergency Medicine 1948 – 2004).* Palgrave Macmillan.

Jones G: (2009) *Targeted for blame.* Nursing Standard April 22 vol 23 no 33 24-25

Jones G: (1997) *Accident & Emergency – A Scoping report* (Report to the Chief Nursing Officer Department of Health)

King's College Hospital: (1993) *New Challenges in Accident &Emergency: Developing the Primary Care Role of A&E Nurses.* King's Healthcare London

NICE: (February 2005) *Managing Disturbed or Violent Behaviour in Emergency Departments.* Guideline CG25. Updated (28th May 2015) as *Violence and aggression: short-term management in mental health, health and community settings.* Guideline [NG10]

National Audit Office: (1992) *NHS A&E Departments in England.* London: HMSO

National Audit Office: (1992) *NHS A&E Departments in Scotland.* London: HMSO

National Audit Office: (2003) *A Safer Place to Work: protecting NHS hospital and ambulance staff from violence and aggression.* London: HMSO

Nursing Standard: (March 1977) *Nurses can't give care if cure still has all the cash.* Royal College of Nursing Publication

Royal College of Nursing: (1986) *Guidelines for dealing with aggression in the Accident &Emergency department.* RCN Publication

CHAPTER 9
PROFESSIONAL DEVELOPMENT

Throughout the history of nursing, nurses have continuously acquired new skills and developed new ways of providing improved care. However, defining nursing has plagued the profession for decades with Florence Nightingale stating, 'The elements of nursing are all but unknown' (Notes on Nursing 1860).

The introduction of models of nursing and philosophies demonstrated that care was not just about skills, it was about the way we viewed the patient as a person and how nursing can provide the support when required.

Professor Dame June Clark in her inaugural professorial lecture at Swansea University in 1997 said, 'The core of nursing practice does not lie in our technical skills, it does not lie solely in our empathy or caring approach to people. It lies in our ability to diagnose and deal with human responses to illness, frailty, disability, life transitions and other actual or potential threats to health, and to do so within a relationship of trust and care that promotes health and healing.' She went on to say that nursing is an intellectual, emotional, moral and political activity and all of these draw on the nursing knowledge that is, in Benner's words (1984) embedded in clinical practice.

Defining Nursing (RCN 2003) described what nursing is and clarified the role of the nurse. The definition of professional nursing was based on a core and six characteristics. 'Nursing is the use of clinical judgement (the document clarified how this is obtained) in the provision of care to enable people to improve, maintain, or recover health, to cope with health problems, and to achieve the best possible quality of life, whatever their disease or disability, until death'.

This was followed a year later with the *Nursing the future campaign* in 2004. The campaign highlighted in the 8th September *Nursing Standard* demonstrated how to 'get to the bottom of this thing called nursing care' by deconstructing nursing from practice to theory. Through a personal experience at my local A&E in 2004 I deconstructed the emergency nursing care provided for my mother. I highlighted in my article in *Emergency Nurse* (October 2004) how a staff nurse used knowledge and understanding of emergency care to provide essential and technical care to my mum. What was demonstrated was emergency nursing at its best: being able to link the doing with the caring, the knowledge with the clinical judgements, yet making it look effortless – even simple.

In the June 1993 *A&E newsletter* the editor reported that the process to outline a definition and philosophy of A&E nursing and to identify a strategy and skills that were specific to A&E was to take place. A working party (of which as Chair of the RCN A&E Nursing Association I was a member) was put together and we consulted members, read through professional and government publications (including those covering generic nursing such as *A Strategy for Nursing and a Vision for the Future*) as well as publications specific to A&E nursing.

The result was *Accident & Emergency - Challenging the Boundaries (RCN 1994)*. The document states, probably for the first time, what the service and emergency nurses are all about.

The mission statement reads *'The Accident & Emergency Service is an interface between primary and secondary care and should be viewed as part of the community and not simply as a department within a hospital. A&E nurses provide an immediate nursing response to meet the full spectrum of human need.'*

Accident & Emergency - Challenging the Boundaries laid out the philosophy, role and scope of practice of the A&E nurse. It identified the A&E specialist nursing practitioner as:

- being responsible for providing immediate care to people who have undifferentiated and undiagnosed problems

- deciding upon the priorities for care, prescribing and initiating appropriate interventions, monitoring, referring or discharging

- taking autonomous decisions with, or on behalf of the patient, to maximise their health potential and promote continuity of care

- having an appropriate education and competency which is continually assessed

These four key statements lead to a number of specific components of an A&E specialist nursing practitioner;

- leading and co-ordinating patient care

- accepting without prior warning any person requiring health care with problems originating from social, psychological, physical, spiritual or cultural factors

- providing immediate contact, rapid and continuing assessment and allocating a priority of care

- is the key decision maker in selecting and prioritising the most appropriate source of care

- makes rapid decisions underpinned by a specialist body of knowledge

- sets short term goals to deal with identified problems

- concurrently evaluates care

Essentials of good practice covered targets for leadership, research, education, protocols and written guidelines, measuring and monitoring care and skill mix.

Accident & Emergency - Challenging the Boundaries formed the basis for future work that the RCN A&E Nursing Association undertook and was undoubtedly one of the most significant documents produced by the Association in its history.

One of my contributions to this work was introducing the working party to the nursing model for emergency nursing that had been developed at Orsett and Basildon Hospitals. By using a practice-based system of design (nursing process) over several months in 1988 and with a great deal of input from the staff of the A&E departments at Orsett and Basildon Hospitals and staff from the School of Nursing at Orsett, the design of the model had taken place. I named it the Components of Life model and the work was published in 1990 by Faber & Faber under the title *Accident & Emergency Nursing - a structured approach*. A brief description of the model was published in the October 1991 *A&E newsletter* and was further published in more detail in *Emergency Nursing Care: Principles and Practice* and in *Accident & Emergency: Theory into Practice*. Although outside the dates of this book it is interesting to note that in November 2017 the model was adopted by the emergency care networks in the Republic of Ireland and is used throughout the country to support the delivery and recording of nursing care.

The Components of Life model is based on the belief and values that all humans are individuals with individual human needs. It is also based on the belief that during their lifespan the individual is engaged in various self-care activities in an attempt to retain independence. Seven components of life comprising physical, human behavioural and social aspects were identified and when in balance maintain health and quality of life. Due to an event (physical illness, mental illness or injury) in the course of the individual's lifespan the balance can be upset and the ability to maintain health and quality of life is disrupted. The individual identifies emergency care staff as the resource to assist them re-balance the components, re-establish independence and thus continue physical, emotional and social comfort. The seven components are:

a) communication, b) airway/breathing/circulation, c) mobility, d) environmental safety, e) personal care, f) eating/drinking/elimination and g) health promotion.

The model includes four universal goals: 1) establishing a partnership with the patient, 2) helping the patient achieve a level of independence appropriate to condition and assist to restore health and quality of life, 3) enable the individual to avoid ill-health or injury through self-care, health education and environmental safety and 4) to ensure optimum effectiveness of medically prescribed treatment. The final part of the model includes the development of knowledge and skills.

From this work a dependency tool (later named the Jones Dependency Tool) was developed to ensure that the patient was allocated to a nurse with the relevant competencies to provide the care required. The dependency tool was later used by other departments in the UK to determine dependency threshold levels and to assist in the calculation of staffing and skill mix (chapter 12).

*   *   *   *

Emergency nurses are not just concerned about the nursing care of patients when ill or injured, they are also concerned about prevention of illness or injury. Throughout this book (particularly in Part One) I have demonstrated how A&E nurses have been at the forefront of accident prevention and have been involved in care of vulnerable individuals. The third edition of the *A&E newsletter* (Winter 1983) reported on the World Health Organisation's (WHO) symposium on accidents in Europe indicating that participants attended from 21 member states (including the UK and the RCN A&E Nursing Forum) and the role of the nurse was considered fundamental in accident prevention. The May 1984 *A&E newsletter* reported further on the symposium highlighting that delegates discussed 25 papers ranging from road accidents, effect of drugs and alcohol on driving, home and sports accidents, accidents and prevention in children and the elderly, the bio-mechanics of injury, the trauma process, standards and design of A&E departments and the role of nursing in accident prevention. From this symposium a whole range of European wide recommendations emerged and many are now enacted in our laws.

The *A&E newsletter* (Winter 1983) reported on the resource centre on accidents to children. It indicated that the Child Accident Prevention Trust (a registered charity) investigated the pattern of accidents in childhood, their causes and relationship to child development and to the social and environmental background in which they occurred. The reference centre based in the University College, London welcomed visitors who were involved/interested in child accident prevention to attend the scientific meetings and seminars and use the library facilities.

A further Department of Health document influencing how staff could contribute to the prevention of injury/illness came in the form of *The Health of the Nation Key Area Handbook – Accidents (1993)*. It identified the need to prevent accidents through education, training and environmental improvements. It identified the age groups and major causes of accidents and set targets to reduce death in all age groups as well as how the NHS and local DHA's (community and acute) could take this forward. Examples included key individuals to be responsible for accident prevention, checklists of good practice, training programmes and audit.

The July 1996 *A&E newsletter* ran a full page article entitled, 'Nurse on the road' explaining a joint safety campaign between the police traffic division and the A&E staff from Bristol Royal Infirmary. A nurse travelled with the police and when motorists were stopped in relation to a motoring offence that had the potential for injury the nurse would reinforce road safety issues including the need to prevent alcohol related incidents.

Further reinforcement of the nurses' role in prevention was reported in the 1997 November edition of *Emergency Nurse* with an article on public education injury prevention and an article on health promotion. In 1999 The Royal Preston Hospital was the first hospital in England to be designated as a Health Promoting Hospital and the A&E's contribution was to identify current trends in accident occurrence in the 0-16 year age group and contribute to their prevention. In 2007 the ECA helped push through a resolution at RCN Congress to lobby the government to ban the sale of most fireworks to the general public.

*   *   *   *

Advancements in clinical nursing care have come both from essential care and through acquiring clinical skills that were traditionally the domain of doctors. Way before the establishment of the RCN A&E Nursing Forum or the Joint Board of Clinical Nursing Studies A&E course, and the document *The extending role of the nurse - legal implications and training requirements HC(77)22'*, A&E nurses were acquiring clinical skills to provide improved care to patients and establish the role of the A&E nurse. In my first book of this memoir series, *It's Not All Blood & Guts: My Amazing Life as an A&E Nurse,* I described how during 1975 the development of my 'clinical nursing skills' in A&E was based on the needs of the patient and the department. Within a few weeks I had been taught how to suture wounds, pass gastric lavage tubes and wash out a patient's stomach, trephine nails, apply plaster of Paris, record ECGs, undertake complex wound dressings and nurse acutely ill and traumatised patients. Although limited in the theory behind the skill I was very soon able to provide care to a whole range of patients.

As mentioned in Part One, the Joint Board of Clinical Nursing Studies (JBCNS) was established in 1970 and the A&E course 199 became available by 1975.

The JBCNS determined the pattern of training and awarded certificates, although the responsibility for clinical training remained with individual hospitals. As time progressed designated hospitals became centres for the A&E course but the demand outstripped the centres available and consequently many departments continued to provide locally based training.

The JBCNS remained in place until the reorganisation of the nursing registration bodies and the establishment of the national nursing boards. In the *A&E newsletter* (December 1983) it was reported that the honorary officers of the forum were to meet with an English National Board (ENB) officer to discuss the ENB clinical course 199 for A&E (formally the JBCNS course). This demonstrated the continued involvement that the forum had with the ongoing development of A&E education.

In April 1985 a study day was arranged by the RCN A&E Nursing Forum to explore the way forward for A&E nursing education. This linked to the study of emergency nursing that I was undertaking through the RCN A&E/3M Health Care award. The findings of my work were published in the *Nursing Times*, 'Behind the times' (October 1986). What I found was that it was impossible to establish what was normal practice for nurses in A&E. Each department varied considerably as to the skills undertaken by nurses. Often skills acquired on the ENB A&E course were not being used or local certification was required. Through a timing study I was able to demonstrate that an increase in direct nursing intervention at triage could reduce patient waiting time. Either by sending the patient directly to X-ray or by treating the patient with a minor injury had the potential to reduce patient waiting time by an average of 30 minutes with as much as 54 minutes in some cases.

As Chair of the A&E Nursing Forum I opened the study day by identifying the purpose of the day which was: to determine the present clinical role of the A&E nurse; to identify advanced nursing care in A&E; to remove post basic training from local restrictions; to ensure common skills were taught on all A&E courses and to have these accepted nationally.

Following the study day a working party was established to present the case for national standards and to develop a more robust A&E course. The need for a more robust course was clearly demonstrated in the October 1986 *A&E newsletter*. Derek Eaves (runner up of the RCN A&E/3M Health Care award) had surveyed ENB A&E courses and found the 14 ENB 199 courses were inundated with applicants. He demonstrated many differences between what was taught on each course and concluded that the course had no consistent significance and each hospital had a casual treatment of the curriculum. He concluded that the hospital nurse educators and the ENB needed to agree a nationally recognised course. This was of course something that the A&E Nursing Forum had grappled with since its inception.

Following months of work the working party proposed the new A&E course, the draft being reported in the January 1987 *A&E newsletter*. It had an extensive curriculum and was based around the nurse working from a basic to advanced level of competency (this was one of the recommendations in my 1985 RCN A&E/3M Health Care award report). The two-level course would start at a basic level (similar to the current A&E course) and progress to a secondary advanced practitioner level. However, by November 1988 the *A&E*

newsletter reported that despite several years of work and meetings with the ENB by the previous and current committee, an advanced A&E course was not being taken forward. The forum officers continued to try new approaches to education including looking at an open learning course.

Because demand for the ENB 199 course continued to grow, the course length was subsequently reduced and course organisers were designing core foundations shared with other critical care specialties. This subsequently caused concern that A&E as a specialty was being eroded. Julia White from Whipps Cross Hospital, London speaking at the April *A&E Nursing 91* conference held in Bournemouth, voiced her concern that the ENB had recently initiated far reaching changes to many courses with the introduction of a common core competency. She pointed out that while elements of 'high tech' post registration courses were common, the proposal to unite two or three courses for a common core and to reduce the length of the courses to six months created a great danger that the branch content may be too radically diluted. Her presentation continued to highlight the vast differences in the ENB 199 course content, with little standardisation of the knowledge and skills gained. 'This was' she said, 'most evident in the areas of extended role and trauma education.'

In his article 'Education: reaching the parts' published in *Emergency Nurse* (Spring 1993) Ernie Botley (lecturer practitioner, A&E, John Radcliffe Hospital, Oxford) pointed out that even with Department of Health funding in 1990 that created more than 30 centres providing the ENB 199 A&E course, by 1993 courses still remained oversubscribed. A few institutions incorporated the A&E course into diploma or degree level programmes. Despite all of these initiatives many A&E nurses still relied on local and national study days and conferences to improve their knowledge base. This was demonstrated well in the April 1995 *A&E newsletter* where a whole page of diary dates covered study days from head and neck trauma, paediatric care, law and the court system, sudden death and major incidents as well as three clinically focussed conferences. This need was one of the main reasons why I was so successful in my consultancy/lecturing and expert witness business (see *It's Not All Blood & Guts: My Amazing Life as an A&E Nurse*).

As more college/university based courses were being developed so more A&E nurses were employed as lecturers and lecturer/practitioners. This led to a small group of nurses meeting at the A&E conference in 1991 and in March 1992 under the auspice of the RCN A&E Nursing Association forming the RCN A&E Education Special Interest Group. The group's purpose was to serve as a means of gathering, sharing and distributing information. The group was open to all registered nurses with an interest in the education of A&E nurses and would provide peer support for A&E nurse educators. By 1993 the group incorporated research into their remit and changed their title to the RCN A&E Education and Research Special Interest Group. This group held many successful conferences and throughout the pages of the *A&E newsletters* and *Emergency Nurse,* regular reports kept members up to date with changes in both education and research.

By the time the autumn 1995 *Emergency Nurse* was published there were so many ways nurses could access A&E education and development it was becoming more and more confusing. The RCN A&E Education and Research Special Interest Group published the first of two articles entitled,

'Educational opportunities'. The first article identified the growing number of educational opportunities and guided the reader through the maze. The group indicated the shift from traditional post registration courses to diploma and degree level studies. They indicated the need for core and specialist knowledge and skills. What is required, they stated, was a 'national standard framework' – A&E nurses educated at the same level and exposed to the same opportunities (this of course had been the intention in 1985). The second article published in the winter of 1995/96 focussed on research. It suggested that specific staff working with academics should be setting research priorities for local units. It recommended research posts and research linked to lecturer practitioner roles and development nurses. It also recommended that research should be disseminated in a user friendly way without lots of jargon.

An additional challenge arrived in 1996, that of clinical supervision. An article by Lynda Holt (*Emergency Nurse*, Winter 1996) indicated that despite various interpretations of the title the UKCC had identified several factors for success including the need for a clinically focused professional relationship between the nurse and clinical supervisor. She concluded by indicating that while the title did not help the understanding of the role it was an opportunity for nurses to further develop their nursing practice, challenge professional boundaries and celebrate the value of nursing.

As even more educational roles developed in A&E, by April 2000 the National Network of A&E Learning Facilitators was successfully launched. Meeting three times a year and facilitating a full day for presentations, updates and discussion, regular reports of progress were published in the *A&E newsletter*. A change of name to the Network of

Emergency Learning Facilitators (NELF) in 2003 linked to the change of name of the RCN A&E Nursing Association to the RCN Emergency Care Association (ECA).

The report of NELF activities in the autumn 2006 *ECA newsletter* reported that at each meeting the group was now running a masterclass looking at common objectives given to practice/professional development nurses and lecturers and then a problem-based learning scenario around resolving common problems.

*   *   *   *

Historically, apart from developing nursing skills nurses have continually acquired skills originally in the hands of doctors and the concern in some quarters was that nurses had simply taken on these skills with little or no acquired knowledge base (as I did in 1975). The introduction of the document, *'The extending role of the nurse - legal implications and training requirements HC (77)22'* in 1977 was to ensure nurses undertaking 'extended skills' had the correct knowledge base linked with the skill. The document also included the need for approval for the nurse to undertake the skill and certification requiring signatures from medical staff and senior nursing staff. The intent was to bring clarity to how nurses correctly acquired clinical skills normally undertaken by doctors.

While the intention of this document was laudable, for A&E and other critical care nurses it caused many developments to slow and often skills already acquired were being curtailed. The guidelines were also used when new skills were being developed that were not directly taken from doctors. An example of this was the new capillary blood tests for glucose that had never been performed by doctors and when introduced, nurses were often the first professional group to undertake the procedure. Despite this, in many hospitals the 'extended skills' document was used and certificates issued signed by a doctor as well as senior nurse. As Ethel Buckles wrote in her April 1987 *A&E newsletter* editorial, 'Ten years ago the experienced nurse would have sutured, taken bloods and put up Intravenous infusion (IVI) 'drips'. Not so now in many places.' In the same newsletter a synopsis of a paper given by Sue Russell (adviser at the RCN) to the A&E conference in 1986 highlighted these issues. She gave an example of a nurse in A&E asking a paramedic to come from the car park into the department to start an IVI on a patient because a doctor was not immediately available and she was not certificated to do this. From my own experience in 1981, having acquired the knowledge and skills in the USA to safely and competently undertake manual defibrillation, cannulate and start IV fluids and intubate a patient's airway, and having a competency letter from the consultant, I was only allowed to practise once I had certificates signed by the chief nursing officer of our district, the A&E consultant and others.

In her *Nursing Standard – special supplement Advances in Clinical Practice* article, 'Developments or extensions' (April 1988), Frances Pickersgill, RCN Assistant Adviser in the Practice of Nursing questioned if the advice given in the 1977 'extended skills' guidelines was ever correct and as she said in the article, 'Even if it was it was certainly not correct in 1988.' Fortunately A&E nurses did not allow the 'extended role' document to completely curtail development as can be seen with the development of the Emergency Nurse Practitioner role (see further in this chapter) and the establishment of the Trauma Nursing Core Course in 1990 (chapter 13).

With the introduction of the document the *Scope of Professional Practice* in 1992 and the withdrawal of several guidance documents on 'role extension' everything changed. Nurses were free of many restrictions and as Lynn Sbaih, lecturer in A&E nursing, North Staffs College of Nursing & Midwifery pointed out in her article, 'Reaching out: nurses' role expansion' (*Emergency Nurse* spring 1993), the Scope of professional practice encouraged 'the parameters of practice' and for A&E nurses this enabled the nurse to provide high standards of holistic care. With the publication of more journals and books specific to A&E there had never been a better time to link knowledge with skill development.

*   *   *   *

At the same time as the debate around 'extended roles' was taking place, so too was the debate around how A&E nurses took on other roles as staff left at 5pm. The editorial of the *A&E newsletter* in November 1987 written by Ethel Buckles used the image of Janus (the porter of heaven commonly represented by two heads looking two ways) to illustrate how A&E nurses were looking two ways. One face was looking forward – developing our role into advancing nursing practice, triage, nurse practitioners, and specialist training. Our other face was looking backwards – we still took over most others' roles at 5pm including ECG technician, plaster technician, clerical work, domestic work and pharmacy. Ethel suggested that if we were to advance we had to ditch the backward stuff and at the same time know our end game (not just taking on tasks). 'We need to complement and enhance the nursing role' she said.

These thoughts reflected my own. During my RCN A&E/3M Health Care award study of emergency nursing in 1985 (Behind the times October 1986) I found that more

A&E nurses carried out reception/clerical duties, domestic work and made drinks for patients than were allowed to suture, record ECG's, administer IV drugs, perform venepuncture or perform defibrillation.

Even in 2003 *The Future Nurse* (RCN) reporting on nurses' views for the future recognised that the shared vision could only be achieved on the basis of improving patient care and patient experience and not picking up the work others leave behind or choose to delegate.

*   *   *   *

With the promises made by Tony Blair for his revolution in A&E care, in March 2001 the CNO for England published *The NHS Plan - an action guide for nurses, midwives and health visitors*. Although focussed wider than A&E, in the summary it stated that patients wanted better quality care especially around fundamental care of hygiene and nutrition, more staff, more time to listen, more time to care. Patients said there was a need for strong nursing leadership (many wanted a return to Matron) and sisters/charge nurses should be more visible and clearly in charge of nursing in their area. The guide demonstrated how these wishes were to be achieved including the introduction of modern matrons, 10 key roles for nurses to work in new ways included ordering diagnostic investigations, direct referrals, admit/discharge patients, manage caseloads, run clinics, prescribe medicines and carry out a wide range of resuscitation measures including defibrillation.

In 2003 the Department of Health and Royal College of Nursing published *Freedom to Practice: dispelling the myths (2003)*. Linked to the *NHS Plan* the purpose of this publication was to provide a resource to nurses and others to clarify what nurses and others were allowed and able to do within their codes of practice. Focussed on first contact, urgent and emergency care, the foreword, signed by Sarah Mullally CNO and Beverley Malone RCN General Secretary pointed out that modernising emergency care also meant modernising education and training and measurable clinical competencies provided a framework for this while safeguarding standards of care. Comments in the document were expressed by Professor Sir George Alberti, National Director for Emergency Access Department of Health and Jonathan Asbridge, Clinical Director for patient experience in A&E, NHS Modernisation Agency.

Six myths (stages in the patient journey) and how they could be unblocked were cited. Examples included nurses not being allowed to refer patients for tests and investigations (myth), nurses not able to make initial diagnosis without referral to medical opinion (myth), nurses not able to refer patients for specialist opinion or discharge patients from hospital (myth). Each myth was explored and examples given of how they were busted. The document pointed out that the RCN Faculty of Emergency Nursing (chapter 10) provided a framework of clinical competencies enabling nurses to identify and move through an emergency care career pathway. In my board's eye view (*Emergency Nurse* March 2004) I indicated how the document could be harnessed to improve patient care.

With these two documents the green light was given for the A&E nursing workforce to take forward many of the developments that for so long had been desired and in 2006, Grant Williams, Chair of ECA made ministers aware at a multidisciplinary emergency services government meeting of the need for nurses to be given more opportunity for continuing professional development. Reporting on the meeting in the July 2006 *Emergency Nurse* a Department of Health spokesperson said, 'We encourage and support A&E staff to work differently and take on new roles to deliver service improvements. Continuing professional development has a part to play in this.' Supportive words but as Jim Bethel, senior lecturer at the University of Wolverhampton indicated in the board's eye view of *Emergency Nurse* (May 2007), NHS funding cuts was reducing training and educational opportunities for emergency nurses. He said, 'It seems that many trusts are intent on achieving solvency, not only by reducing or freezing staffing levels, but also by slashing nurse training budgets'. Due in part to the reduced educational budgets emergency staff looked at other ways of continuing staff development. In Leeds, trust emergency staff in 2006 pioneered professional development with on-line learning programmes.

Emergency Nurse Practitioners (ENP)

The concept of an emergency nurse practitioner within a district hospital's A&E department first came to the attention of the RCN A&E Nursing Forum at the 1986 A&E conference. Sonia Head A&E Nursing Officer at Oldchurch Hospital, Romford, Essex presented the work that had been undertaken in her A&E department. This was followed with an article by Peter Kohn, Charge Nurse in the A&E department at Oldchurch writing in the January 1987 *A&E newsletter*. Peter explained that the scheme started after a three year preparation period. During this period district and regional health authorities, the Department of Health and Social Security, the RCN and local community health councils and GPs had all been contacted. A protocol was drawn up by a steering committee comprising the A&E nursing officer, A&E consultant, Director of Nursing and others. The purpose was to reduce waiting times by the ENP providing assessment and treatment for a range of minor injuries. Thirteen items were identified, some that most nurses routinely provided in most A&Es such as removal of rings and removal of sutures. More controversial was being able to send patients for x-ray and treating minor lacerations and burns. In June 1988 the hospital produced an information leaflet highlighting the role of the nurse practitioner in the A&E department (BHB HA June 1988).

Although none of the interventions by those early pioneers may appear controversial today, in the 1980s the opposition to emergency nurse practitioners and especially ENP's requesting x-rays was high. Many nurses and doctors were opposed to nurses stepping into the world of medicine and most radiographers and radiologists were so against accepting requests from nurses that the RCN A&E Nursing Forum with the Royal College of Radiologists and College of Radiographers often met to try and resolve this issue. An article in the February 1999 edition of *Emergency Nurse*, 'Key issues in nurse requested x-rays' pointed out that the Audit Commission in 1996 recommended triage nurses to request certain x-rays and a study by the RCN, Royal College of Radiologists and the BAEM had shown it was safe. The conclusion of the article was that nurse requested x-rays was a new and exciting development.

Despite the 1996 recommendation, like most advancement to nursing roles it took a long time to resolve the x-ray issue, in fact guidance on nurse requested x-rays were eventually drawn up and published by the RCN, Society & College of Radiographers and NHS Alliance in November 2006 (20 years since that first presentation on ENPs). The 2006 guidance was to prevent the problem of having x-ray requests refused by some x-ray departments who had traditionally been reluctant to accept referrals from anyone other than doctors. In 2007 revised guidance on nurses requesting x-rays were published (*Clinical Imaging Requests from non-medically qualified staff*).

Following the presentation at the A&E conference in 1986 and that first article in 1987 the speed at which the development of the emergency nurse practitioner role and all the controversy surrounding it was fast. Almost immediately concerns were being raised - was it a specific role or a collection of extended skills? It did not appear to follow the philosophy of a nurse practitioner working in GP practice where the emphasis was on acting as an alternative consultant, managing minor and chronic ailments and the practice of health maintenance and promotion. What was the difference between a clinical specialist in A&E and an ENP?

Margaret Lee, RCN adviser in the practice of nursing, pointed out in her 1987 A&E conference presentation that the RCN document *New Horizons in Clinical Nursing* (1976) described the development or extension of the nurse's role as a means of developing the role of nurses whose prime commitment was to nursing care. Margaret was not sure that the emerging ENP role was really an alternative to or enhanced the care of a patient, but rather was a mix of triage and extended role. However, she believed the ENP could emerge from the current role and, 'Patients should be able to choose the ENP as an alternative primary therapy.' She pointed out however, that 'to enable the patient to do this the role needs to be defined and especially what the role offers the patient that others do not. It should not be a stop gap service due to a reduced number of junior doctors.'

Nurses working in GP community hospitals had often provided minor injury care in the absence of medical staff well before emergency nurse practitioners were introduced into district hospital A&E departments. Highlighted by K Wolfenden, Sister in charge of the minor injuries department of Whitworth Hospital, Matlock, Derbyshire (*A&E newsletter* November 1987) she indicated that, 'such a service had been in operation for 12 years (full training and recognised role) yet little was known of this service within the wider A&E specialty.'

The RCN A&E Nursing Forum quickly set up a working party to identify where the ENP role was being developed and to produce guidance to members. The forum organised a discussion day at the RCN and many nurses attended to both learn more and participate in the debate. By 1988 a position statement had been produced and a definition of an ENP agreed. The definition of an ENP was – a nurse specialist who has a sound nursing practice base in all aspects of A&E nursing with additional skills in physical diagnosis, psychosocial assessment, the prescribing of care, preventative treatment and the promotion of health.

By January 1989 the *A&E newsletter* indicated more ENP programs were being developed and Anthony Potter, an A&E course 199 student from A&E, Leicester Royal Infirmary provided an article on his research into the potential role of the ENP. He believed the ENP was the opportunity for nurses to develop their own professional and autonomous role. His research aimed to identify if nurses had the ability to request x-rays, prescribe tetanus immunisation, treat minor injuries correctly and the effect the role had on waiting times. The conclusion was all areas appeared to prove the ENP could carry out the care effectively.

A guidance leaflet was published by the RCN A&E Nursing Forum in early 1990 (*Emergency Nurse Practitioners...guidelines*) which further detailed the role and training requirements and clarified the difference between the triage nurse who was responsible for assessing the priority for care and the ENP who was concerned with the prescription of care. The leaflet referred the nurse to a plethora of DHSS circulars setting out legal implications for extension of roles and made clear that there was no legal requirement for patients to be seen by a doctor merely because they presented in A&E. Training was suggested as covering four modules including assessment and diagnosis; treatment and prescribing; communication skills; health behaviour and prevention of injury and illness.

Emergency Nurse (March 1992) featured two articles describing the development of the Emergency Nurse Practitioner in A&E. The article written by Peter Howie, Senior Nurse Manager, A&E Lincoln County Hospital reported that following a study that showed the experienced nurse with additional training could provide a safe service, all first level nurses had been trained as ENPs. The second article described the ENP service in A&E Derbyshire Royal Infirmary. Like the first article it described the training undertaken and the way the role was expanding to include knee and hip injuries, elbow injuries, acute eye problems and appropriate care and treatment of children.

In the same way as the lecturer and lecturer/practitioners had seen the need for a special interest group within the RCN A&E Nursing Association so too did the ENPs. The special interest group was established in March 1992 with the purpose of supporting the development of the ENP role and influencing the education and training for the role, including trying to ensure standardisation and national credibility. The group worked to establish regular meetings, study days and these were published in the *A&E newsletter*. By 1993 updated guidelines of the role were published by the group and by 1994 study days on developing the future practice of the ENP had been held. Roadshows and study days continued and in the July 1996 *A&E newsletter* it was reported that due to the reduction of junior doctors' hours more trusts were moving to employ ENPs.

Throughout the latter part of the 1980s and into the early 1990s, more ENP roles were developing in the community setting because of the move to replace some A&E departments with minor injury units. My article in *Nursing Standard* (February 1993) described how following the closure of Orsett Hospital's A&E department, we set up a community minor injury unit by training a small number of nursing staff to provide minor injury care. Following an ENP approach, internal training comprised a range of assessment and treatment skills and each ENP was assessed for competency. Managerially I managed the unit that was linked to the newly centralised A&E department at Basildon Hospital.

In August 1993 the RCN held the first UK conference on Nurse Practitioners. Speakers included nurse practitioners from a variety of specialties and A&E featured prominently over the three days of the conference. An article by John Beales, nurse practitioner, St Charles' Hospital minor injuries unit, London in the spring 1994 *Emergency Nurse* questioned why patients were waiting and the need for nurses to contribute to minor injury care. It indicated that ENPs continued to be developed and that minor injury units were growing fast, mainly because of the continuing closure of A&E departments due to the economic pressures of the internal market. The article also demonstrated how ENPs were overcoming nurse prescribing, by prescribing by protocol, an agreed statement by doctor and nurse detailing each particular drug and dose from an agreed list and circumstances in which it can be given. It also mentioned the ongoing issues around nurses requesting x-rays.

By the summer of 1995, with the continuing success of developing ENPs there was a need to clearly provide a purpose statement. This statement had to include the need for the ENP to provide independent but accountable treatment and management services to ambulatory A&E patients with minor injuries and non-acute conditions. This need was highlighted in *Emergency Nurse* (Summer 1995) where it was stated by the author Mike Walsh that the independence from the A&E SHO was fundamental, as it made the role different from the more traditional nursing role where the doctor retained control of the medical care. This was a fundamental shift from the traditional view of the ENP.

Further support for the role was demonstrated in the Spring 1996 *Emergency Nurse* when the journal scan reported that the *Journal of A&E Medicine* (1996) had shown that nurse practitioners trained in X ray interpretation were at least as good as SHOs in recognising the need for x ray and were as competent in their interpretation of a limited range of x-ray views of patients attending minor injury units. The authors believed that the results should encourage more nurse-led minor injury units.

A further move to the autonomy of ENPs was highlighted in an *Emergency Nurse* article, 'Nurse practitioners in A&E: a literature review' (Summer 1996). The authors pointed out that a literature review of nurse practitioners in A&E showed that ENPs provided a new complementary minor injury service to that currently provided by A&E medical staff. Patient satisfaction was high and patients appreciate the more relaxed style of consultation offered by an ENP.

By the summer of 1996 (10 years since the first presentation at the A&E conference) the *Emergency Nurse* editorial pointed out the hottest topic amongst A&E nurses was nurse practitioners. Brian Dolan pointed out that the term nurse practitioner was interpreted differently in different areas. Some people he said confused the nurse practitioner with the clinical nurse specialist. Some medical staff believed nurse practitioners were employed simply to reduce junior doctors' hours and some nurse managers believed that anyone could be a nurse practitioner even at D grade (junior nurse). The editor pointed out that if the professions had such a poor understanding of the concept, what hope did the public have of understanding it and more important, what protection did they have if things went wrong.

The RCN sought to clarify the difference between a Clinical Specialist and a Nurse Practitioner. The clinical nurse specialist demonstrated a high level of clinical practice, wealth of experience and superior expertise and knowledge in a specific field of nursing. A nurse practitioner practised autonomously but was accountable and providing care to patients independently of direct medical supervision.

Hoping for some clarity from the nursing registration body, the UKCC, was short lived. The May 1997 *Emergency Nurse* reported that nurses have welcomed the UKCC's decision (March 1997) not to set standards for advanced practice, but concern has been raised that the status of the nurse practitioner still remains unclear. This was not the last report on this subject as in June 1997 *Emergency Nurse* again reported that the UKCC was looking to how it could include nurse practitioner courses in a category of recordable qualifications for specialist practice. However, in June 1998 an article in *Emergency Nurse* indicated the UKCC was still struggling with the role of nurse practitioners.

Articles on how to implement a nurse practitioner service continued throughout the latter part of the 1990's as demonstrated in the November 1998 *Emergency Nurse*. John Beales, Senior Nurse Practitioner, Primary Care/Minor Injuries Unit, Homerton Hospital, London indicated (by using figures from a 1996 survey) that 98 A&E departments in the UK (36% of the total number) claimed to offer such a service. The article covered how to set up the service, why it was needed, where to locate the nurse, how to finance the role and what training was required.

To try and clarify the added value of the nurse practitioner service, Bernie Edwards in the June 1999 *Emergency Nurse* pointed out that the nurse was not a doctor substitute and he indicated that the service was complimentary to medicine rather than antagonistic. The concept of caring was the central ethic and a necessary condition of therapeutic practice. This issue of nurse or doctor substitute was further illustrated in the November 1999 *Emergency Nurse* article entitled, 'Autonomous practitioner or handmaiden?' The conclusion was that ENPs were neither totally autonomous but also nor a doctor's handmaiden. The author pointed out that yet again the local obstacles caused the most issues and a call for a standardised national ENP training and education was required.

As health care moved into the new millennium, and ENPs were becoming a common feature in many A&E departments and minor injury units, the ongoing debate around definitions and education continued. There were still many academics who considered the ENP to be a nurse with a range of extended skills rather than the nurse practitioner who practiced autonomously within a wide range of specialties. Concern also continued around the issue of no regulation and numerous nurses calling themselves nurse practitioners or ENPs, yet the training and roles were very different across many A&E departments. Also the on-going debate regarding the need for a degree education versus experience in practice continued. These debates can be seen in numerous editions of *Emergency Nurse* (December 2000/January 2001, February 2004, April 2004). They cover a whole range of issues linked to the ongoing development of the ENP including Teleconsultation by ENPs and see and treat - the emphasis being on treatment of the patient with minor injury as they arrive.

During the 2000s some ENPs were moving into treating major cases and acquiring percussion and auscultation skills while others were running review clinics. Others were undertaking masters degrees so becoming advanced practitioners and assessing and treating a whole range of conditions. In the October 2001 *Emergency Nurse* an article demonstrated how an ENP was working with paramedics to provide care in the patient's home.

Patients definitely liked the ENP role as demonstrated in the March 2001 *Emergency Nurse*. The article by Ruth Walsh, A&E staff nurse at the Royal Alexandra Hospital, Paisley showed through a literature review a high level of satisfaction. This reflected a much earlier report by the Audit Commission in 1996 showing that patients liked ENPs.

Brian Dolan, Editor of *Emergency Nurse,* summed up the situation in his February 2003 editorial, pointing out that in 1998 he told delegates at a conference that the UKCC let nurses and the public down by refusing to recognise the growth of nurse practitioners and with no core requirements for the post anyone could call themselves a nurse practitioner. Five years on, he pointed out nothing had changed. The NMC (that replaced the UKCC) had still not taken the role on board. Eventually towards the end of 2004 the NMC put out a consultation document on the definition of a specialist nurse practitioner and the minimum qualifications, competencies and proficiencies required.

As part of the government's initiative to reduce waiting times in A&E and to achieve the 4 hour target, see and treat had been introduced. In 2004 a report from the Department of Health Care Group Workforce Team for Access advised that at least 1,000 more ENPs were required to make see and treat work and this led towards the idea of a more generic advanced practitioner. In the April 2004 *Emergency Nurse* an article covered the extended skills required to become an Emergency Care Practitioner (ECP). This was part of the modernisation programme aimed at developing roles of nurses, paramedics, physiotherapists, occupational therapists and pharmacists and expanding the role between hospitals, primary and acute care (chapter 15). At the same time with the development of the Medical Care Practitioner (MCP) as a means of compensating for reduced junior doctors' hours, many nurse practitioners vented their anger in the December 2005 *Emergency Nurse* indicating that they believed they already filled this role.

The issue of who does what (ENP, ECP, MCP) was not going away and in the *Emergency Nurse* (September 2006) it was reported that a turf war had broken out between ENPs and ECPs with one lecturer suggesting that the way forward was to get rid of ENPs and paramedics and to simply have one level of advanced emergency care practitioner in both the emergency department and on the ambulances.

This of course was not the first time this idea had been suggested. Back in September 1998, Robert Crouch for his guest editorial in *Emergency Nurse* suggested the development of an integrated emergency care system from roadside to recovery, and highlighted role development being discussed by the Joint Royal Colleges Ambulance Liaison Committee (JCALC). Exploring the future provision of paramedic training had led to suggestions of the development of a 'generic emergency care worker' or 'practitioner in emergency medicine'; an individual who could work both in the A&E setting and pre-hospital arena and that the educational basis for this role would be nursing.

In the December 2006 *Emergency Nurse,* an article by Sue First, advanced practice learning facilitator and Erica McGregor, practitioner development programme manager, reported on the success of the Salford ECP service indicating that it was complementing not replacing existing services from GPs and Nurse Practitioners. ECPs were able to work in the patient's home or walk- in centres out of hours, to deliver care, rather than the person being transported to A&E.

The ENP special interest group within the RCN A&E Nursing Association continued to report on successful study days and how the role continued to expand within the UK. As many ENPs were now working in the ever expanding community minor injury units, a special interest group was established in 2001 and in 2004 the ENP group and minor injuries group merged.

Nurse prescribing

Nurse prescribing was first proposed in the Cumberlege report in 1986. It was suggested that treatment in the community would be enhanced if community nurses were able to sign prescriptions. The *A&E newsletter* January 1990 reported that nurse prescribing would become reality in the 1990s with the report being considered. The Prescriptions by Nurses Act came into force in 1992 although it did not apply to all nurses and it was restricted in the range of medicines the nurse could prescribe.

For most ENPs, in the early days any drugs that the nurse considered appropriate would have to be prescribed by a doctor. This included anti-tetanus injections. With the introduction of Patient Group Directions (PGDs) in 2000 (current guidelines on the NICE website), ENPs were able to supply and / or administer a medicine directly to a patient with an identified clinical condition without the need for a prescription. Strict rules applied and the PGD had to be signed by a medical prescriber.

During the 2000s extensive reviews of nurse prescribing and the expansion to other groups of nurses meant it was coming closer for A&E ENPs to prescribe. The June 2001 *Emergency Nurse* reported that government ministers had agreed that nurses in emergency care would be able to prescribe independently for minor injuries under the extension of nurse prescribing. However the July/August 2002 *Emergency Nurse* editorial indicated that a decade after the nurse prescribing act was passed emergency nurses were still unable to formally prescribe and the RCN A&E Nursing Association Chair Grant Williams hit back at claims by *The Lancet* editorial suggesting that plans to roll out nurse prescribing was a dangerous, uncontrolled experiment. Grant described the editorial as 'demeaning'.

Although nurse prescribing still remained a no go area for emergency nurses, changes to the Misuse of Drugs Act 1971 came into effect in October 2003 and this allowed emergency nurses to administer diamorphine to treat chest pain and to administer all Schedule 4 & 5 drugs under patient group directions (PGDs). In the December 2005 *Emergency Nurse*, Chair of the ECA Grant Williams said he planned to call for a re-write of PGDs to allow nurses to administer controlled drugs in any care settings. He also indicated his delight that the extended formulary for nurse prescribing was liberating nursing practice.

Eventually nurse prescribing in emergency departments became a reality to the point where appropriately trained nurses could prescribe codeine and a range of other drugs for pain relief at triage. Independent prescribing followed in 2006.

Consultant Nurse
Tony Blair announced the introduction of the consultant nurse in September 1998 at the *Nursing Standard's* Nurse 98 awards ceremony, the first ones coming on-line in 1999. In the September 2000 *Emergency Nurse* the guest editorial by Robert Crouch reflected on the announcement. He pointed out consultant nurses were not as new as one might think as back in the 1980s development of nurse led units had taken place though the titles were different or not used. Others felt this was a rebadging of clinical nurse specialist, however Robert argued that the description of the role suggested it was a new breed rather than a rehash. He pointed out disparity between consultant nurses already existing with marked ranges in salary, expectations and academic level.

In the April 2001 *Emergency Nurse* an article by Chrystal Fox and Bob McMaster, both consultant nurses at Leeds General Infirmary, demonstrated the experiences of the two in A&E. They pointed out the role was designed to allow expert clinical practice 50% of the time with the emphasis being on professional leadership and consultancy, education and training, service development, research and evaluation. The nurse should be educated up to or beyond master's degree, have senior experience and a track record of practice development and scholarship. The two pointed out that initially there was a degree of confusion and scepticism from many disciplines of health care professionals concerning the role. I can understand that concern because in the title of the article 'Nurse consultants in A&E' and throughout the article, the term nurse consultant is used while the authors' actual title is printed as consultant nurses.

By 2003 there were a number of consultant nurses in post around the UK and attention started to focus on the next generation as outlined in the November 2003 *Emergency Nurse*. The article by Robert Crouch, Ruth Buckley and Katherine Fenton described a pilot programme between three trusts in southern England to develop consultant nurses in emergency care. The article reflected on the roots of consultant nurse development and the role that had been laid out formally in the nursing strategy document, *Making a Difference* (Department of Health 1999). The strategy was to improve career prospects, strengthen education and training, and boost the status of nurses, midwives and health visitors. Its goal was to enable nurses to make a greater contribution to health and health care.

The pilot programme enabled five trainee consultant nurse posts to be established. Based in the three emergency departments, they had a 25 percent professional, educational and personal development component, a 50 per cent service delivery component and a 25 per cent service development component to prepare them for the consultant nurse role. The article went on to indicate the recruiting of trainees would take place over the following few months.

During the 2005 RCN ECA research conference and reported in *Emergency Nurse* (May 2005) concern had been raised over the consultant nurse role needing more clarity. Research showed 80% of consultant nurses in emergency care had no competency framework in which to operate and many lacked preparation and support. Marie Davies-Gray who held one of the five nurse registrar posts on the pilot programme mentioned above, told delegates at the conference that the disparity between consultant nurse posts was the 'biggest challenge' to the initiative. She said, 'People have had to create their own pathways. One of our recommendations is that this needs to be nationally agreed.'

In the October 2007 *Emergency Nurse,* Nancy Fontaine, Consultant Nurse, A&E, Whipps Cross Hospital, London and three colleagues from other hospitals in the UK explained the functions of the consultant nurse. In the article they indicated that partly as a result of strategy documents published over the period 1999 – 2002 the purpose of the role, to support improvements in healthcare delivery and strategy, became better understood. The authors pointed out that the role encompassed four key functions –

> Clinical: helping to develop expert practice;
>
> Strategic: providing professional leadership and consultancy;
>
> Educational: training and developing staff and

Evaluative: integrating research with practice and service development.

The functions had to be closely inter-related parts of a coherent whole and examples of how these were achieved were provided. They pointed out that the consultant nurse must remain in clinical practice and they demonstrated how consultant nurse trainee programmes were being constructed.

Modern matrons

Prior to the loss of the title Matron within the NHS in the early 1970s, the matron was seen by the public as the figurehead of nursing. Despite a raft of titles for a senior nurse of a hospital, between then and the millennium, the public still called for the return of the matron. Responding to the call for the return of matron the government introduced 'modern matrons' in 2001. Rather than overseeing a whole hospital the modern matron had a number of wards or a department in which to improve standards of clinical care, in my view the return of the nursing officer role of the 1970s and 80s.

By 2003 the roll out of modern matrons to all emergency departments in England was underway (by June 2003 there were around 30 in place) and it was announced by the Health Secretary that every modern matron would receive £10,000 to improve standards of cleanliness, hygiene, comfort and patient information. The RCN A&E Nursing Association gave a cautious welcome to the roll out. The May 2003 *Emergency Nurse* included a news item – A&E modern matrons given £10,000 as a one off to improve the A&E environment including extra cleaning or drinks and snack machines for patients and carers. Chair of the RCN A&E Nursing Association, Lynda Holt was disappointed that the money was tied to the title modern matron and not going to the department per se. As time progressed the senior nurse of the emergency department either took the modern matron title or retained a senior nurse title. When I reflect back on my own role as the nursing officer of A&E at Orsett Hospital I had the managerial clout to make things happen and standards of clinical care was my number one priority.

References

Cumberlege J: (1986) *Neighbourhood nursing: a focus for care* [Cumberlege Report]. London: HMSO

Department of Health: (1977) *The Extending Role of the Nurse - legal implications and training requirements HC (77)22.* London: HMSO

Department of Health Nursing Division: (1989) *A Strategy for Nursing.* London: HMSO

Department of Health (1993) *A Vision for the Future.* NHS Management Executive. London: HMSO

Department of Health: (1993) *The Health of the Nation: Key Area Handbook – Accidents.* London: HMSO

Department Of Health: (1999) *Making A Difference - strengthening the nursing, midwifery and health visiting contribution to health and healthcare.* London: HMSO

Department of Health: (2001) *The NHS Plan- an action guide for nurses midwives and health visitors.* London: HMSO

Department of Health (2003) *Freedom to Practice: dispelling the myths*. London: HMSO

Dolan B Holt L Accident & Emergency: (2008) *Theory into Practice*. Baillier Tindall Elsevier

Havering and Brentwood Health Authority: (June 1988) *The Role of the Nurse Practitioner in A&E services at Oldchurch Hospital Romford*. Leaflet published by the Health Authority

Jones G: (1986) *Behind the Times*. Nursing Times Oct 15 30-33

Jones G: (1990) *Accident & Emergency Nursing: A Structured Approach*. Faber & Faber London

Jones G: (1993) *Minor injury care in the community*. Nursing Standard: February 17/volume 7/number 22/ 35-36

Jones G Endacott R Crouch R: (2003) *Emergency Nursing Care: Principles and Practice*. Greenwich Medical Media Ltd London

Jones G: (2019) *It's Not All Blood & Guts: My Amazing Life as an A&E Nurse*. Self-Published available through Amazon

Medicinal Products: Prescription by Nurses etc. Act 1992

Notes on Nursing 1860 Dover publications Constable & Co Ltd, London (1969)

Nursing Standard: (week ending April 23 1988) *Advances in Clinical Practice*– special supplement pages 14-15

Nursing Standard (8th September 2004) RCN Nursing the future campaign. RCN Publication

National Institute for Clinical Excellence (NICE): Patient Group Directions: Medicines practice guideline [MPG2] Published date: 02 August 2013 Last updated: 27 March 2017

Royal College of Nursing: (1976) *New Horizons in Clinical Nursing*. RCN Publication

Royal College of Nursing: (1990) *Emergency Nurse Practitioners – guidelines leaflet*. RCN Publication

Royal College of Nursing: (1994) *Accident & Emergency - Challenging the Boundaries*. RCN Publication

Royal College of Nursing (2003) *The Future Nurse*. RCN Publication

Royal College of Nursing: (2003) *Defining Nursing* RCN Publication

Royal College of Nursing: (2007) *Clinical Imaging Requests from Non-Medically Qualified Staff*. RCN Publication

UKCC (1992) *Scope of Professional Practice*. London: UKCC

CHAPTER 10
THE FACULTY OF EMERGENCY NURSING (FEN)

Throughout its history, the A&E officers have put forward course curriculums to the regulatory bodies of the day. As described in previous chapters the RCN A&E Nursing Forum was key to the first A&E course and in chapter 9 I described how as early as 1987 a basic and advanced A&E course was proposed. Prior to 1990, as part of a proposal for Association status within the RCN, the officers had indicated that one of the objectives was to provide post basic education and role development of the A&E nurse.

The Faculty of Emergency Nursing (FEN) could have been the ultimate success story in the early development of emergency nursing. Inspired by Robert Crouch who had the vision for a faculty within the RCN, it was launched at RCN Congress in April 2003. Despite widespread support from both the RCN Council and a government health minister at the time, by 2006 the faculty had been 'watered down' to such an extent that the FEN governing board decided to run the faculty independently of the RCN. It never achieved the status within emergency nursing that the pioneers envisaged.

Robert Crouch first suggested the idea of a faculty to me in 1995. He had the vision of integrating education, competency development, a career pathway and standards of practice. A meeting between Robert, Alison Kitson (then Director of the RCN Institute) and me proved very positive and the first step was for me as an RCN Council member to convince Council to support the idea, which fortunately they did.

Following the agreement by RCN Council, a series of key player meetings within the RCN A&E Nursing Association took place and after many drafts a structure for the faculty began to emerge. By April 1997, Robert reported in the *A&E newsletter* that several meetings had taken place between the Association, RCN staff and council and that the idea of developing a faculty structure within the RCN for other membership groups was mooted. A&E would be the first pilot and a faculty steering group was being formed to take forward this initiative.

Although the membership of the RCN A&E Nursing Association were aware of the work through the *A&E newsletter*, it was our first joint article in the autumn 1997 newsletter and the follow up more detailed article in *Emergency Nurse* (October 1997) that brought the faculty to the majority of A&E nurses' attention. Robert and I pointed out that with the tendency over recent years to develop generic 'critical care' courses, these in some ways had detracted from the specialty of A&E nursing and failed to recognize the uniqueness and diversity of A&E practice. We pointed out that it was the publication of the RCN A&E Nursing Association's document *Accident & Emergency: Challenging the Boundaries* (RCN 1994) that had sown the seeds for the proposed faculty.

The article explained that the proposal was the development of a faculty of the RCN dedicated to the education and research needs of A&E nursing. The faculty would aim to develop a national educational framework to facilitate career development at all levels in the specialty, a programme to recognise specialist practice, advanced practitioners in the specialty and a number of clinical research posts at regional level. It went on to explain the faculty would establish national standards of clinical competency through the monitoring and accreditation of education, seek funding to commission and co-ordinate national A&E research and co-ordinate and provide a structure for educational activities currently undertaken by the RCN A&E Nursing Association. The proposed educational route was illustrated as a linear pathway between expertise and time and included a number of boxes representing modules that would eventually emerge. Three clinical/academic attainments were shown as associate, member and fellow. It would act as an advisory group to statutory bodies on issues pertaining to A&E nurse education and research, as well as acting as an advisory group to trust boards in the development of A&E services and appointments to senior nursing posts. Finally it would assess and validate training posts for the faculty.

The article demonstrated what the faculty would mean for the patient and the A&E nurse as well as what it would mean for the trust, the university and the specialty of A&E nursing. It concluded by indicating informal discussions had taken place with key stakeholders; discussions had taken place at two RCN A&E Nursing Association conferences and welcomed views from members.

The proposal was not without its critics as the *Nursing Times*, 'Clear passage to A&E' (October 8 1997) report by Rob Garbett illustrated. Barbara Vaughan, programme director for nursing development at the King's Fund was reported as saying, 'the idea reinvents the wheel, they're proposing to do what the national boards purport to do.' David Benton regional nurse director for NHS Executive Northern and Yorkshire suggested in the report that the proposal was out of step with government policy on how health services should be shaped by what patients want. He felt it was a reductionist idea and isolationist. Others however supported the proposal such as Jonathan Asbridge, Chief Nurse at the

Royal Hospitals Trust in London, saying in the report that, 'it would benefit patients' and Pippa Gough, assistant director for policy and practice at the RCN reported as saying, 'It would fill a gap between minimum standards set by the UKCC and national boards and best practice that should be provided by specialist practitioners.'

By the end of 1997, the Faculty had reached its feasibility stage. Through focus groups and as part of the development, emergency nursing was defined as 'the provision of immediate nursing care to people who have identified their problems as an emergency or where nursing intervention may prevent an emergency situation arising'.

At the annual A&E conference in November 1997 and reported in the December 1997/January 1998 *Emergency Nurse*, Robert Crouch demonstrated concern that A&E was being broken down into subspecialties and was losing the recognition of the A&E nurse as a specialist of A&E. The development of a faculty he said would provide a national framework for education and career development leading to recognised specialist and advanced practice.

Throughout 1998 members were kept updated on the progress of the faculty. The RCN published a leaflet in April 1998 – *Shaping the future of nursing - the faculty concept.* The first paragraph set out the aim - to develop nursing practice in a way which ensured patients received the highest standards of care. It pointed out that while the initial project would focus on A&E, other faculties would be developed. The leaflet explained how the faculty would link into a number of other RCN projects such as those of expert practice, promoting ward leadership and setting priorities in research and development. The leaflet laid out a number of reasons for the faculty and the six key stages to the project. It was clear that the RCN Council and the organisation backed the faculty, indicating in the leaflet that the concept had many benefits including the development of recognised standards of care to safeguard patients. It also indicated that nurses would also benefit from the introduction of career development frameworks; RCN members would have greater confidence to influence nursing and those nurses working in a particular specialty would have greater representation and authority.

In the September 1999 *Emergency Nurse*, Ruth Endacott who was now engaged by the RCN as the Faculty Project Evaluator/Facilitator and nine others including myself wrote an update article highlighting the progress that had been achieved. In particular the domain of emergency nursing had now been established comprising four key elements, nursing, environment, person and health. The linear pathway illustrated in the 1997 article had now developed into a concentric model with five levels and eight areas of practice covering the broad clinical range that forms emergency nursing. The five levels represented by the letters V-Z showed how a nurse could move from V (newly qualified or new to A&E) to Z (consultant nurse). The article continued to provide an in-depth explanation of the core activities for the various levels and competency statements. The authors concluded by emphasizing the work that was still to be undertaken to refine the clinical competency framework and to develop a national educational framework to support its implementation.

By March 2000 the faculty was ready to pilot the competencies in five sites; two in England, and one each in Scotland, Wales and Northern Ireland. In April 2000 RCN Council wrote an open letter to all members via *Emergency Nurse*. The letter indicated that many of the competencies would be used across the whole family of nursing so what had been developed had far greater significance than any of us could have envisaged when the feasibility study began. Council felt the project was exciting, challenging and would ensure the RCN of a leading edge position. Council unanimously supported the pilot study.

The Autumn/Winter 2000 *A&E newsletter* reported the pilot stage and the appointment of Rachel Rowe as the national projects manager to facilitate the pilot sites and work closely with project facilitators. A report by Sarah Goodgame, lead facilitator for the pilot study at Neville Hall Hospital, Abergavenny, Wales in the autumn *2001 A&E newsletter* demonstrated the work and commitment that was required by both the local facilitators and the A&E nurses to achieve developing the portfolios. 'Nurses themselves had no idea that they knew so much' was the headline of her piece. For me her final paragraph summed up what the faculty was all about, 'This project celebrates the fact that despite the trolley waits, threats of violence and the other negative aspects of our work, emergency nurses are making a difference for patients. Making practice visible in this way has been inspiring and has reinforced all the reasons why I still want to be an emergency nurse after all these years'!

Throughout 2001, 2002 and 2003 numerous articles, reports and conference presentations continued to inform members of the progress of the faculty. The pilot site update was reported in the September 2001 *Emergency Nurse* indicating that the core competencies had been tested in all five pilot sites and portfolios would be assessed by review panels once the specific competencies had been completed. At the November 2001 A&E conference the RCN General Secretary told the delegates she considered the faculty represented an exemplar for nurses in other specialties.

An article in *Nursing Times* by reporter Nikki Daly, 'Hands up for Hands-on' (February 2002) explored one of the aims of the faculty - to develop practical A&E skills. Interviewing Garrett Martin, regional facilitator for Northern Ireland and me, Garrett said, 'It will revolutionise nursing. It is a groundbreaking transformation process that will require a new way of thinking. In the past, a lot of value has been placed on technical skills in A&E. There is nothing wrong with that, but there are other skills that nurses use day in, day out in dealing with difficult situations. For the first time a value will be put on these.' I said that, 'the original aim was to introduce clear career pathways and standards in emergency nursing to enable people to develop their knowledge and skills. There has been too much emphasis on academic training, with little or no recognition of nurses' clinical skills in practice.'

A reflective view was how Garrett Martin offered a critical reflection of his journey through the development of FEN in the May 2002 *Emergency Nurse*. His conclusion was, 'The FEN will change the shape and character of A&E nursing. My experience of facilitating the FEN pilot while working in a practice development role reinforced my belief that A&E nursing is a leading edge in nursing specialism.'

More detail of the pilot phase was made available to members in the February 2003 *Emergency Nurse*. Rachel Rowe and Robert Crouch described the background, aims, processes and findings of the faculty pilot. It described the two-year phase that had taken place including the first year's work defining emergency nursing, an articulation of the values and beliefs around emergency nursing, the development of the core and patient specific competencies and the model for career development with explicit levels of practice. The description of the second year included the feasibility study and the award of monies to facilitate the testing of competencies across the UK through the pilot study. The article continued to explain in detail the methods used during the two year process, and how the pilot sites had been selected and the results of that work.

With a successful launch of a shadow faculty at RCN Congress in April 2002 the door was open for members to apply to join. To gain foundation status nurses had to apply before January 2004 by submitting an extended CV with supporting statements from colleagues and pay a flat fee of £50 for the first year. An application pack for founding membership was produced clearly indicating that the faculty was structured around an integrated clinical competency and career framework. It enabled clinical competency to be recognised through professional accreditation against standards. The standards were developed by emergency nurses for emergency nurses across the areas of emergency care of the older person, major incident planning, pre-hospital care, major trauma management, emergency care of the adult, child and young person, the person with minor injury or illness and with psychological needs.

The pack included background information on the faculty, a question and answer sheet, guidance notes of how to join, a self-assessment tool to ascertain the individual's level of practice, an application form, a CD-ROM containing the A&E competencies and an invoice form. Around 13,000 A&E nurses were expected to join within five years, the majority entering at associate level. RCN Council announced that three other specialties would move to faculty status and I was elected by Council to chair a new faculty steering group.

Although Council had financed the work to date, concern by the council treasurer and one or two other council members regarding long term funding did emerge. It was hoped that either nurses themselves or the employing trust would finance membership. This issue would start to overshadow the project and would be the long term challenge that was never resolved. My personal concern during this period was that costs being reported as those of the faculty project were possibly linked with a number of other RCN projects interrelated with expert practice. I could never prove it.

At the January 2003 Council meeting it was agreed that the faculty would be launched officially at RCN Congress in April. Although the majority of council members approved there was still ongoing concern around the long term financing and during the April pre congress council meeting the director of finance and council treasurer attempted to abort the launch. Emergency meetings between the two, the General Secretary, director of the institute and I enabled the launch to proceed and Sylvia Denton, RCN President and longtime supporter of the faculty, launched FEN as planned.

Reporting the launch, *Emergency Nurse* (June 2003) included the RCN President's wish that emergency nurses everywhere would show their support for the endeavour. However, there was concern from many of us regarding the £75 a year fee that RCN members would need to pay. This was 50% higher than envisaged the previous November and again led me to believe that more than the faculty was being financed, though this was impossible for me to prove. Having to persuade the members that this fee was required if the faculty was to survive long term was a blow for all those who had worked so hard to develop the faculty.

Despite the financial concerns the RCN named the four pre-faculty specialties that would now follow FEN - gastroenterology and stoma care forum, mental health, care of older people and paediatrics. Due to my term of office on council coming to an end in October 2003 the RCN president took the Chair of the faculty steering group. This group of which I was still a member now included representatives from the four pre-faculty specialties. Our task was to begin the development of a faculty structure within the college.

Health Minister Rosie Winterton in her keynote address to the A&E conference in November 2003 gave FEN her backing saying, 'I have been very impressed by the work of the RCN Faculty of Emergency Nursing on a framework of clinical competencies, to help provide a career pathway that supports lifelong learning tailored to individual learning needs.' It was also reported in the November 2003 *Emergency Nurse* that the Department of Health supported the faculty as a 'framework of clinical competencies enabling nurses to identify and move through an emergency care career pathway'.

By November 2003, 244 emergency nurses had bought a membership package and 26 had applied for accreditation with 20 of those becoming fellows, 4 members and 2 associates.

To help support nurses financially, the faculty was to become easier to join with the introduction of a fourth tier of affiliate status. Although joining FEN as an associate, member or fellow would continue to cost £75 the new affiliate level would be as little as £12 and would entitle the person to the faculty resources and access to the FEN network.

Having steered the faculty from its inception to its launch both Robert and I decided that it would be appropriate for others to form the new foundation board of the RCN Faculty of Emergency Nursing. Jill Windle, Lecturer and Practitioner at Hope Hospital (now renamed Salford Royal), Salford, Manchester was appointed Chair and Phil Downing, Nurse Manager, A&E, Gloucestershire Royal Hospital appointed Vice-Chair. In her first Chair's message in *Emergency Nurse* (December 2003/January 2004), Jill laid out her plans for the coming year including extended CV guidelines, competencies adopted across all grades and her final wish that FEN became synonymous with emergency nursing.

A position statement published in the autumn 2004 *ECA newsletter* indicated the RCN Emergency Care Association strongly supported the faculty and believed that it benefitted patients through good evidence based care, it benefitted NHS Trusts with reduced clinical risk and increased the ability of nurses to provide effective care and achieve key performance indicators, it benefitted emergency care managers as there were national benchmarks to assist in the employment process and it benefitted nurses giving a coherent framework which guided development in practice and career structure.

Elizabeth Bennett, Emergency Nurse Practitioner at Leicester Royal Infirmary A&E became the 1,000th member of the Faculty and by September 2004 there were more than 1,000 affiliated members who had paid for the starter pack. An article in *Emergency Nurse* (September 2004) from the FEN board gave information to members regarding completing extended CVs and the revised competency and career framework. The article also provided guidance for managers, lecturers, researchers and practice developers. The final thoughts in the article summed up where FEN was in the autumn of 2004, 'The Faculty epitomises lifelong learning and provides tools to demonstrate a nationally recognised and professionally driven career and competency framework. This extraordinary achievement firmly shapes the future course of emergency nursing as we all strive to develop and maintain high standards of competence and professional integrity.'

The December 2004 edition of *Emergency Nurse* reported that while RCN Council backed the development of the faculty of emergency nursing and outlined moves to make it central to the college's future membership services they agreed it should be linked to proposals for a 'professional development framework'. At that point in time it did not suggest to anyone involved in the faculty development that this could mean a fundamental change of direction. Throughout 2005 FEN continued to develop and the shadow faculties were well on course in developing their competencies and structures required to become future faculties within the RCN. FEN linked with Agenda for Change (2004) and the NHS (England) document *Reforming Emergency Care*.

A tremendous amount of work continued to be undertaken with numerous workshops provided for emergency nurses to develop their extended CVs. In addition, major reviews of the competencies were undertaken, with edition two of the core competencies being completed and launched in spring 2005. During the summer of 2005 all the core competencies were linked with all current initiatives such as agenda for change and the knowledge and skills framework. All members were indebted to the tremendous amount of work undertaken by the board members and others.

Linking education with practice was always key to FEN's success and in April 2005, *Emergency Nurse* published an article by Joss Kitching, senior lecturer emergency nursing, and Chris Thomas, lecturer practitioner emergency nursing, both of Thames Valley University describing how they had used FEN to address the overriding political agenda towards training nurses who are 'fit to practise.' It was done by enabling the service providers of emergency care to have more influence over the training and development of nurses. From this joint working the FEN eight areas of clinical practice were used in the two specialist emergency care modules. The first module correlated to five and the second to the remaining three.

By 2006 everything seemed to be going well. FEN was on track with members and the newly formed Malta Emergency Nurses' Association indicated they wished to work with FEN on professional educational programmes. FEN was working with the BAEM (emergency medical staff) on a number of projects and was formally linked with all the work that the Department of Health and the National Director for Emergency Access was undertaking on care pathways. The three pre-faculty specialties were well on their way to preparing to launch.

However, without warning the RCN stopped accepting any further applications for accreditation. Also, without any warning, while attending a faculty steering group meeting chaired by the President, we were all told the steering group was to be disbanded. Even the President had not been given any warning of this decision by the staff of the college.

This move appeared to be linked to the future of RCN specialty entities (forums, associations, societies). The RCN Council had voted in February to adopt a new 'professional development framework' that had originally been proposed in late 2004. Under the plans the College's 76 forums including the Emergency Care Association would be replaced with eight divisions. FEN was even more vulnerable and it was reported by one commentator 'FEN has had the plug pulled on it'. The report of this radical change to the forum structure within the college indicated that the new framework was not due for implementation until 2008 and consultation would continue at congress and through various meetings with the forums.

Despite this timetable FEN appeared doomed and the FEN board decided to step away from the RCN and become independent. The FEN board issued a statement indicating that 'following the decision of the RCN council to no longer support stand-alone entities and their recent unilateral decision to cease accreditation to the RCN faculty of emergency nursing, from 31st March 2006 FEN would become an independent body'.

Although FEN was now outside of the RCN it was hoped that emergency nurses, NHS Trusts and the government would continue to see FEN as a major player in emergency nursing. Initially this seemed to be the case with FEN and the College of Emergency Medicine holding a scientific meeting in November 2006. FEN also continued to work with the RCN ECA developing a computer based skill mix calculation tool and jointly ran the 2006 annual conference. As mentioned in Part One, it was at the 2006 conference that I was honoured with the first Honorary Fellowship of the Faculty.

By September 2007, due to widespread criticism, the controversial plans to replace the ECA and other college forums with 'virtual entities' and local networks (the eight divisions) had been shelved. Ironically had these proposals never been put forward in the first place and staff decisions on FEN accreditation and the steering committee not been taken unilaterally, the Faculty of Emergency Nursing may still be a reality within the RCN.

Although outside of the dates of this book FEN has continued to provide a service to emergency nurses and the following information is taken from the FEN website:

'Our primary goal is to improve patient care through the provision of education and competencies along a career pathway from registrants new to the specialism to senior nursing staff, autonomous practitioners and consultant nurses. We have three levels of competencies Associate Level (AFEN), Member Level (MFEN) and Fellow Level (FFEN). We are entering an exciting time. From 15th September 2020, FEN will be delivering a 2-Yr webinar programme to support AFEN development. We will also be holding monthly webinars to support Assessors as well as other monthly webinars too. All of which are included in FEN Membership. Individual or Corporate Membership is now available. Soon, the competencies will be accredited with an awarding body which can be mapped to the European Qualifications Framework – so in essence members can be awarded with credits for their practical work and underpinning knowledge.'

Reading this statement makes me feel that the hard work so many of us put into FEN was not completely wasted. Unfortunately the RCN missed out on what could have been a major success for the organisation.

References

Agenda for Change: https://www.nhsemployers.org/-/media/Employers/Documents/Pay-and-reward/AfC-Handbook-Version-1.pdf?la=en&hash=D2D451D330A220A11503DC07E0892B88FB92BAE3

Department of Health: (2001) *Reforming Emergency Care*. London: HMSO

Faculty of Emergency Nursing https://fen.uk.com/

Nursing Times: (Oct 8 1997) *Clear Passage to A&E* Vol 93 No 41

Nursing Times: (February 7 2002) *Hands up for hands-on*. vol 98 no 6 (11)

Royal College of Nursing: (1994) *Accident & Emergency - Challenging the Boundaries*. RCN Publication

Royal College of Nursing - Faculty of Emergency Nursing: Application pack for founding membership. RCN Publication

Royal College of Nursing: (1998) *Shaping The Future of Nursing - the faculty concept*. RCN Publication

CHAPTER 11
NURSING ASSESSMENT & TRIAGE

Prior to the 1980s very few, if any, A&E departments had a formal system of assessing and prioritising all patients who came through the doors. Ambulance patients would be assessed and a crude categorisation would be used such as the patient needs to be seen immediately or can wait a short while. Patients who walked in were normally seen by a receptionist and booked in. Unless they looked very ill, were bleeding all over the floor or complaining of chest pain it was usual for them to be directed to the waiting room and to wait.

Gradually a more formal assessment on arrival started to emerge. At the A&E conference in May 1983, the 1982 RCN A&E/3M Health Care award winner Peter Blythin spoke on triage systems he had observed in American hospitals and encouraged their use in UK departments. In my own department at Orsett Hospital, following my 1980 scholarship tour and observation of triage practice in Canada and the USA, I had introduced nursing assessment of all walking patients and this was followed by a formal triage system in 1983/84.

Triage means to sort or select. In the A&E department it refers to the category (priority) to which a patient is allocated following initial nursing assessment. As triage was introduced during the 1980s each department developed their own categories and waiting times. The system that we set up at Orsett in 1983/84 consisted of four categories – immediate, within 30 minutes, within 1 hour, can wait longer (though our waiting times did not normally exceed 2-3 hours). For us it was more than just the categories, we also encompassed a range of activities that was part of the complete triage package including early patient assessment, first aid, control of patient flow, assignment to the correct area of the department, diagnostic measures, explanation to the patient and priority rating. The whole focus was on the patient receiving safer care in a timely fashion *Nursing Standard,* 'Top Priority'(12th November1988).

As more departments were moving towards triage it was important to try and establish some national consensus around how it should be implemented. The May 1985 *A&E newsletter* indicated a working party was established to produce guidance on both triage & the nursing process in A&E. By January 1986 the RCN A&E Nursing Forum had produced introductory guidelines that were available through the RCN and by January 1989 the editorial of the *A&E newsletter* indicated triage was becoming well established throughout the UK. Members also used the *A&E newsletter* as a means of establishing links with departments that had established nursing assessment/triage. My own department received many visits from A&E managers who wished to introduce the system.

With nursing assessment/triage having become well established throughout the 1980s it was in the 1990s that the system started to be refined. One of the key influences on this was the introduction of *The Patient's Charter NHS 1992*. Charter standard 5 indicated that the patient could expect to be seen immediately and have their need for treatment assessed. By introducing this standard all A&E departments were required to set up some form of immediate patient assessment. Although the charter standard did not mention triage the vast majority of departments that were used for demonstration events and depicted in *The Patient's Charter* video provided a triage service. Consequently following the need to change, many departments that had not set up formal triage systems during the 1980s were now doing so.

It was also in the 1990s that the need to link the dependency of the patient for nursing care with early patient assessment was formalised. As previously stated in chapter 9, at Orsett we developed a dependency tool from the Components of Life model. The purpose of the tool was to ensure that all patients were assessed for dependency as well as urgency and that the appropriately skilled nurse was linked to the patient dependency level. Following a number of minor changes and research by Crouch and Williams (2001) the tool was named the Jones Dependency Tool (chapter 12).

Research was also being undertaken into what was considered 'best practice' and one of the early papers of the 1990s was an article in the October 1991 *A&E newsletter* by C Churchward, staff nurse at Epsom A&E department, Surrey. Ms Churchward discussed the different interpretations of triage and how the systems had been set up in 40 randomised A&E departments. Her article contained a brief history of triage and how it had moved from selection of produce at a market to its use in the two world wars and then into health care. It went on to describe her methodology and her review of published work including articles from Peter Blythin, M Palmer & E Hewitt, and me. Her findings showed there were two methods in use - reception first, followed by nurse assessment/triage (all 40 randomised departments in her study), and through the literature search she reported some nurse first systems. Areas for undertaking triage varied from designated areas to designated rooms. All hospitals provided some form of education for those undertaking triage but this varied in length and content. All the hospitals involved in the survey indicated that triage improved patient care through communication and information and the provision of first aid treatments. Her final sentence summed up where we were in the late 1980s/early 1990s – 'There is still a great deal of work to be undertaken in the development of this important Accident & Emergency function.'

Following the introduction of *The Patient's Charter* standard the need to submit audit returns led to the issuing of a NHS guidance letter in December 1992. This letter indicated that 'as a general rule of thumb we are content to accept a good performance against a challenging target of 5 minutes within this standard as a satisfactory position to achieve'. This led many departments to reconsider the way they introduced initial (immediate) patient assessment. It was further complicated by The Patient's Charter group considering initial assessment and triage as separate activities whereas most departments linked the two as one overall process. What this led to was some departments creating what became known as 'hello' nurses doing no more than eye balling the patient but complying with the 5 minute standard time. Other departments had patients taking a ticket system so 'accurate timing' could be achieved.

Further articles appeared in *Emergency Nurse* including an article – 'Triage decisions: how are they made' (Spring 1993). Chris Jones, Senior Lecturer at Sefton College of Health Studies pointed out that A&E units implement different triage systems; however the process usually concentrated on early patient assessment, priority rating, first aid and control of infection. He went on to explain that in triage the principle of first come, first served had been replaced by a principle of assessing patients' needs. 'Need' he said, 'is decided by nurses, the patient's own perception of need is not a guiding principle of any triage system'. Chris highlighted the fact that any system of patient prioritisation gives some urgency to the treatment of one patient while denying the same urgency to another; however, the system had been implemented with little or no controversy. It was recognised that a patient with crushing chest pain is in more need of attention than someone with a finger injury but the article did question how some systems looked at need in different ways. Should for example age, social class, poverty and dependants all be included during the assessment before allocation of a priority is made?

The following year in the spring 1994 edition of *Emergency Nurse* Robert Crouch gave a short history of triage development, then the article mainly looked at models in practice and linked this with *The Patient's Charter* Standard 5. He argued that little indication existed as to what constitutes assessment. Robert suggested a two-stage assessment - immediate to determine if resuscitation was required, and if not, further assessment should be undertaken pre or post registration. He also indicated that training was required for the role.

By 1994 there was a great deal of concern regarding the initial assessment standard, the timing and methods deployed in some A&E departments. Meetings between the RCN A&E Nursing Association and The Patient's Charter Unit took place and this led to the research that I undertook on behalf of The Patient's Charter Unit in 1995.

Initial assessment study 1995
Following the 1994 meetings between the RCN A&E Nursing Association and The Patient's Charter Unit I was engaged on a consultancy basis to determine the value of

initial (early) patient assessment within the A&E department and the most effective way of achieving this activity. The study undertaken during the first few months of 1995 involved visiting 44 departments in England, receiving information from two others, interviewing patients and staff and obtaining views from both patient and staff organisations. Patient attendances per department ranged from 30,000 to 120,000.

The main findings were that methods of providing assessment to non-ambulance patients in many departments had changed from an informal system to formal. The majority of departments provided initial assessment as part of triage and not as a separate activity. The majority of departments had a room where patient assessment took place. Others had triage desks and some had nurses based in clinical areas or at the reception desk.

Training and experience of staff providing assessment varied, with over 50% of staff having 9 months – 1 year A&E experience. The assessment in most cases included chief complaint, and a brief history with the provision of first aid prior to waiting. Triage was operated in every department visited. Although all departments achieved *The Patient's Charter* standard for ambulance patients, the achievement for non-ambulance patients varied considerably, mainly due to the length of assessment and treatment provided.

Department managers were keen to assure me that the audit time of five minutes from arrival to nursing assessment was achieved in their department. In reality, it seldom was. In many departments, it took me five minutes to reach and speak to a receptionist so I knew it would be longer to see a nurse. In other departments the 'hello' nurse was ticking a box indicating the standard had been achieved.

Nurse first versus receptionist first did play a part in the assessment time process, however although nurse first appeared to achieve the Charter standard in more departments than registration first it was not always the main reason for success. Many other factors were identified as being responsible for a speedy or slow process including the location of the room/desk, the length of time the nurse spent with the patient, the volume of arriving patients and the availability of the nurse at any given time.

Overall, while staff and patients were happy with the Charter standard, most realised that a 5 minute target was unachievable unless any meaningful assessment was abandoned when more than two patients arrived simultaneously. This was an important issue as I found that patient satisfaction came from the patient seeing the nurse early and feeling that an assessment of the injury/condition had been made. Dissatisfaction came when the assessment was rushed with little if any physical assessment. I highlighted this further in my article in *Nursing Times* 'Ways of reducing waiting times for patients in A&E' (March 1996) pointing out that one patient had said 'The nurse did not look at my foot. My toe could be hanging off.' A staff member remarked 'I feel sad that, having developed a good service, I am now just playing at it to keep people happy with figures.'

Another important issue that was identified was that the standard had no bearing on the time to see a doctor or nurse practitioner, therefore an overall waiting time would have been more useful. My lasting memory from one patient interview was his words: 'Don't tell us lies, tell us the truth.' He pointed to the scrolling information sign on the waiting room wall. It said: 'waiting time for doctor 30 minutes'. But he told me: 'I've been here an hour and still not seen a doctor.' The patient went on to say he understood his injury was not serious, and he knew he was not a priority but his message was that he did not want a false promise about the waiting time.

From this work my report *The value of initial patient assessment within the A&E department and the most effective way of achieving this activity* contained 19 recommendations. These were put to the Charter Unit including early patient assessment to continue as part and not separate from triage. A national triage scale should be developed and supported by all bodies and the initial assessment standard should be 5-15 minutes (80% within 5 minutes, 90% within 10 minutes, 100% within 15 minutes). The Charter Unit published my findings in the September issue of *The Patient's Charter News*.

By the spring of 1996 it was reported in *Emergency Nurse* that all departments were now complying with the initial standard (before the standard only 35% of departments had initial assessment of non-ambulance patients on arrival) however many reduced quality to achieve the 5 minute target. This was picked up by Baroness Jay, Health Minister, who in 1997 condemned the 'hello' nurse in A&E saying they were covering the letter of the charter but not the spirit.

Following much discussion within The Patient's Charter Unit and government, by May 1996 draft papers were circulated with my main recommendations for a better quality initial assessment and a 15 minutes audit time.

In her July 1996 *A&E newsletter* editorial, Kathie Butcher, while reporting the latest annual league table results, indicated more A&E departments were achieving the assessment within 5 minutes but questioned if it had improved the overall standard of care when many patients wait long periods for other interventions.

*   *   *   *

The need for a national agreed triage scale was moving forward and by 1996 an article in *Emergency Nurse* (Autumn 1996) by Robert Crouch (RCN) and Jonathan Marrow (BAEM), 'Towards a UK triage scale' indicated that across the UK the variation in the number of categories, nomenclature used and time frames attached to them was of concern. The article demonstrated a jointly agreed UK triage scale consisting of 5 categories with time scales for each. Immediate - resuscitation included all patients to be seen on arrival and usually met by a team standing by; very urgent – the patient being seen within ten minutes; urgent - the patient being seen within one hour; standard - the patient seen within two hours and non-urgent - the patient should not have to wait more than four hours. The article made reference to a pilot system being undertaken in the North West by the Manchester Triage Group. The authors considered the work by the Manchester group to be a reproducible and promising method that was soon to be piloted in several parts of the country.

The work by the Manchester Triage Group was highlighted in a presentation by Jill Windle at the 1996 RCN A&E Nursing Associations annual conference. Jill highlighted the development of the triage scale and the launch of the training packages in Feb/March 1997. She also explained that the work based on rigorous methodology would underpin the proposed National Triage Scales.

In October 1998 the RCN A&E Nursing Association put out a position statement encouraging the use of the national triage scale with additional information on the process, documentation, training, the environment where triage should be undertaken and an overall reference to good practice. The position statement recommended as good practice the administration of analgesia to waiting patients and the triage nurse being able to request radiographs. Despite the promotion of the national scale, by 1999 the Manchester Triage System was being widely used in the UK.

Two articles in 1999 reflected concerns around how triage was progressing. In the first article, 'What's wrong with triage?' (July/August 1999 *Emergency Nurse*) Bernie Edwards, Lecturer at Bournemouth University questioned triage in its current form asking, 'Does it live up to the espoused benefits?' He recommended that if triage was an attempt to improve patient care, what was needed was a change that rejects medical and organisation driven models and builds a service that can fully realise these aspirations. Using the example of what Bernie calls a move away from the hourglass model to one that recognises the client base, he suggests that if most patients attend with minor injury or primary care needs (often given category 4 status) then it could be argued that activity, resources and staffing should be directed to meeting those needs.

In the second article, in the September 1999 edition of *Emergency Nurse*, Cherine Woolwich, Nurse Practitioner, Colville Health Centre, Ladbroke Grove, London and an early pioneer of triage questioned how things had changed in triage. She particularly disliked the fact that nurses were mainly in rooms rather than walking the waiting room. She felt that triage had moved to a one off encounter rather than ongoing review. She also questioned both the National Triage Scale and Manchester Triage as being too rigid and inflexible. She felt that the expert nurse under the triage systems adopted was not being allowed the use of judgement or intuition.

Despite the move to immediate nurse assessment, during the 2000s many articles in *Emergency Nurse* demonstrated there was still a whole range of practices including receptionists still being involved with triage and giving advice, a lack of standardisation of triage and the role was highly variable. The February 2002 *Emergency Nurse* reported that 25 trusts were going to use the clinical assessment system currently used by NHS Direct and many walk-in centres to help triage patients.

By April 2002 *Emergency Nurse* was reporting on the RCN A&E Nursing Association's research conference which showed that triage using Manchester Triage was used in 80% of departments in the UK plus it had been rolled out to Ireland, Portugal, pockets in Australia, Canada, Japan and New Zealand.

The editorial by Brian Dolan in the May 2002 *Emergency Nurse* picked up on triage and how it had turned into a 'see you now, or see you later' system. However, the journal's board editorial by Jill Windle demonstrated how triage had a dramatic effect on the practice of emergency nurses, putting them in the front line of care, heightening assessment skills and developing the ability to manage a changing patient caseload. 'Triage gives a sense of organisation' she said, 'the waiting room is no longer an unknown entity.'

Despite Jill's comments in 2002, in May 2005 (*Emergency Nurse*) she asked in her board's editorial – 'To triage, or not to triage?' This was not a sudden change from someone who had spent years as a major player developing the Manchester Triage System but rather recognition that with the introduction of patient streaming and see and treat it was not clear where clinical assessment and application of clinical judgement occurred. Streaming and see and treat, introduced by central government was a method to provide fast, fair and convenient access to health care. There should be no wait for this care, with the right clinicians matched to the right patients at the right time. As Jill put it, 'These are great aspirations but, for most departments, somewhat unrealistic.' She emphasised, 'Where such models existed and waiting times were a distant memory then it is clear triage is not needed, but where such services were absent, the reasons for triage remains - to ensure patients are assessed and directed to appropriate services while ensuring that they are managed safely and effectively.'

Despite streaming and see and treat, triage was still required in many departments and during 2005 an updated Manchester Triage was launched (first published in 1997). It was also reported that the Manchester Triage System had been implemented in every department in Portugal.

The success of the Interventional Assessment Teams in the emergency departments in Leeds General Hospital was reported in the September 2005 *Emergency Nurse*. Experienced triage nurses assisted by HCAs were responsible for early assessment, identification of patient needs, early intervention and investigations and streaming major patients to the most appropriate areas.

So triage was to stay and despite some departments banishing it as a shameful activity and others heralding it as the gold standard for all patients (Jill Windle May 2005), in the February 2007 *Emergency Nurse*, health minister Andy Burnham believed emergency care staff should have 'more clearly defined powers' to refer on patients at triage from

A&E. Mr Burnham published a series of recommendations including the case for considering whether A&E staff need more clearly defined powers to refer patients on to more appropriate providers as part of the initial triage process. Although it was not clear from the article who the more appropriate providers were, it did follow earlier references to reasonable use of ambulances and A&E. It did feel to me a bit like déjà *vu*.

References

Department of Health: (1992) *The Patient's Charter*. London: HMSO

Jones G (1988) Top Priority. Nursing Standard week ending November 12, issue 7 vol 3 (28-29)

Jones G: (1995) *A Study of the Value of Initial Assessment Within the A&E Department and the Most Effective Way of Achieving this Activity*. The Patient's Charter Unit.

Jones G (1996) Ways of reducing the waiting times for patients in A&E. *Nursing Times* March 13, vol 92, no 11 1996 (31-32)

Patient Charter News: (21 September 1995 7) *Action in A&E: Good Practice on Immediate Assessment*. The Patient's Charter Unit Publication.

CHAPTER 12
STAFFING & SKILL MIX
INCLUDING THE JONES DEPENDENCY TOOL

Staffing of any ward or department cannot be achieved by just counting the number of patients and staff; it also requires a skill mix of knowledge and clinical ability. Throughout the history of A&E nursing one of the most contentious issues has been the required numbers and skill mix of nursing staff to provide safe and efficient care. To try and achieve this, a whole range of ideas, plans and mechanisms have been deployed with some degree of success. In the 1970s the skill mix was fairly straightforward. There were a small number of sisters/charge nurses who brought both management and clinical ability to the workforce. The majority of qualified nurses were staff nurses and enrolled nurses. Student nurses made up the rest of the staffing complement with a small number of nursing auxiliaries. The first *A&E newsletter* in January 1983 reported that following a joint conference with A&E medical staff in Dublin in April 1982, a working party had been set up to examine staffing levels and make recommendations. Unfortunately, apart from a note in the May 1984 newsletter indicating that the honorary officers had received a draft report no further reference is made in subsequent newsletters.

With the emergence of triage to assess and sort patients into categories for care, extended or advanced skills incorporated into nursing practice, as well as a need for paediatric and mental health nurses in A&E and the emergence of the emergency nurse practitioner in some departments, fundamental changes to the skill mix of the 1970s had occurred. The change in workload and professional development during the 1980s necessitated the need for a fresh look at staffing and particularly skill mix.

Until the late 1990s, most departments continued to base staffing on what the senior nursing staff believed they required and the money available. The problem was that money was in short supply and as I pointed out in my article, 'A&E nursing: all change ahead' (*Emergency Nurse* Spring 1993) senior nursing posts were disappearing or being downgraded. I indicated that the effects of devaluing A&E nursing in these ways were yet to be seen, but they may be seen both in the short term - senior staff leaving the specialty or facing compulsory redundancy, and in the long term – senior nurses employed at a much lower grade.

The *National Audit Office reports (England & Scotland 1992)* concluded that staffing was a local issue for clinical managers but further research was required to develop a practical tool for assessing the required number of staff and skills needed. Andrew Carr, Charge Nurse in A&E at Addenbrooke's Hospital, Cambridge presented a nurse workload measurement tool at the Pan Pacific Emergency Nurses Conference in Singapore in 1992. Known as GRASP (Grace Reynolds Application of a Study by PETO), Andrew explained how the tool used the clinical nurses' assessment of the patient's needs to accurately measure the hours of nursing care each patient had received. Clinical nurses entered data into microcomputers where it was analysed. GRASP provided the hard data enabling the nurse manager, administrators and accountants to better plan staffing and skill mix.

In 1993 the RCN A&E Nursing Association published the document *Skill mix in A&E nursing: a framework for managers.*

Much of the content came directly from the North East Thames Regional Health Authority document *Accident & Emergency Services – a guide to good practice* (1992) and went some way to help address the need for a staffing tool. It recommended staffing levels based on five key department areas and a number of posts from nurse manager to the novice nurse. Each post was described, as well as what was expected of the role holder and a set of practice, education and research skills linked to each one.

The *Emergency Nurse* editorial (Spring 1994) highlighted that A&E had become an employer's market and unless the nurse had an A&E course qualification, employment was often not offered. The editorial went on to point out that with the changing nature of A&E it was essential that nurses with RMN (mental health), RSCN (children), CCU/ITU (cardiac and intensive care) and other qualifications were considered for a specialty that thrives on diversity and flexibility.

The report *By Accident or Design – improving emergency care in acute hospitals. Audit Commission England/Wales 1996* looked at doctor and nursing numbers in some detail and while it referenced the BAEM medical staffing formula in its findings no such formula was shown for nurses. This was despite the publication of the North East Thames Regional document and the RCN A&E Nursing Association document *Skill mix in A&E nursing: a framework for managers 1993*. The report showed a wide variation in numbers of nurses in departments with similar numbers of attendances but the only recommendation was for hospitals to ensure they had enough nurses. It did advocate expanding nursing practice and ENPs but not at the expense of traditional nursing roles.

Two factors during the 1990s that influenced staffing numbers and skill mix were a move in some units to 12 hour nurse shift patterns and the reduction in junior doctors' hours. Traditionally full time nurses had always worked an 8 hour shift but during the 1980s and early 1990s 12 hour shifts were being introduced, liked by some, hated by others. The November 1994 *A&E newsletter* requested information on 12 hour shifts and the impact on nurses and nursing care. The debate continues to this day. In 1996 a discussion at RCN Congress considered the implications for nurses when reduced junior doctors' hours came into force and the representatives from the RCN A&E Nursing Association contributed to the debate. This was not the last time that this subject would be debated as during the 2000s whole rafts of changes were implemented.

Accident & Emergency – A Scoping report (G Jones March 1997) undertaken for the nursing division of the Department of Health showed that only six nurse managers out of the twenty six departments surveyed for the report considered their establishment to be reasonable. Discussion at the A&E conference on staffing in 1999 reflected the need for a new approach. Views from delegates included: staffing and skill mix should be about the best skill mix not the minimum; there was a need for a valid dependency tool; the layout of the department needed to be taken into consideration; training, professional development and sickness needed to be built into the establishment. The spring 2000 *A&E newsletter* continued this debate reporting that a RCN snapshot of emergency pressures showed staffing levels varied considerably both in terms of numbers and grade mix.

The National Patient Access Team (NPAT) which was part of the government's strategy to deal with modernisation of the NHS, while drawing up guidance regarding 'trolley waits' included a need to focus on clinical and managerial leadership, matching capacity with demand and tailoring staffing levels and skill mix to requirements including using staff to their full potential (*Emergency Nurse* May 2001).

The Audit Commission report 2001 reported that nationally the numbers of patients were growing by about 1% per annum; however, nursing numbers remained fairly static. The number of junior doctors had increased but the number of nurse practitioners had not increased much since 1998. The Audit Commission considered this a missed opportunity. The report also pointed out that more departments had children's trained nurses than in 1998 but numbers were still low.

The December 2001/January 2002 *Emergency Nurse* published a news item indicating that government advisers were considering the merits of the Jones Dependency Tool (JDT) to assess patient dependency in emergency settings. Interviewed for the news item I said 'We are still measured on how many patients come through the door. If you can measure dependency and link that with the number of patients in the department and link this with competencies of the nurse, you have got for the first time three parts of being able to say 'This is the establishment and skill mix we need.'

The Jones Dependency Tool (JDT) was seen as central to establishing adequate levels of staffing. The JDT was designed at Orsett Hospital, Essex in 1989 and was originally published in 1990 (*Accident and Emergency Nursing: A Structured Approach*). Throughout the years 1992 – 2001 the dependency tool was modified and through further work with staff at Oldchurch Hospital, Essex changes were again made to the original design. Further changes occurred as the result of a Delphi study during research into the tool by Crouch and Williams (2001). It was at this point when the refined tool had been established that Crouch named the tool the Jones Dependency Tool (JDT).

The main purpose of the JDT is:

>1 To ensure that the patient is allocated to a nurse with the relevant competencies to provide the care required.

>2 To provide a dependency rating across the department that can be calculated and actions taken if the threshold level is reached

>3 To be used to determine nursing numbers and with dependency/competency factors determine skill mix.

The tool - Key components
The JDT comprises six key component headings (with relevant statements to guide the user)
>Communication
>Airway Breathing Circulation
>Mobility
>Eating/drinking/elimination & personal care
>Environmental safety, health and social needs
>Triage

Each one has three ratings. On arrival and subsequently throughout the stay in the A&E department this tool provides the overall ratings that determine which of four dependency levels the patient falls into. Dependency levels range from low dependency = 0, medium dependency = 1, high dependency = 2, total dependency = 3

The research by Crouch and Williams (2001) demonstrated that the JDT is a valid tool and is transferable and they recommend it for the measurement of adult patient dependency in the emergency department. The research also found a highly significant correlation between the JDT dependency scores and the nurse's subjective rating of patient dependency suggesting nurses will find the tool easy and quick to use. Publication of the research to the Department of Health was followed by an article in *Accident & Emergency Nursing*. Further publication of the JDT included chapters in the books *Emergency Nursing Care: Principles and Practice* and in *Accident & Emergency: Theory into Practice*.

Evidence from work undertaken by Heather McClelland (2002) showed that the JDT correctly captured the dependency of patients when compared with outcome. All the low dependency patients in her study were discharged. Some moderately dependant patients were discharged but the majority were admitted. The majority of high and total dependency patients were admitted with all the patients who died and the vast majority of those admitted to ITU coming from the total dependency group.

Research undertaken in the emergency department of Bristol Royal Infirmary (A O'Brien and J Benger 2003 published 2007) showed the JDT to be an effective tool that can be used with minimum difficulty and inconvenience. The conclusion to the publication indicated that patient dependency is one of the essential determinants of nursing grade mix and with further work and adaptation the Jones Dependency Tool can be used to predict workload, resource use and the optimal staffing levels that will provide safe and effective patient care. Dependency can be readily and repeatedly assessed and we recommend this approach to other Emergency Departments.

Although outside of the dates of this book a further study in the Prince of Wales Hospital in Sydney, Australia in 2010 (Varndell et al 2013) demonstrated the reliability, validity, and sensitivity of the JDT for the first time in an Australian adult emergency department. It showed patient dependency can be measured in a hectic environment and enabled improved patient placement in the department and capacity planning.

Much work has also been undertaken in Portugal and the JDT is used as an integral part of patient assessment in a number of departments. In 2014, I was invited to meet with senior nurses from emergency care in Portugal and speak at their international conference. I also visited two emergency departments where the JDT is in use. In 2015, I presented a joint paper with the Portuguese A&E nurses at the International Council of Nurses (ICN) conference in South Korea. I also wrote an article in *Nursing Standard,* 'Measuring Patient Dependency in the Emergency Department' (9th September 2015). The *NICE safe staffing guideline (draft for consultation, 2015)* recommended that when determining A&E nurse staffing, patient dependency should be considered using for example, the Jones Dependency Tool.

*   *   *   *

The news item, 'How many staff is enough' (*Emergency Nurse* November 2004) highlighted a report from the National Audit Office indicating that understaffing represented one of the remaining obstacles to modernising emergency care. Despite this, due to ongoing financial deficits in most NHS Trusts during the 2000s, *Emergency Nurse* (June 2006) reported that 60 NHS Trusts were reducing the number of nursing posts and this had a direct effect on emergency departments. However, taking a proactive approach Gerard

Cronin, Matron, A&E, Basildon Hospital, Essex emphasised in the board's eye view of the July 2006 *Emergency Nurse* that caring for colleagues and supporting permanent staff was essential to retention. He also emphasised the need for supporting students as this would encourage them to return when qualified. His views went on in support of flexible working practices, self-rostering, reduction in the number of night rotas and the need for stress management programmes. Gerard believed that all these interventions and more would help improve staffing levels.

All the surveys and reports led the RCN A&E Nursing Association to start work on new guidelines and link this with a computer based system. By October 2005 the work was ready for piloting and included two main factors (patient numbers and dependency). The tool was launched at the ECA conference in November 2005 and delegates were invited to test run the latest proposals. Departments that piloted the tool showed results to be 'extremely promising and although a temporary delay occurred after this initial pilot study, the ECA and FEN resumed the development in the autumn of 2006 indicating that the plan was to test it on a greater range of sites. However, due to the issues that occurred between the ECA and the RCN management and the internal ECA issues that lead to the eventual resignations of three ECA members (see Part One) the skill mix tool was put on hold. It was not until some six years later that a computer based skill mix calculation tool was launched. The Baseline Emergency Staffing Tool (BEST) uses total attendance numbers and the Jones Dependency Tool. These are then linked with competency levels from the FEN competencies to calculate recommended staffing and skill mix numbers. I would highly recommend this tool to all managers of emergency departments.

The Nursing Auxiliary & Health Care Assistant

Throughout the history of nursing there has always been the debate around what role if any an assistant to the nurse should take. Prior to the formal training of what became the enrolled nurse there were just registered nurses and assistants. The first enrolled nurses emerged from the assistants being recorded as State Enrolled Assistant Nurse (SEAN). Once the enrolled nurse was fully established there was the registered nurse, enrolled nurse and nursing auxiliary who was the assistant to both the registered and enrolled nurse.

In A&E departments the number of nursing auxiliaries was, like nursing numbers, established locally. The role was also a local decision, as was any training, therefore the role varied quite considerably. The May 1984 *A&E newsletter* reported on a list of duties compiled from responses to a questionnaire sent to members. The list demonstrated that in most departments the role was one of support and did not suggest the auxiliary was undertaking tasks that should be undertaken by a registered nurse. However, in some departments it was felt some duties were in the remit of the registered nurse and concerns were raised that the overlapping of skills could mean more untrained staff employed to provide nursing care.

With the introduction of a completely new way an individual would be educated to become a registered nurse (Project 2000) and with discontinuation of enrolled nurse training in the 1990s student and pupil nurses started to disappear from the workplace and a replacement had to be found. The Health Care Assistant (HCA) emerged. Although some came from the nursing auxiliary role others came in as new recruits. Initially there was little difference between the auxiliary role and the new HCA but as time moved on and the skills required of the HCA became more complex, local and national training programmes were introduced.

Despite a change of emphasis from auxiliary to HCA and the introduction of formal training it is important to recognise that the term assistant was because the individuals assist the registered nurse and should not replace the nurse. There were concerns raised in the June 1993 *A&E newsletter* over the emerging roles of the health care assistant and with their NVQ training there was wide held concern that this could lead to the government deskilling the NHS workforce. Further concern was raised by the comprehensive study conducted by Ann Boyes and published in the summer 1995 edition of *Emergency Nurse*. Her study showed HCAs performing procedures involving very ill, unstable patients, assessing patients on arrival before they were seen by a registered nurse, deciding on wound dressings and in some cases planning nursing care. Conclusions drawn from the data included employment of some HCAs was necessary to free qualified nurses for direct patient care but there was no consensus on the role of the HCA in A&E nursing across the UK and as seen throughout history, there was never consensus over the role of the auxiliary either. Five recommendations were made in the report including the need to identify when the patient required qualified nursing care versus HCA care and consensus as to the role of the HCA.

In the Autumn 1997 *A&E newsletter*, the RCN A&E Nursing Association published a position statement on HCAs in A&E. Anecdotal and research evidence had shown that some HCAs were working outside their perceived remit and with insufficient levels of supervision. It pointed out that

HCAs are employed to support and complement professional nursing practice. The statement listed a range of good practice recommendations probably best summed up by the opening bullet point – HCAs should work only with patients who have been assessed as stable by the qualified nurse. The conclusion stated that lack of supervision of HCAs was unacceptable and skill mix must allow high standards of nursing care to be maintained and monitored.

Despite this position statement *Emergency Nurse* (December 1999/January 2000) reported that HCAs were still undertaking a large range of activities with inconsistent training and in some departments HCAs were replacing trained nurses. Similar concerns were reported in the spring 2000 newsletter. There was a need for role clarification, standardised practice and possible UKCC registration and development. The debate continues!

References

Audit Commission: (1996) *By Accident or Design – improving emergency care in acute ho*spitals. London: HMSO

Audit Commission: (2001) *Accident & Emergency - Review of National findings.* London: HMSO

Crouch R, Williams S, (2001) *Patient dependency in A&E: validation of the Jones Dependency Tool (JDT).* Report to Department of Health, England.

Crouch R, Williams S, Jones G: (2006) *Patient dependency in emergency department (ED): reliability and validity of the Jones Dependency Tool (JDT). Accident & Emergency Nursing 14, 4, 219-229*

Dolan B Holt L: (2008) *Accident & Emergency: Theory into Practice* Baillier Tindall Elsevier

Jones G: (1990) *Accident & Emergency Nursing – a structured approach.* London: Faber & Faber

Jones G: (1997) *Accident & Emergency – A Scoping report* (Report to the Chief Nursing Officer Department of Health)

Jones G et al: (2003) *Emergency Nursing Care: Principles and Practice.* Greenwich Medical Media Ltd. London. Digitally reprinted by Cambridge University Press Cambridge 2007.

Jones G: (2015) *Measuring Patient Dependency in the Emergency Department.* Nursing Standard 30, 2, 38-43

McClelland H: (2002) *Nursing Dependency and Workload in the Resuscitation Room.* Unpublished MSc dissertation. University of Sheffield

North East Thames Regional Health Authority: (1992) *Accident & Emergency Services – A Guide to Good Practice.* NETRHA publication.

National Institute for Health & Care Excellence (2015): *Safe Staffing for Nursing in A&E Departments.* NICE safe staffing guideline. Draft for consultation

National Audit Office: (1992) *NHS A&E Departments in England.* London: HMSO

National Audit Office: (1992) *NHS A&E Departments in Scotland.* London: HMSO

O'Brien A, Benger J: (2007) *Patient dependency in emergency care do we have the nurses we need?* Journal of Clinical Nursing. 16, 11, 2081-2087

Royal College of Nursing (1993) *Skill Mix in Accident and Emergency Nursing: A Framework for Managers.* RCN Publication

Royal College of Nursing: (2015) *Baseline Emergency Staffing Tool (BEST)* tinyurl.com/rcn-best

Varndell W, MacGregor C, Gallager R, Fry M: (2013) *Measuring patient dependency—Performance of the Jones Dependency Tool in an Australian Emergency Department.* Australasian Emergency Nursing Journal
Volume 16, Issue 2, Pages 64-72

CHAPTER 13
CLINICAL DEVELOPMENT & PROFESSIONAL CARE

By reviewing the pages of the *A&E newsletters*, *Emergency Nurse*, significant reports and my own practice, in this chapter I cover a range of conditions/practices that have changed over the period this book covers.

From the first publication of the *A&E newsletter* in January 1983, clinical updating through short news reports or longer articles has enabled emergency nurses to keep updated. The production of the *Emergency Nurse* and *Accident & Emergency* journals gave the opportunity to continue with clinical news updates and journal scans. They also enabled the majority of pages to focus on in-depth clinical articles. As clinical development and professional care evolved the need for further training and development was essential and conferences, study days and formal A&E courses have all played their part.

Trauma

War, conflict and terrorist attacks, while appalling are often the key to improved trauma care. The paramedic and trauma care seen in the US and Canada during my scholarship tour in 1980 developed from the lessons learnt in the Vietnam and Korean wars. The Afghanistan war of the 2000s led to further advancement in trauma management. In Northern Ireland during the troubles a great deal was learnt and that has improved trauma care across the UK and many other countries. Although the NI troubles did affect mainland Britain with such incidents as the bombing of the City of London and Docklands, it was the 7th July 2005 (7/7) terror attacks in London that encouraged the NHS to ensure that all emergency care staff were prepared for mass casualty incidents, especially related to terrorism.

Of course preparation for major incidents was nothing new; in fact major incident planning had been recognised since the early 1950s when the Department of Health issued guidelines to district general hospitals providing A&E services. From then on many hospitals regularly practised in some form or another. In my own department at Orsett we regularly held exercises linked with the Port of London Authority. A major incident usually involving a ship at one of the major oil refineries along the Thames enabled us to practise our pre-hospital and in-hospital response.

The latter part of the 1980s certainly put the A&E service into the public's eye. This period saw some of the most horrific major incidents of our time. There was the King's Cross underground station fire, Clapham rail disaster, Lockerbie and Kegworth air crashes and the Hillsborough and Bradford City football stadium disasters. The Troubles continued in Northern Ireland including in 1987 the Remembrance Day bombing in Enniskillen, County Fermanagh. In Hungerford, in August 1987, a mass shooting took place with 16 people killed and 15 others seriously injured. Many lessons were learnt from these disasters and they became key subjects for presentation at A&E conferences and study days for years to come.

The publication by the Home Office Emergency Planning College of the *Easingwold Papers No 8 'A digest of some well – known disasters'* provided a quick overview from a selection of disasters. Ranging from the Aberfan disaster of 1966 to the Towyn floods of 1990, as well as some overseas disasters, the papers provided salient features and offered some suggested lessons learnt, including preventative as well as operational recommendations. The *Nursing Standard* (July 2, 1988) reported on a successful full-scale disaster exercise in London where for the first time underground trains were used to ferry 'casualties' from Heathrow airport to St Mary's Hospital, Paddington.

In 1995 the NHS added to the 'Emergency Planning in the NHS' guidebook, indicating that medical and nursing staff attending the scene of major incidents must be clearly identified by appropriate clothing and headgear and this had to be implemented by March 1997.

*   *   *   *

Following a road traffic accident, having received a call from the ambulance service the trauma room (theatre) was prepared and three trauma team nurses and the emergency department physician arrived. The paramedics had established airway and circulatory support en route to the hospital. On arrival the patient was quickly assessed and trauma team doctors were called from other parts of the hospital. The man was unconscious and bleeding from both ears and mouth. Essential airway care and assisted breathing was quickly achieved. Intravenous fluids were started and X-rays ordered. Distension of the neck veins was observed, blood pressure was low and muffled heart sounds were heard. It was suspected that the patient had blood around the heart and so drainage was undertaken (pericardiocentesis). Chest drains to relieve a pneumothorax, oral gastric tubes and a urinary catheter were all inserted. A blood transfusion commenced and the neurosurgeon ordered a CT scan and EEG.

This man was not being treated in our local hospital at Orsett, this was in the emergency department of Vancouver General Hospital, Canada in 1980. The idea of such paramedic treatment and emergency department intervention in most of the district A&Es in the UK at that time was many years away. At Orsett, especially in the evenings, nights and weekends the on-call surgical/orthopaedic teams had just one registrar and two house officers (junior doctors).

Until the recent introduction of organised trauma care, many reports highlighted an under-provision of facilities and inadequate staffing for the care of severely injured patients, with many small hospitals struggling to provide an effective service.

The Osmond-Clark report of 1961 *Accident Services Review Committee of Great Britain and Ireland* recommended a tripartite scheme of peripheral casualty units, district general hospital accident centres and a regional major injury unit serving a population of one to two million.

Two reports were published in 1988. The first looked at coroners' reports of one thousand deaths due to injury (Anderson et al 1988). Four expert assessors concluded that if the patients had been admitted to a fully staffed and equipped trauma centre 20% of deaths would have been preventable. The second report from The Royal College of Surgeons of England *The Management of Patients with Major Injuries* raised awareness of inadequate trauma care. The report identified that approximately 40 deaths from trauma occurred each day, 14,500 deaths per year and trauma accounted for 545,000 inpatients per year. The report also highlighted that of the 1,000 trauma deaths 17% were preventable and 30% of the trauma deaths that occurred in hospital could have been prevented. The report concluded that there were significant deficiencies in the management of seriously injured patients and on the basis of the previous study they made the following recommendations:

- the majority of patients should be managed in large district general hospitals with a wide range of facilities and appropriate senior staffing.
- life-threatening injuries should be transferred if their management was beyond the capabilities of the district general hospital.
- enhanced training for ambulance staff was required.
- an improvement in communication between ambulance and hospital receiving staff was necessary.
- more sophisticated methods of transport would save lives.
- support for a major trauma outcome study would be welcome.
- there was a requirement for improved training for all staff dealing with major injuries.
- investment into trauma research was overdue.

The Department of Health responded by supporting the development of a pilot regional trauma service in North Staffordshire Royal Infirmary, Stoke on Trent funding the pilot site for three years. It commissioned an in-depth analysis of its performance compared with the orthodox British model of care in two other centres in Lancashire (Preston) and Humberside (Hull). There was also funding for two other demonstration projects at Peterborough and

Southend. Reviews were also undertaken of the cost effectiveness of helicopter ambulances in London & Cornwall and nurse triage and nurse practitioners. Probably one of the most comprehensive booklets covering all aspects of setting up a complete trauma service is the *Royal London Hospital Daily Express Helicopter Emergency Medical Service*. From the helicopter to the emergency room, the trauma team to the nurse's role and data collection to evaluation, this is a very comprehensive read and many aspects are still pertinent today.

The government also contributed funding for Professor David Yates' department at the University of Manchester to continue the audit of trauma care under the Major Trauma Outcome Study (MTOS). Although trauma scoring was first developed in the USA in the 1960s, it was not commonplace in most UK A&Es until the introduction of MTOS in the early 1990s. Trauma scoring combines a number of scoring methods together to provide an overall trauma score. It provides a measure to determine if a trauma patient has received the best care, spent the minimum of time as an inpatient and has the minimum of residual disability from the trauma. MTOS figures for 1992 showed trauma being the fourth leading cause of death in all ages and the leading cause of death in persons aged between 1 year and 44 years of age. The figures showed that in 1992 there were 16,676 deaths due to trauma, an increase of over 2,000 since 1988.

The British Orthopaedic Association report of 1989 *The management of trauma in Great Britain* also recommended that services should be concentrated. There were too many small units and too few consultants with a special interest in trauma care. Further, the report indicated that any rationalisation of trauma services could not occur without an expansion of consultant numbers. Importantly, the report proposed that any trauma system should also provide a better service for the more numerous, serious, complex but non-life-threatening injuries. The report recognised the considerable resource implications of trauma centres, based upon the American model.

The Institute of Economic Affairs Health & Welfare Unit booklet 1991 - Saving Lives: The NHS A&E Service and how to improve it focussed on the direction to a more efficient and cost-effective care system for accident victims. Three authors gave their respective views of how services should be configured in the future. One author suggested that due to the mortality and cost of injury deaths being four times that of cancer and six and a half times that of cardio-vascular disease, a redirection of money from cancer and cardiovascular disease to trauma should occur. He also proposed the development of some 25 major trauma centres in the UK. The second author took a different view and recommended concentrating accident services on district hospital services and regional centres. The third author suggested an improvement in pre-hospital care including increased paramedic skills, pre-hospital medical care and mobile hospital teams all with helicopter evacuation. When I look back at that publication, in a sense all three views are reflected in today's services.

The British Orthopaedic Association report of 1992 reviewed trauma care in 283 hospitals in the UK, identifying many which were inadequately staffed and ill-equipped. The delivery of trauma services had not kept pace with technical advances and many units were too small to sustain an adequate standard of care. The report expressed a view on trauma organisation and set standards for the facilities required in a district general hospital. Smaller hospitals would treat major injuries according to agreed protocols. The report described the regional trauma centre with its multi-disciplinary arrangements. It was recommended that orthopaedic surgeons in training should be encouraged to specialise in trauma.

In the Spring 1993 edition of *Emergency Nurse* Simon Davies, Research Fellow, Keele University/Staff Nurse, emergency department, North Staffordshire Royal Infirmary (pilot trauma centre) wrote an article covering a range of issues that required attention if trauma centres were to become the norm. Issues highlighted included the need for trauma scoring in the pre-hospital setting so ensuring the correct patients are transferred to the trauma centre, communication systems between the trauma centre and paramedics was essential as were firm links between the ambulance service, trauma centre and local A&E departments.

Accident & Emergency – A Scoping report (G Jones March 1997) indicated that trauma care had developed considerably since the publication of the Royal College of Surgeons report (1988). Only four of the 26 respondents to the survey indicated progress was slow while the rest highlighted good progress including many staff attending one of the recognised trauma courses. The report also demonstrated a number of initiatives taking place including the development of trauma response teams and protocols for trauma care. At Hope Hospital (renamed Salford Royal), Salford, Manchester the first UK research based trauma nurse co-ordinator had been appointed to co-ordinate care of the trauma patient from admission to discharge.

The British Orthopaedic Association report of 1997 *The Care of Severely Injured Patients in the United Kingdom* reviewed the care of severely injured patients in the UK. The report concluded that patients in the UK were not receiving the quality of care available in many other developed countries, including Germany, Switzerland and the USA. An integrated approach based upon a hub and spoke model was recommended. The American model of a level 1 trauma centre was not recommended and the bulk of trauma would still be treated in district general hospitals. Standards of care should be defined. The report enthusiastically supported a national strategic plan for the management of severe trauma. In the Association's view, the quality of care would only be achieved by:

- the rapid transfer of severely injured patients to hospitals most suited to their need
- concentrating expertise in the management of severe injuries
- a multi-disciplinary team approach with the integration of hospitals into a system of care
- the direct involvement of senior clinicians

As trauma care was improving so it was that trauma scoring systems were continuing to develop. Lynne Dadley, Major Trauma Outcome Study project co-ordinator for six trusts in the South West of England explained the methodology, scoring systems and purpose of scoring in the November 1998 *Emergency Nurse*. Her conclusion was that the main outcome measure in 1998 was dead or alive; however, this was very crude and a measure of morbidity or injury impairment would be of more use. Lynne reported that work was underway to develop such a scoring system.

Trauma Nursing Courses

The October 1990 *A&E newsletter* contained an article from Simon Davies describing his experience as a participant in an adapted advanced trauma life support course for nurses in Baltimore, USA. The course had been developed in 1983 by the Maryland Institute for Emergency Medical Services Systems (MIEMSS) and the American Association of Critical Care Nurses (AACN). This course for nurses had been developed from the original American College of Surgeons Advanced Trauma Life Support course (ATLS) designed for medical staff. Simon made reference to the content and Trunkey's work (1983) on trauma deaths occurring in a trimodal fashion. The first peak was immediate deaths due to spinal cord or disruption of the heart and major blood vessels. The second peak due to major internal haemorrhage of the head, respiratory or abdominal systems (these deaths occurred within the first few hours after injury). The third peak was the late deaths occurring days or weeks after the initial injury, 80% being due to either systemic infection or multiple organ failure. It is in the second peak that deaths can be avoided with improved trauma care in the emergency setting, hence the need for trauma training. A further article in the same newsletter described a visit by Abigail Hamilton in July 1990 observing six different nursing trauma courses each one varying in length from one day to a two year master's degree programme. She reported the most common courses lasted two to three days and consisted of lectures and skill stations. This was similar to the two-day course I participated in during my studies in Canada and the US in 1980.

The RCN A&E Nursing Association, through the negotiating skills of the Vice-Chair Ethel Buckles, linked with the US Emergency Nurses Association (ENA) to provide the ENA international Trauma Nursing Core Course (TNCC) in the UK. On 8th October 1990 in Chicago, eight UK nurses undertook the course consisting of reading and digesting a very comprehensive manual, studying on the course for three days of lectures and skill stations and then undertaking the written and practical exams. It was also planned that if successful all eight nurses would undertake a one day instructor course. All passed as TNCC instructors and as Chair of the RCN A&E Nursing Association I signed an agreement on behalf of the RCN A&E Nursing Association with the Chief Executive of the Emergency Nurses Association to enable us to provide the course in the UK.

The first Trauma course in the UK commenced on Monday 29th October 1990. It was held at the Lord Daresbury Hotel four days before our A&E conference. Twelve A&E nurses went through the course, including me. To enable the first UK instructors to become verified three instructors came over from the US, Susan Buddasi-Sheehey, Sue Hoyt and Karen Kernan Bryant. The 1991 ENA President, Lynne Gagnon, also accompanied them. As it was the first course in the UK, the nursing press wanted photos and interviews. Being a hotel, there were no patient trolleys so we put mattresses on the floor and during all of the trauma care skill stations we were on our knees. On the afternoon of Wednesday 31^{st,} October we all took the assessment (MCQ and four skill stations) and in addition four (one being me) went on to the instructor day. Fortunately, we all passed and so there were now twelve instructors to take the trauma training forward in the UK. Sandra Buckley, Senior Nurse of the A&E at Stoke on Trent was appointed the Chair of the newly formed TNCC committee and Ethel represented the link between the RCN A&E Nursing Association and the Trauma committee. The first TNCC course run entirely by UK TNCC instructors was held at the North West Regional Ambulance Headquarters & Training School. In 1994 the first newsletter from the TNCC committee was published, it reported 215 provider passes and 26 instructors. By 1996 providers had reached almost 1,000. Two of the original US trained instructors have been committee members since the original committee was formed in 1990. Gabby Lomas and Jill Windle have continued to move TNCC forward and have become essential to its continued success as a limited company within the UK (https://www.traumanursing.uk/). In 2020 TNCC celebrated 30 years of providing the trauma nursing course throughout the UK and Eire.

A second trauma nursing course was launched around the same time as TNCC. The Advanced Trauma Nursing Course (ATNC) was developed jointly between emergency nurses and doctors and links the medical advanced trauma life support (ATLS) with a bespoke nursing syllabus. The course held over 5 days had the first two and half days focussing on nursing issues with the following time spent covering the ATLS. Both courses provide the trauma nursing skills required for today's trauma services.

The editorial of *Emergency Nurse* (December 1998/January 1999) reflected the fact that trauma remained the leading cause of death in people under 40 years of age in developed countries which in the UK translated as 25,000 fatalities per annum as a direct result of trauma, with 500,000 sustaining major injury per annum. It highlighted both the TNCC and ATNC courses as moving trauma care forward but regretted that some individual nurses had to fully fund themselves. The editor noted that while medical colleagues saw training as an investment there were still many employers who saw training for nurses as a perk.

Lee Patient, Practice Development Nurse in the emergency department at University Hospital, Lewisham, London provided a comprehensive review of trauma training for emergency department nurses in the November 2007 *Emergency Nurse*. Using a range of references that covered the established trauma courses and the effectiveness of trauma training his conclusion was that evidence suggested that there were many advantages in developing an abbreviated one-day trauma course.

*   *   *   *

With the introduction of trauma training into the UK in the 1990s doctors and nurses significantly changed the clinical care of the trauma patient. Apart from the systematic approach there was also the introduction of the high concentration oxygen mask and a change in fluid resuscitation. Throughout my time as an A&E nurse the crystalloid - v- colloid debate had raged. Under the trauma guidelines crystalloid was used initially followed by blood transfusion. This was not the first reference to fluid resuscitation. As far back as 1983 a report in the third *A&E newsletter* (winter 1983) indicated that an infusion box had been designed to facilitate the pressurisation of plastic infusion containers for procedures that required rapid IV infusion. Known as the Norfolk and Norwich Infusion Box this was the forerunner of today's high-volume systems. In the September 1985 *A&E newsletter* auto transfusion was reported as becoming more common in American emergency departments. Being used mainly with patients suffering with a haemothorax, the patient's own blood was transfused from the chest via the auto transfuser into a vein. It was suggested in the newsletter this technique could become common place in UK hospitals but this has not been the case.

During the 1990s great emphasis was placed on cervical spine and full spine immobilisation. The use of rigid neck collars and spinal boards became almost a daily routine. The April 1995 *A&E newsletter* contained a summary of a study from the USA on Cervical Spine injuries and guidelines for immobilisation. The study showed that 17% of patients that walked into emergency departments with neck pain were found to have unstable cervical spine fractures. The study continued with a number of recommendations as to when spinal immobilisation should be instituted. Having been encouraged to 'collar and board' all trauma patients, during the late 1990s concern was building around the length of time patients were immobile and the risk of pressure sore development. The article in *Emergency Nurse* (February 1999) by John Sexton, 'Can nurses remove spinal boards and cervical collars safely?' changed the way nurses in the UK were able to determine if boards and collars could be removed prior to medical intervention. The guidelines also enabled nurses to determine if there was a need to fit collars in the first place. Although not universally practised at the time, more departments now practise this care process.

Head Injury
While the majority of head injuries are minor, many can be significant and life threatening. A range of causes can be identified and often the social trends of the day play a part. As far back as 1983 it was reported in the winter edition of

the *A&E newsletter* that 50% of head injuries in A&E had high blood alcohol.

In the October 2002 edition of *Emergency Nurse* an article on the CRASH (Corticosteroid Randomisation After Significant Head Injury) trial described a large-scale trial of adults with significant head injury. During both the pilot phase (1999-2000) and the main phase (2001-2005) emergency nurses played a significant role. Gabby Lomas, Sister, A&E, Salford Royal, Manchester as the lead trial nurse and member of the main committee headed a team of nurses who were engaged as trial managers and regional co-ordinators. The main phase of the trial continued until 2005 with over 100 hospitals worldwide taking part. In June 2005, a further article in *Emergency Nurse* updated the reader on the CRASH trial. It showed that the use of corticosteroids after head injury increased the risk of death or severe disability and did not decrease it as many had thought - and for more than 30 years this had been the way head injuries were treated. These findings significantly changed the way serious head injured patients were treated.

In June 2003 new guidelines were launched from the National Institute of Clinical Excellence (NICE) on the management of head injuries. The focus was on triage, assessment, investigations and early management. The guidelines covered both pre-hospital care as well as A&E. A wider use of CT scanning was recommended with 11 recommendations for when a scan should be requested. Any patient admitted should be under the care of a consultant trained to manage head injured patients and in a ward where staff are used to observing head injured patients. The guidelines also recommended the length of time various observations should be undertaken as well as advice on what should be on any discharge advice cards.

Further guidance on the care of head injured adults and children was reported in the October 2007 *Emergency Nurse*. The National Institute for Health and Care Excellence (NICE) had updated their guidelines (first issued 2003) on head injuries pointing out that 750,000 people with head injuries are seen in A&E each year and while many are minor some are moderate or severe and there was a need for quicker access to CT scans and for transfer of serious head injuries to neurological units irrespective of the need for surgery.

Orthopaedics
The treatment for a fractured shaft of femur was traditionally to insert a metal pin through the patient's tibia and then attach weights to the pin and with the use of a Thomas splint, apply counter traction and leave the patient suspended in bed for three months. As a student nurse and then the charge nurse of the orthopaedic ward, many of the patients I nursed were treated this way. Although external fixators can be traced back centuries many were unsuitable for fractured femur often associated with unacceptable high mortality rates attributed to fat emboli. With the design of the dynamic axial fixator in the late 1970s bones such as the tibia were being fixed in this way (although not on the scale of today) and towards the late 1980s and into the 1990s the use of external fixators moved to the femur.

Application of plaster casts in some A&E departments was the sole duty of nurses trained in the procedure and they ran the plaster room. In others, application of plaster casts only became the nurse's role in the absence of the plaster technician. My own experience as a night staff nurse in the early 1970s is typical of how things were at the time. Only after a few nights of working in the department I was shown by a nurse colleague how to apply back slabs, Colles' and scaphoid plaster casts. From that night on I did my best! Although individual departments developed training packages and nurses on A&E courses were taught more effectively than I had been, it took until the early 2000s before a news article appeared in the December 2001/January 2002 *Emergency Nurse* on the move by the RCN A&E Nursing Association and British Orthopaedic Association to develop casting courses for emergency nurses. This move was due to concern that half of the casts applied in six large A&Es were unsatisfactory and legal action could take place if injury occurred.

Before the popularity of regional blocks in the latter part of the 1980s it was common place for a general anaesthetic (GA) to be administered in A&E for the purpose of fracture manipulation. The *A&E newsletter* (October 1989) reported that the Royal College of Anaesthetists were concerned that anaesthetists working in A&E did not have proper assistance when giving GAs. There was also criticism of the lack of monitoring equipment that they considered put patients at risk. The report recommended anaesthetists should have fully trained assistance and adequate monitoring equipment and preparation.

The increased use of Bier's block was highlighted in the November 1987 *A&E newsletter* with some cautionary notes regarding toxic reaction, clinical criteria and the need for close monitoring. The October 2005 *Emergency Nurse* reported in the clinical article on managing Colles' type fractures in emergency care settings that haematoma block (direct infiltration of the fracture haematoma with local anaesthetic) was one of the most commonly used methods of pain relief for reduction in the UK.

Wounds
A&E wound dressings were often limited and based on tried and tested results over many years. Despite many new dressings on the market A&E appeared to be set in the traditional ways of working. The article in the summer 1995 *Emergency Nurse* challenged the need for A&Es to expand the range of dressings used and move away from every wound is ok with either Tulle Gras, Mepore or Melolin. This was followed up by a further article in *Emergency Nurse* (July 1998) that demonstrated how practice continued to change from keeping wounds moist to keeping wounds dry to keeping wounds open and back to keeping wounds moist. A further article in the March 2007 *Emergency Nurse* continued to support the use of modern dressings over the traditional ones. Guidelines on managing patients with partial thickness burns endorsed by the European Burns Association emphasised the use of more modern dressings that did not need to be changed as often and did not stick.

Having trained in ophthalmic nursing in 1975 I always ensured that eye care in our A&E was of a high standard. I always insisted that all corneal abrasions were treated using chloramphenicol ointment and the double pad method. However despite the successful outcomes I realised research changes practice and the *Emergency Nurse* (April 1998) article emphasised the change to treating corneal abrasions without the use of eye pads.

Probably one of the major changes in A&E wound care management during this period was moving from almost every patient receiving a tetanus toxoid injection to accepting the 1990 Department of Health changes that recommended five vaccinations were enough to give lifelong immunity (*Emergency Nurse* September 1997).

Other emerging trauma
Although gun and knife injury has always been part of the trauma world and certainly from my experience in 1980 in Canada and the USA was almost a daily occurrence, the use of such weapons in the UK was limited. Unfortunately with the increased use of guns and knives, and as we know today this is extremely high, and a general increase in crime related trauma against the police, the use of 'Tasers' were introduced during the 2000s. Guidance on managing patients who had been 'tasered' (*Emergency Nurse* September 2006) indicated that Taser guns delivered a 50,000-volt electric current causing temporary loss of voluntary muscle control and causing the individual to freeze on the spot or fall to the ground. The guidance reminded emergency staff to look for injury due to the fall as well as for the need to remove the Taser darts. The Taser darts or barbs were described in the article as like removing fishing hooks (a common treatment in most A&Es).

Resuscitation for Cardiac Arrest

Resuscitation guidelines have changed considerably since the days of the Holger Nielsen, Silvester or Schafer methods which were still published in the Red Cross first aid manual in 1969. Alongside these historical methods was the preferred option of mouth to mouth and chest compressions. The following were the guidelines available for this method of resuscitation in 1969:

> For resuscitation – give four breath inflations, check carotid pulse, if present continue ventilating the lungs. If there is no response and pupils are widely dilated, the colour becomes or remains blue-grey, a carotid pulse is absent, strike the chest over the heart smartly. If still no response, start external cardiac compression, ratio of one inflation of the lungs to six or eight compressions to the sternum. Check the effectiveness of compression of the heart by noting the size of pupils, feeling for a carotid pulse, watching for improvement in colour.

In the hospital scenario, resuscitation of a patient in cardiac arrest was determined by the on-call medical registrar following guidelines produced locally. With some basis of research sodium bicarbonate 8.4% and adrenaline was given IV, chest compressions (not too quickly as the heart needs to fill) and ventilation continued. This situation was the norm until the Resuscitation Council UK was established in 1981. From that time guidelines based on International and European research have been followed throughout the UK and updated every 4-5 years.

As the national guidelines started to be used throughout the UK training was necessary and hospitals started to appoint resuscitation training officers. In the November 1987 *A&E newsletter*, Jaqui Hawkrigg, nurse tutor and resuscitation training officer for Birch Hill Hospital, Rochdale described the training for doctors and nurses using a 'mega code' simulated cardiac arrest scenario. Jaqui pointed out that at that time very few hospitals carried out that type of training and few had the full range of resuscitation equipment available. Her results indicated a vast improvement in the management of cardiac arrest moving from what she described as a situation of chaos to one of control. Her final paragraph perhaps summed up the situation in the UK at the time 'We have been lukewarm about resuscitation for far too long.'

The article by Lucy Belson, resuscitation training officer and co-director of advanced cardiac life support at the John Radcliffe Hospital, Oxford in *Emergency Nurse* (Spring 1993) indicated how dramatic advances had been made in the treatment of cardiac arrest in the past 30 years due to the modern techniques of resuscitation and the advanced cardiac life support course being introduced in the USA in 1973. She indicated that the first UK advanced cardiac life support course had been held at St Bartholomew's Hospital in the mid-1980s and the course was now available in a number of centres throughout the UK. The article described in detail the three day course and use of the 'mega code'.

Advisory defibrillators were introduced in the 1980s and although common place now, very few would have been found in public places. The November 1987 edition of the *A&E newsletter* highlighted a report in *The Times* newspaper 20th July 1987 reporting that defibrillators were being introduced as part of a research project funded by the British Heart Foundation at Victoria, Waterloo and Brighton railway stations. In the report they suggested that lifesaving equipment for heart attack victims could be as readily available as fire extinguishers. *The Independent* newspaper 17th July 1987 reported the introduction of 'defibrillating machines' in *British Caledonian* jumbo jets. Having the Port of Tilbury within our catchment area, and supporting the police who provided the ambulance service within the docks, during the mid-1980s we introduced the first automated defibrillation-training programme for the police.

In a message from Virginia Bottomley, Secretary of State for Health, to the RCN A&E Nursing Association in 1990 she stated that £3.8 million was being made available to provide defibrillators to all front line ambulances in England, some 2,350 vehicles. This linked with the continuing development of ambulance personnel towards paramedic status.

A multidisciplinary group from Britain having completed the first Paediatric Advanced Life Support (PALS) provider and instructor course in 1992 held in Europe, went on to set up the course in the UK. The Spring 1994 *Emergency Nurse* reported on the course held under the auspices of the Resuscitation Council UK describing the content and criteria for success.

Relatives witnessing resuscitation was considered good practice by the 1995 working group from the RCN & BAEM *Bereavement care in A&E departments* but many doctors and nurses were sceptical of this new way of involving the relatives. Judith Morgan, Teaching & Development Sister, Hammersmith Hospital, London highlighted a range of positive and negative reasons behind the controversy of relatives being allowed to witness the cardiac arrest procedure as well as presenting suggested guidelines to enable good practice (*Emergency Nurse* May 1997).

The June 1997 *Emergency Nurse* reported that the motion to allow relatives to witness the resuscitation process had been debated and rejected by RCN Congress that year. During the debate the RCN A&E Nursing Association participated and many delegates argued for and against the resolution. Still an issue for debate even in April 2007, the article, 'A final question: witness resuscitation' by Kieran McLaughlin, Specialist Nurse Practitioner in A&E at Altnagelvin Hospital,

Londonderry and Mark Gillespie Lecturer in Nursing at the University of Ulster (*Emergency Nurse* April 2007) examined the literature pertaining to witnessed resuscitation, and recommended that emergency departments implemented policies to improve and clarify the practice. Using a number of references and displaying both sides of the debate, the conclusion drawn was that it remained a complex and controversial issue. For it to be introduced successfully emergency nurses had to act as leaders and catalysts to deliver the ultimate package of holistic care to patients and their families.

The May 1997 *Emergency Nurse* reported that the UK was the first country to adopt the latest international guidelines for resuscitation based on statements from the International Liaison Committee on Resuscitation (ILCOR). Guidelines were published by the Resuscitation Council UK after the launch at the international conference in Brighton - CPR 97- Towards a Common Goal. The Resuscitation Council UK were also tasked with the assessment of the guidelines on behalf of the European Resuscitation Council. Changes included more emphasis on assessing breathing and signs of life and less on checking for a central pulse. A new rate of 100 chest compressions a minute was also introduced.

Throughout the 1990s resuscitation continued to advance yet in the September 2000 *Emergency Nurse*, Jane Lambert, (Resuscitation Officer) and Gillian Heath (Sister A&E) both from Milton Keynes General NHS Trust indicated their concern that despite the increased ability to provide more advanced airways and defibrillation and ALS training, many nurses were reluctant to use the skills.

Further advances in resuscitation followed including an article in the July/August 2002 *Emergency Nurse* on the use of the Laryngeal mask. First available in the UK in 1988, it gained widespread acceptance during the 1990s having distinct advantages over the bag/valve/mask normally used by nursing staff. In the same year the November *Emergency Nurse* contained an article indicating that the introduction of the biphasic defibrillator in the 2000s allowing a lower DC shock to be administered caused less damage to the myocardium. A guide to implanted cardioverter defibrillators (ICD) was highlighted in the May 2007 *Emergency Nurse* indicating that more and more patients were being fitted with them and yet many emergency care staff were less aware of how to manage them. The guide provided a range of information from what an ICD was through to safety issues.

Myocardial Infarction & Thrombolysis
Before the introduction of thrombolysis in the latter part of the 1980s, any patient who suffered a myocardial infarction was treated by several days of bed rest, cardiac monitoring and they may have been administered anticoagulants depending on the individual consultant's instructions. As the days progressed, the size of the infarct would develop but if the area of heart muscle that had been destroyed was small and it did not cause any life threatening arrhythmia the patient had a chance of survival and would be discharged after a couple of weeks.

With the introduction of thrombolysis all that changed. In the Spring 1995 edition of *Emergency Nurse* an article on thrombolysis indicated how its use had expanded during the 1990s and a further article in the December 2000/January 2001 *Emergency Nurse* pointed out that during the 1980s and1990s numerous trials showed good results and thrombolysis had become the accepted treatment. By the early part of 2002, ambulance services and hospitals were set to receive £40 million to help reduce deaths from heart disease and strokes. Funding was targeted at the ambulance service and would pay for new defibrillators and ECG equipment linked with training of staff to give thrombolysis on the way to A&E or soon after arrival. It was also reported that A&E nurse practitioners could move to take on administering thrombolysis. By April 2004 *Emergency Nurse* was able to report on the success of decreased deaths due to heart attack with 4 out of 5 patients receiving thrombolysis in 30 minutes of hospital admission compared with 2 out of 5 in 2000. These results demonstrated that the sooner a patient attended a hospital the more chance they had of survival so the British Heart Foundation launched a campaign in November 2006 encouraging patients who experience chest pain to seek clinical attention quickly.

Oxygen therapy

As I mentioned in Part One, *Emergency Nurse* introduced a major new series in conjunction with the RCN Institute of Advanced Nursing Education in 1993. This enabled nurses to earn continuing educational points through reading and undertaking a series of activities based on clinical articles. The first was an article I wrote on oxygen administration. The aim of the article was to increase the nurses' knowledge of this procedure.

Since my early days in nursing I had seen the guidelines on oxygen administration change several times. In my early years the emphasis was caution with oxygen administration. The fear was too much oxygen, especially with patients suffering from chronic respiratory conditions where it could cause more harm than good. This concern often led to many patients who required increased oxygen being deprived. By the time I worked in A&E the emphasis was changing and there was a greater move to increasing the oxygen percentage, though with the popular MC mask the highest percentage was around 60%. At the time I wrote the article in 1993, the high concentration mask with reservoir bag had been introduced. This mask became popular almost overnight due to trauma training being introduced into the UK in the early 1990s.

With the introduction of the high concentration mask the emphasis moved to almost everyone having higher concentrations of oxygen, often to the detriment of some patients. Eventually, although just outside of the dates of this book, national guidelines were introduced in 2008. The British Thoracic Society (BTS) published guidelines for *Emergency Oxygen Use in Adult Patients*. A whole range of Royal Colleges and other professional groups endorsed these guidelines. The guidelines encouraged the use of pulse oximetry (introduced in the UK during the mid-1980s) and the patient's condition (critical, serious without chronic obstructive airways disease, serious with chronic obstructive airways disease) as the basis for oxygen administration. The guidelines also discouraged the use of oxygen in patients suffering from myocardial infarction (heart attack), stroke and some other neurological disorders with normal oxygen saturation levels.

Overdose
One of the many skills I quickly learnt when I first went into A&E as a night staff nurse back in 1975 was how to pass a gastric lavage tube on a patient who had taken an overdose and how I should lavage the stomach with water until the return was clear of tablets. This method dating back to 1812

was by the mid-1980s being questioned. The article by Pat Valladares, Emergency Nurse Practitioner, Northampton General Hospital (*Emergency Nurse* Spring 1996) described how the use of drugs changes over time. Barbiturates were common during the 1950s-1970s, and then they were replaced in the 1990s by tricyclic antidepressants. The way to manage overdose was also changing and although it still included gastric lavage in the adult or oral administration of ipecacuanha syrup (ipecac) mainly in children, gastric lavage was not being used routinely for overdose and ipecac was also going out of favour. Like the lavage, ipecac was not shown to significantly prevent absorption. Charcoal was being used far more and was shown to be more effective than lavage or ipecac however the main disadvantage was its administration (black horrible mess, my words).

Further support for the discontinuing of lavage was found in the June 1997 *Emergency Nurse* with an article on acute poisoning. The National Poisons Information Service (NPIS) indicated that gastric emptying was probably only worthwhile up to 2 hours post ingestion and emesis was best avoided as a means of gastric emptying with activated charcoal being preferred. They did indicate that there were some exceptions to all of this and early presentation of severe poisoning may require gastric lavage. The article also indicated that the use of ipecac especially in children was also declining. Overall the NPIS no longer recommended emesis as a means of gastric emptying and advocated activated charcoal in the majority of cases. Further articles over the next few years continued to advocate the use of activated charcoal over gastric emptying including a further article from the NPIS in the October 2000 *Emergency Nurse*.

The British Medical Journal (1996) included an article dismissing the idea that the government should limit the availability of designated drugs by reducing pack size or making larger amounts only available on prescription as a way to reduce overdoses. The authors were unconvinced this would deter overdose. However, by 1998 the size of paracetamol packs available over the counter was limited by law and figures on the NHS website before and after the legislation (1993 to 2009) showed the number of paracetamol-related deaths had reduced by 43%. There was also a 61% reduction in the number of people needing a liver transplant as a result of a paracetamol overdose.

HIV/AIDS
These conditions changed clinical practice beyond anything that anyone could have imagined. As student nurses we were always discouraged from wearing gloves for routine care as this may imply to the patient that they were dirty or infected. Apart from barrier nursing patients, suturing wounds or when in theatre, there were very few occasions when gloves were worn. Wound dressings were performed using forceps so no need for gloves and often in A&E, blood and body fluids came in contact with the nurse's skin and clothing. Watch many of the trauma videos of the 1970s and early 1980s and you see doctors and nurses treating seriously injured patients without any protective clothing or gloves. HIV/AIDS changed all of that.

Considering how care has changed over the last 30 plus years it may be difficult for some of the younger readers of this book to appreciate how traumatic this virus was, not only for the patient but also for the public and health care staff. Like Covid-19 in 2020, for us in the early 1980s AIDS was scary as we did not fully understand the transmission. Although we knew it was primarily a blood borne/body fluid transmission, to what extent it could be transmitted through the skin was unclear. Infection control measures were put in place and if the patient died, protective body bags were used. AIDS transformed the way we handled blood and body fluids forever.

As I said in Part One, in May 1985 I wrote a short piece in the *A&E newsletter* picking up on the anxiety of nurses around AIDS. HIV at that time was not mentioned in the media but the tombstone advert on the television was very graphic and suggested AIDS equalled death.

The September 1985 *A&E newsletter* reported that Kenneth Clark, Minister for Health announced in June that an AIDS blood test would be introduced. The test would screen all donated blood for antibodies to the virus. By July 1986 the *A&E newsletter* reported that in 1985 out of 43 needle stick injuries involving patients with HIV in the UK only 1 health worker (nurse) developed antibodies after accidently injecting several millilitres of infected blood into her skin. Despite this, anxiety remained and Margaret Carron, Sister in A&E, Walton Hospital, Liverpool wrote a guest editorial in the April 1987 *A&E newsletter* recognising the fear of AIDS since it was first identified in the US in 1981. She pointed out that the patient required care, sympathy and understanding and the nurse should be fully informed about the true facts of the disease. Margaret reemphasised the guidelines the RCN had published and also pointed out that the RCN had organised a series of day courses.

Cerebral Vascular Accident (Stroke)
Progress to improve professional and public understanding of stroke moved a stage further in 2005 with the launch of

the FAST acronym. Initially FAST was described as Facial weakness, Arm weakness, Speech problems, Test all three symptoms. More recently this has been refined and indicates only one problem is enough to warrant action and the T became Time to dial 999.

References

Accident Services Review Committee of Great Britain and Ireland (1961) (Chairman: Sir Henry Osmond-Clarke). Interim Report. London: British Medical Association

Anderson et al: (1988) *Retrospective analysis of 1000 deaths from injury in England and Wales.* British Medical Journal 296 1305-1308

British Thoracic Society (BTS): (2008) *Emergency Oxygen Use in Adult Patients.* BTS publication

Easingwood Papers No 8: (1994) *A digest of some well-known disasters.* Home Office Emergency Planning College, Easingwold, York. UK

FAST acronym https://www.stroke.org.uk/what-is-stroke/what-are-the-symptoms-of-stroke

Jones G: (1997) *Accident & Emergency – A Scoping report* (Report to the Chief Nursing Officer Department of Health)

Nursing Standard: (Week ending July 2, 1988) *Full-Scale Disaster Alert: From Heathrow to Paddington.* (11)

National Institute of Clinical Excellence (NICE): (2003) *Management of Head Injury.* London: HMSO

NHS website - Re Paracetamol packs
https://www.nhs.uk/news/medication/smaller-paracetamol-packs-may-have-reduced-deaths/

Resuscitation Council UK https://www.resus.org.uk/#

Royal College of Nursing & British Association for Accident and Emergency Medicine: (1995) *Bereavement Care in A&E Departments.* RCN Publication

Royal College of Surgeons: (1988) *Report on the Management of Patients with Major Injuries.* London, Royal College of Surgeons

Saving Lives: The NHS Accident & Emergency Service and how to improve it. (1991) The IEA Health and Welfare Unit, London.

The Royal London Hospital: Daily Express Helicopter Medical Service. Saldatore publication, Bishops Stortford, Herts. UK

The British Orthopaedic Association. London: (1989) *The Management of Trauma in Great Britain.*

The British Orthopaedic Association. London: (1997) *The Care of Severely Injured Patients in the United Kingdom.*

Trauma Nursing UK https://www.traumanursing.uk/

CHAPTER 14

SPECIAL POPULATIONS

Children

In the mid-1970s, when I first worked in A&E there were no registered children's nurses in our department. I was taught early on that when a child was being sutured I had to wrap the child in a blanket, dismiss the parents from the room and get the job done. Thankfully that has now changed and much of the change came about because registered children's nurses working in A&E took on the battle for improved child care and won.

Although registered children's nurses have always been part of the family of nursing very few had specialised in A&E. During the 1980s there was a movement to improve the care of children in general A&Es, both in the facilities available and the staff caring for children. It is fair to say that sometimes views conflicted, especially around staffing and who should care for children in the general departments. Following work between representatives of the RCN A&E Nursing Association and the RCN Paediatric Society, guidelines on the care of children in A&E were launched in April 1990 at a joint Paediatric Society, Child Accident Prevention Trust and RCN A&E Nursing Association conference. Reported in the July 1990 *A&E newsletter* this 1990 booklet set the foundation for standards of paediatric care in A&E.

The Children in A&E Special Interest Group (SIG) was formed in March 1992. As a specialist group within the RCN A&E Nursing Association, the group worked to establish regular meetings and study days and these were published in the Association's newsletter. By March 1993 the first formal meeting took place and Susan McGuiness, from University College Hospital, London was elected the first Chair. A range of issues were identified that were to be addressed over the following 12 months including what facilities were available for children in A&E departments in the UK. The 1993 spring edition of *Emergency Nurse* published an article on the Children Act 1989, which was implemented in October 1991. The article pointed out that the act included the need for adequately trained nurses in child care but did not specifically state RSCNs, though it was interpreted by many that the act indirectly supported more RSCNs in A&E depts. Others took a slightly different view and felt child care could be provided by general registered nurses with the addition of a child specific module. The article also indicated how the act provided key information on such issues as how to define a child in need, and for the nurse to be aware of various acts and court orders related to child care.

By 1994 the Children in A&E SIG had held two international conferences and had been involved with numerous agencies regarding care for children in A&E, these included action for sick children, child accident prevention trust and children protection group. In 1995 the group was 250 members strong and working with the RCN paediatric groups on updating the children in A&E booklet.

Activity of the special interest group continued and by July 1996 the group was holding quarterly members meetings in various venues throughout the UK and had established international links in Australia and America. The group published comprehensive guidelines in the July/August 1997 *Emergency Nurse*. These covered numerous areas including recommendations on facilities such as the need for a separate clinical area available throughout the 24 hour period and what to include in the way of play facilities and equipment. On the issue of staffing it recommended the ideal would be all staff looking after children being registered children's nurses, however they recognised at that time that was not feasible. What was promoted was a registered children's nurse at senior level leading child care and general nurses having appropriate training and knowledge in child care. The guidelines also included the need for family involvement throughout the child's care and appropriate pain assessment tools. Continuity of care with health visitors, and paediatric wards was also essential.

In the same edition of the journal it was reported that The National Charity, Action for Sick Children had issued a report with recommendations. The news report indicated that *Emergency Health Services for Children and Young People* (June 1997) offered practical advice to trusts and health authorities including audit checklists. The report recommended similar guidelines as those from the Children in A&E Special Interest Group.

In October 1998, the Children in A&E SIG published a survey in *Emergency Nurse* showing that overall facilities for children had improved, however 21% of departments did not have sufficient child focussed facilities. 73.5% of departments had at least one registered children's nurse with 11.3% having at least one throughout the 24 hour period. The conclusion was that substantial improvements in facilities and improved provision of registered children's nurses had been achieved but more was required.

The Children in A&E SIG were advisers for the Children's Charter and progress continued including annual conferences and being involved with others to develop the National

Service Framework. *The National Service Framework for Children* was published in 2004 as a 10 year plan to improve the health and social care of children, young people and maternity services from birth, through adulthood and was aimed at all professionals who came into contact with children including the need for adequately trained and educated staff. In the May 2006 *Emergency Nurse* Gerard Cronin and Sarah Barton reviewed the framework and its impact on emergency services. The article, 'Reaching the target' concluded a lack of progress had been made and indicated that it was clear that the framework had been overshadowed over the previous two years by the reorganisation of emergency services in light of the 4 hour target. Managers and staff needed to be aware of the need to develop safe environments, child, family friendly and high quality, evidence based care and significant investment was needed.

In line with the change of name of the parent group to the RCN Emergency Care Association in 2003 the RCN A&E SIG was renamed the RCN Paediatric Emergency Care group.

With the continued lack of available RSCNs, general A&E departments struggled to meet even the basic guideline of one registered children's nurse. Donna McGeary - pointed out in *Emergency Nurse* (June 2005), 'Although for more than a decade the Department of Health has advised that there should be at least one registered children's nurse on duty at all times in the emergency department the reality is that many could not provide this.' She questioned the current system of training regarding the competency in emergency care of children. Referencing the Faculty of Emergency Nursing, Donna encouraged adult trained nurses to demonstrate competency of emergency child care through attending a number of shorter courses focused on children.

The Healthcare Commission in 2007 suggested that emergency care networks should be developed to help NHS organisations provide better care for children in A&E (*Emergency Nurse* March 2007). The report *Improving Services for Children in Hospital* was drawn up after a review of 157 NHS foundation trusts in England which called into question the sustainability of emergency services in some NHS Trusts.

As a conclusion to this section, the editorial by two paediatric emergency nurses (*Emergency Nurse* September 2007) reflecting over 10 years of paediatric development in A&E shows that improvement had been achieved. They indicated that 10 years before most children waited with adults and in time order. Few staff were children's trained or had paediatric APLS training. Following a number of publications on improving services for children much had improved both around facilities and staff.

Elderly

Reflecting on my own nursing career I recall in 1969/70 how two of the wards at Orsett Hospital in what was the old part of the hospital were occupied with elderly patients who considered it a bed for life. The same applied to Thurrock Hospital a few miles from Orsett where all the wards were for elderly patients and many considered it their final home. Although from 1935 pioneering doctors started to transform elderly care it was not until the early/mid 1970s that real progress in care of the elderly came about with the setting up of professorial posts. More full time consultants were engaged and a move to care in the community rather than a life in hospital was instituted.

As my A&E life progressed I watched as the elderly wards at Orsett and Thurrock changed from long stay wards to wards for rehabilitation and the increasing number of elderly people coming into A&E required a modern approach. Over the period that this book covers more A&E nurses became involved with not only providing elderly care in the department but also with the safe discharge of the elderly person as reported in chapter 8.

One of the first articles on the elderly in A&E appeared in the October 1986 *A&E newsletter*. Written by Rosamund Griffiths, Staff Nurse in A&E, St James's University Hospital, Leeds. Rosamund pointed out that at the turn of the century anyone living past the age of 45 was considered elderly but in 1986 elderly was mainly confined to those in their 70s or 80s. The article highlighted some of the common reasons that elderly patients attended A&E, these included hypothermia, loss of family/community support, dementia, stroke and fractures. Rosamund also highlighted a joint study between two hospitals in Edinburgh which compared the level of function and dependency of 100 elderly patients after admission and discharge. A part of the study showed scant consideration had been given to function, dependency and support arrangements in the elderly while they were in A&E. Her final paragraph, now read again in 2020, is extremely relevant today and I will leave the reader to decide if her wish has been achieved! 'I would like to consider the future of our ageing population. The number of people over 65 is increasing and we hope that more resources and more finance will be made available to enable us to provide the high standard of compassionate care that we ourselves would wish to receive in our mature years.'

An initiative to overcome the concern of elderly patients being discharged alone was highlighted at the Pan Pacific Emergency Nurses Conference in Hong Kong in 1989. Phyllis Robson from Cumberland Infirmary, Carlisle, Cumbria presented a paper entitled, *'Homeward bound'*. Phyllis described a project in her A&E to identify problems associated with discharging elderly patients and the outcome of the project that led to setting up an emergency intervention team. The project was prompted by the death of an elderly patient who, after discharge, was found dead the next morning due to hypothermia. The intervention team was made up of a number of volunteers who would accompany the elderly person home and ensure warmth and food/drinks were available and they were safe to be left. The GP and social services would be contacted to continue on-going care.

The article, 'Blue light patients: resuscitate or not' by Andrew Cook, Senior Staff Nurse, A&E, Bromley Hospital, Kent (*Emergency Nurse* Autumn 1995) focussed on the whole issue of decisions being made in the back of an ambulance, concerns that were also picked up by the Editor of the journal in his editorial. Andrew suggested that it was often elderly patients who were not taken in from the ambulance to resuscitation. 'It cannot be denied that their age is an influence in this decision' he said. Brian Dolan in his editorial pointed out that it paints a vivid picture of all of us being equal, until that is, we get old. He then continued his editorial exploring why such decisions are made, 'Do older people have less to offer society'? And 'Are their lives not worth saving?'

Accident & Emergency – A Scoping report (G Jones March 1997) indicated that all the departments in the survey reported a large increase in the number of elderly patients attending and although many departments had improved care for this group of patients others felt they often 'got the rough end of the deal'. Many managers highlighted initiatives such as pressure risk assessment tools, use of pressure relieving mattresses, fast tracking of patients with a fractured neck of femur and in-depth discharge planning with some of the departments having nurses appointed specifically for care of the elderly.

As the 'trolley wait' problems continued to increase during the 1990s and early 2000s it became even more imperative that care of the elderly person while in A&E was not compromised. Nicola Wickham, Staff Nurse, A&E, John Radcliffe Hospital, Oxford undertook a literature review published in *Emergency Nurse* (June & July 1997). The review indicated that there was very little literature specific to A&E and pressure area care. Nicola indicated that although pressure sores were not traditionally viewed as an A&E problem she wished to dissipate this belief and show that pressure area care was everyone's responsibility. Through referencing numerous papers Nicola concluded that there was the need for local contingency plans, extra equipment, pressure area care policies, local protocols, use of risk calculators and strategies appropriate to the level of risk. As she said 'Since A&E nurses are often the first point of contact when a patient enters the health care system, it is they who must instigate pressure care measures'.

Two years on from Nicola's article, Karen Spilsbury, Research Assistant, St Bartholomew School of Nursing & Midwifery, City University, London and colleagues described their research into the narrative accounts of older patients retelling their experiences in one A&E department. The article in the October 1999 *Emergency Nurse* demonstrated that from the data collection older people and their carers did not have high expectations of care. They came prepared for long waits. Key messages from older patients to health care professionals under what was termed 'the little things count' included:

- attempt a more comprehensive assessment
- give information
- ensure patients are aware of time to prevent disorientation
- be aware of physical and sensory problems
- be aware of inappropriate comments
- consider privacy, comfort and safety
- consider the patient's view
- attempt to understand circumstances that brought the patient to A&E
- patients are observant and categorise staff based on their caring ability
- attendance may be the first sign that the patient is not coping at home

The RCN A&E Nursing Association in the same edition of the journal launched a position statement which contained a mission statement and identified specific age related needs. It addressed some of the key areas of care including communication, risk assessment, elderly abuse, health promotion, referral/discharge and reflected good practice. The statement concluded by emphasising the need for quality standards and regular audit of the care provided.

Despite all the improvements that many A&E departments had put in place concern still remained as Marie Davies-Gray, lecturer practitioner, A&E, King's College Hospital, London indicated in her article, 'Nurse led fast track' (*Emergency Nurse* September 2003). Marie pointed out that in a BBC news report in December 2000, the charity Help the Aged accused A&E departments of discrimination and administering poor care to elderly patients. The article reported on a multidisciplinary team project set up to explore ways of improving the care of older people in the A&E department. It showed how improvements could be made by staff using the King's A&E over 75 risk assessment tool and the fast track pathway. This pathway included nurses directly referring patients to on-call medical teams.

In the June 2007 *Emergency Nurse* an article by Gerard Cronin, Emergency Care Matron, Basildon Hospital, Essex reported on the increased number of elderly abuse victims and how they should be managed by emergency nurses. Referencing the Department of Health paper *No Secrets* (March 2000) which suggested that 500,000 older people are abused in the UK each year, the article presented typical signs and symptoms of abuse including physical, psychological, sexual, neglect, familial and financial. Guidance was included to help emergency nurses detect abuse and provide appropriate management.

Mental health/Learning Disabilities

Throughout the period covered in this book, care of patients with mental health problems and learning disabilities was a challenge and often care fell short. *A Guide for Good Practice* (NETRHA 1992) recommended 24 hour access to psychiatric and specialist social work support, education of A&E staff as well as registered mental health nurses appointed or made available to A&E. It also recommended psychiatric units develop assessment areas for patients who are in crisis and to be used as a place of safety rather than the current position of police using A&E.

The Audit Commission Report (1996) indicated that in general, mentally ill patients received poor care in A&E. Few nurses and doctors were trained in psychiatric care and psychiatric support was often lacking. The report recommended as a priority the development of good psychiatric crisis intervention services which were not accessed through A&E. It also recommended psychiatric liaison nurse links with A&E.

During my research for the *Accident & Emergency – A Scoping report* (G Jones March 1997) one area that troubled most of the respondents was the large number of patients attending A&E because of a lack of emergency psychiatric services. The report demonstrated that things were improving although slowly. Three of the twenty six departments surveyed had registered mental health nurses on staff but twenty three did not. Fifteen reported good links with psychiatric services, four had fair links and four were poor.

The June 2001 *Emergency Nurse* contained an article on how at West Middlesex University Hospital, London the presence of mental health liaison nurses taking referrals straight from triage as well as from the department after medical assessment improved care. The authors recommended caution and flexibility in setting up such a scheme as the liaison nurse can be overwhelmed by the workload.

Following the government's announcement that NHS Trusts responsible for providing mental health services should show evidence of progress in achieving effective, co-ordinated

24/7 crisis services, modern matrons working in A&E met with the health minister in 2004 (*Emergency Nurse* March 2004). During the summit concerns were raised by several matrons regarding the inability to refer patients to appropriate care staff, and A&E being designated as a place of safety to which police can bring people with mental health issues. Following this the Department of Health launched a mental health checklist for emergency care. The checklist offered practical advice to emergency care staff in all areas of emergency mental health in an attempt to improve care of patients with mental illness.

The *Mental Capacity Act (2005)* came into force in April 2007. Simon Baston, Mental Health Liaison Nurse at Northern General Hospital, Sheffield provided a very comprehensive article in the March 2007 *Emergency Nurse*. Giving a brief history of a number of previous acts/guidelines from consent to self-harm, the article then set out the *Mental Capacity Act*. He indicated that the Act put the rights of individuals with reduced capacity, and the duties of staff to protect vulnerable individuals, into statute law. The Act provided clear guidance for healthcare staff facing situations where patients refuse care or cannot make their own decisions about care. Simon went on to list the four conditions that people with incapacity must fulfil and the importance of documenting decisions made on behalf of the patient. Pointing out that until the *Mental Capacity Act* was in force staff should have been following the guidance of the previous acts/guidelines and he highlighted the NICE 2004 guidelines on self-harm. The article continued to cover an internal audit he had undertaken in his own department on compliance to the NICE guidelines.

At the RCN A&E conference in 1999 Ruth Buckley and Judy Thornley from North Staffordshire presented a paper outlining an innovative project which improved the quality of service for people with learning disabilities attending the A&E department. Referencing the paper *'Signposts for Success'* (NHSE 1998) they demonstrated how they had achieved this in their department. By establishing links between the learning disability services in the community trust and the A&E department they had set up a rolling programme of teaching, direct weekly input from the learning disabilities liaison nurse plus access to the on-call service, proactive use of triage to reduce waiting times, guidelines which formed a care pathway and established a resource file, poster and leaflets about the service.

References

Audit Commission: (1996) *By Accident or Design – improving emergency care in acute hospitals.* London: HMSO

Department of Health: (2004) *The National Service Framework for Children.* London: HMSO

Jones G: (1997) *Accident & Emergency – A Scoping report* (Report to the Chief Nursing Officer Department of Health)

Mental Capacity Act (2005) Government Legislation UK

North East Thames Regional Health Authority: (1992) *Accident & Emergency Services – A Guide to Good Practice).* NETRHA publication.

CHAPTER 15

PRE-HOSPITAL CARE

Throughout the history of emergency nursing there has always been a link between emergency nursing and pre-hospital providers. More recently nurses have moved to working with ambulance staff in the pre-hospital setting, either through the provision of direct clinical care or the community telephone helpline.

The ambulance service

The ambulance service, like the casualty/A&E service, developed over time. From a simple transport service devised to remove the wounded from the battlefields, through to horse drawn vehicles of the First World War, the service moved on to mechanically driven ambulances and the paramedic service we know today.

It was the Battle of Solferino on Friday 24th June1859 when casualties numbered some 40,000 that inspired Jean Henri Dunant to form a band of helpers that was the forerunner of the Red Cross movement. On that night, men lay dead and dying and it took three days to collect all of them from the battlefield. From that encounter Jean Henri Dunant and four other Geneva men set up the International Committee for Relief of the Wounded, later in 1863 to become the International Committee of the Red Cross. The following year 12 governments adopted the first Geneva Convention. The International Federation of Red Cross and Red Crescent Societies was founded in 1919 in Paris in the aftermath of the First World War creating closer co-operation between the societies. The British Red Cross was established in 1870 and celebrated its 150th year in 2020. I joined as a cadet, aged 11 years, in 1964 and was awarded Life membership in 1983.

Until 1966 training of ambulance personnel was through the individual attending a first aid course run by the local Red Cross or St John Ambulance service. Major change occurred in 1966 with the development of the Millar training though in some areas, including my own, the ambulance staff were still attending Red Cross First Aid training in 1969. Under the Millar training (Ministry of Health), regional training schools were established and a residential 6 weeks programme of training was instituted. Ambulances were still basic with two stretchers plus canvas sheets and poles, blankets, splints and first aid equipment. Oxygen was introduced and in the early 1970s Entonox was available for the first time.

As time progressed local pilot extended training was developed leading to the establishment of the Association of Emergency Medical Technicians (AEMT) in 1978. In Thurrock, some of the ambulance staff led by Rob Dodson were keen to expand their knowledge and skills and formed a local AEMT branch. Invited to join and help develop the ambulance staff we would meet at Rob's home and that started what was to be a very long journey to improve patient care. In Essex I was heavily involved in the development and training of the local AEMT group and the development of the Essex ambulance services extended training programme. Essex ambulance service, like many other services in the 1980s, developed a locally based extended training programme that moved staff towards paramedic status. Eligibility to undertake the extended training in Essex required the ambulance staff to have a minimum of 18 months post-qualification experience in front line work and to pass an entry examination. The course comprised three stages, pre-clinical training, clinical training and clinical practical experience. A self-study package (Essex Ambulance Service Extended Ambulance Aid) was linked to formal classroom lectures and skills development.

The success of AEMT triggered the move to full paramedic training in the UK through the National Paramedic Development Group and then the Joint Royal Colleges Advisory Group. I was privileged to have been a member of these groups until 1995 and much of the Essex training programme became part of the national paramedic training programme. By 1988 local schemes came together under the National Health Service Training Authority. Currently a paramedic degree qualification is available through universities.

With the move to Trust status for hospitals and community health care in 1992, ambulance services also became NHS Trusts. Maintaining the previous structures, in our area the Essex Ambulance Service NHS Trust continued to serve the local population and to work closely with police and fire as well as our local hospital A&E departments. Under the *Taking Healthcare to the patient: Transforming NHS ambulance services (2005)* one recommendation was to reduce the number of ambulance trusts and in 2006 it was reported in the June edition of *Emergency Nurse* that the Health Minister had confirmed the number would be cut by more than half from 29 to 12. Essex became part of the Eastern Ambulance Service NHS Trust.

Taking Healthcare to the patient: Transforming NHS ambulance services (2005) not only focussed on ambulance trusts it also contained recommendations on telephone assessment and advice, especially encouraging self-care at home or visiting minor injury units. The policy required more ambulance trusts to treat people in the community. Much more emphasis was placed on ambulance services co-ordinating mobile health care services, including urgent care and diagnostic services and local urgent care provision. Welcoming the roll out of the Emergency Care Practitioner initiative (ECP), Grant Williams, Chair of the RCN Emergency Care Association said in *Emergency Nurse* (July 2005), 'It's a welcome initiative and something that offers opportunities to nurses as well as paramedics.' Nurses did become more involved as emergency care practitioners or paramedics and many provided a range of treatments in the home. In the March 2006 *Emergency Nurse*, Lisa Ashley, Emergency Care Practitioner, South Yorkshire Ambulance Service featured in an article during her ten hour shift demonstrating this relatively new role.

Pre-hospital care: medical & nursing

Dr Ken Easton, a Yorkshire GP developed the concept of a professional pre-hospital care service. Having had experience of such care during the 1940s, in 1967, he set up the Road Accident After Care Scheme of the North Riding of Yorkshire. This led to other such schemes being set up across the UK and by 1975, there were numerous local systems that in 1977 were formalised into the British Association of Immediate Care Schemes (BASICS).

The nurses' role in both the ambulance service and BASICS has been sporadic and was often dependent on what was happening locally. From my own experience, our A&E department at Orsett Hospital ran a pre-hospital mobile medical/nursing team, something I became very aware of soon after joining the A&E team on night duty in 1975. Although our mobile care service ran from the hospital it was linked into the Chingford Major Accident Scheme and in later years this became the London branch of BASICS. Dr Ernst (A&E consultant) was a member of this group and apart from providing care from the hospital he was also on-call from his home in Ilford. This service led me to engage early on in my A&E career with the ambulance staff and service, spending time riding with the crews and understanding the pre-hospital environment. It also connected me with many of the occupational health services in both local industry and the Port of Tilbury. I also attended many of the local BASICS meetings and participated in many of the mock major incidents as well as providing care with the BASICS doctors at many events. One of the advantages of pre-hospital care apart from the obvious lifesaving was that the nurse was able to care for the patient at the scene and then continue that care whilst in A&E.

Fortunately being ahead of the 1995 guidelines on appropriate clothing (chapter 13), when Dr Ernst set up the service in the 1970s he ensured that protective clothing was available for all staff attending a pre-hospital event. Even when hospitals did provide pre-hospital care at a disaster the clothing was often inadequate. The nurses and doctors who attended the Moorgate tube disaster in 1975 went to the incident in full uniform, nurses wearing dresses, aprons, and large linen caps, the doctors in white coats.

Pre-hospital care: nurse training

Courses for nurses in pre-hospital care were proposed in the early 1990s with the *A&E newsletter* (November 1992) reporting that the RCN A&E advisor had met with representatives of BASICS to discuss establishing a short course for nurses in pre-hospital care. The two day training course would be loosely based on a similar course for doctors. Following this news item, the *A&E newsletter* (June 1994) reported that six Pre-Hospital Emergency Care (PHEC) courses had been conducted at five different locations in England and Scotland with a course planned for Wales. Following the underlying principle of shared learning the course included doctors, paramedics and nurses. Unfortunately very few nurses attended but from those who did the majority were from A&E.

By 1996 things had moved on a pace with the *A&E newsletter* (April 1997) reporting the launch of the Faculty of Pre-Hospital Care in January 1996. A Faculty of the Royal College of Surgeons (Edinburgh), the RCN A&E Nursing Association was represented by Simon Davies who had considerable input into the design of the multidisciplinary Pre-hospital Emergency Care course and the development of the Faculty.

In 1998 the A&E Nursing Association established a sub-group to review issues around nurses and pre-hospital care. Andrew Kent who was now representing the RCN A&E Nursing Association on the Faculty of Pre-Hospital Care indicated in the winter *A&E newsletter* (1998) that the prime aim was to determine the role of the nurse in the pre-hospital setting. A medical representative of the Faculty was also a member of the sub-group. It was also reported that the Diploma in Immediate Care was now open to A&E nurses, paramedics and medical staff.

By the early 2000s and the push for more emergency care in the home, *Emergency Nurse* (October 2001) reported on a study conducted by St Martin's College, Carlisle, Cumbria. The study involved a graduate nurse practitioner with extensive A&E experience working in a paramedic role. Working with a paramedic, the trial involved seeing if treatment at home was safe and could be achieved by the nurse working within the paramedic role. The conclusion was that the basic idea was successful and a larger study was justified.

In a further article (*Emergency Nurse* March 2002), it was reported that a pilot degree programme could be used as an academic foundation for a role of Practitioner in Emergency Care. This inter-professional education with a shared learning programme was for emergency nurses and paramedics. By 2005 the government went ahead with plans to increase the number of emergency care practitioners in the ambulance service in an attempt to reduce the emergency department workload by having more people treated at home.

Pre-hospital care was included as one of the eight modules that made up the career and competency framework of the Faculty of Emergency Nursing (chapter 10).

References

Department of Health: (2005) *Taking Healthcare to the patient: Transforming NHS ambulance services.* London: HMSO

Essex Ambulance Service: Extended Ambulance Aid (self-study package) undated

Ministry of Health: (1966) Report by the working party on ambulance training and equipment. (The Millar report). London: HMSO

REFLECTION

In the introduction to this book I invited the reader to imagine emergency care without a whole raft of national guidelines, training courses and advanced nursing practice. Throughout this book I have demonstrated how those early pioneering emergency nurses in the 1960s and early 1970s, working with others, achieved so much and historically in such a short period of time. When I look back to the huge task those early pioneers had, to convince a sceptical medical and nursing profession as well as the public that A&E nursing was more than simply following what a doctor ordered, I have learnt so much from their sheer determination and strength of purpose.

Brian Dolan in his foreword and Joanna Sloan in her chapter pay tribute to my work in emergency nursing. Like them, I had my mentors both in the A&E department at Orsett Hospital and in the RCN A&E Nursing Forum. Kate O'Hanlon, our third forum Chair, was a great mentor. Not only did I gain such a vast amount of information from her through the A&E Nursing Forum, I was also privileged to know her as a friend. In 1985 I visited Kate in her Senior Sister role and undertook study at the Royal Victoria Hospital, Belfast. Thirty six years later Joanna, working in the same department (well the modern version), has written the final chapter to this book. From a very personal perspective, written in the first person and with great passion she demonstrates how the hard work of her predecessors has paid off.

Of course not everything has been achieved and it is interesting to read in Joanna's chapter that while professional and clinical developments have made great strides, workload, staffing and violence to staff still remains a huge challenge. From the very first A&E conference and the first *A&E newsletters* staffing, violence and increased patient attendance have been recorded. Having first worked in A&E as a night staff nurse in 1975 I have witnessed these challenges and probably no more so than the increase in patient attendance. During the 1970s and early 1980s patient attendance in our department at Orsett, whilst increasing year on year, still allowed for many periods during the day and especially at night when the department was void of patients. Changes in society, especially the 24 hour life style rapidly led to increased attendance, especially at night. While these and other challenges are important to resolve, they should not overshadow the many key pieces of work that have emerged over the last 50 plus years. The development of the first A&E course, advanced emergency nursing practice, triage, trauma care and training, the emergency nurse practitioner, the faculty of emergency nursing and articulating what emergency nursing was, through the publication in 1994 of *Accident & Emergency: Challenging the Boundaries*.

As I read through all the literature to compile this book, the one thing that really struck me was that not all developments appeared new. Rather, it was often a remodelling of past work and past activities. Triage comes from way back when it related to sorting produce and then we saw it in some form in 1898 in St Bartholomew's Hospital. Modern Matrons reflect the Nursing Officer role of the 1970s and 1980s and these in turn came from the Assistant Matrons. Emergency Nurse Practitioners legitimised what many A&E nurses in the past were doing, especially on night duty when the doctor who had worked all day and was going to be on duty the next day was having a well-earned sleep. The Faculty of Emergency Nursing was developed from all the work done throughout the 35 years on developing emergency nursing courses. All of this demonstrates that the development of emergency care and emergency nursing has been, and probably will continue to be, an evolution and not as often said (even by me), a revolution. As the words from ABBA's Waterloo states *'The history book on the shelf is always repeating itself'*.

As I reflect on the many battles we all fought in trying to achieve the evolution, none more so than the Faculty of Emergency Nursing, another quote comes to mind – *'Great spirits have always encountered violent opposition from mediocre minds'* (Albert Einstein). I am not sure why new ideas or developing emergency nursing often made it feel like we were fighting against the tide and why those who put obstructions in our way could not see it from the patient's point of view. I will leave you, the reader, to decide where the quote best reflects within the chapters of the book.

Looking at both the past and the future I believe the unique role of the emergency nurse is more than the sum of the parts. The uniqueness lies in the combination and emergency nurses need to continue to demonstrate and articulate that uniqueness. There are many challenges ahead and many of the previous challenges have re-emerged, no more so than 'trolley waits'. Also as I write this reflection, emergency departments have been transformed due to the need to address the Covid-19 pandemic. However, like the nurses before, I am confident that today's emergency nurses will excel and continue the important work of providing excellent care based on sound knowledge and skills.

For today's emergency nurses, especially those in senior positions, I invite you to consider how in the same 35 years the emergency medical consultants have travelled from the Casualty Surgeons Association to the Royal College of Emergency Medicine; yet emergency nurses are still a small cog in the big wheel of the RCN. In 2022, emergency nursing will celebrate 50 years since it became a group in the RCN. My challenge to today's emergency nurses is to continue the legacy of their predecessors and move towards the next 50 years.

FROM PICKET LINES TO PANDEMICS EMERGENCY NURSING IN 2020

Joanna Sloan

> *"How very little can be done under the spirit of fear"*
> Florence Nightingale.

I am very pleased to have the opportunity to compare and contrast parts of the book with today's emergency care provision. I met Gary through the TNCC course when I was a candidate and then again through the faculty network after I became an instructor myself, a course which I have grown to love teaching. I had no idea of the history of Gary's nursing career until I read his first book *It's Not All Blood and Guts* and the manuscript for this book. I had very little appreciation of the work and effort that has been achieved by so many to empower nurses like me and my colleagues and the advancement of the roles and opportunities we have now.

For me 2020 has no doubt been one of the most difficult years for emergency nursing in Northern Ireland. January began with all our nursing staff and multidisciplinary colleagues on picket lines, out on strike to fight for parity. Not just on pay issues (although that remains unresolved and we are still in industrial action) but parity with regards to safe staffing levels, skill mix and educational opportunities across all nursing specialities. What we have achieved this year is phenomenal. In the midst of a global pandemic we became heroes in the public eye, we watched with teary eyes and full hearts as the public stood outside their doors and workplaces and clapped for us. Being recognised for our hard work to keep everyone safe and well as Covid-19 loomed over us all. In the international year of the nurse and midwife and Florence Nightingales bicentennial year (2020) we have, through the fight against Covid-19, sadly lost over 1500 of our nursing force globally (ICN 2020). And that's what we are, a force. We have proven that we get up and go to work each day, knowing the occupational hazards, because nursing is not just a job. Nursing is a vocation that many have now given their lives for.

In the introduction to this book Gary states a range of things that were developed over the 35 year period 1972-2007. I can now give insight into what emergency care looks like today compared to then.

Workload (chapter 8). Nursing assessment and Triage (chapter 11)

There were many changes and adaptations to emergency care in 2020 in the context of Covid-19. Our ability to manage the pandemic has been due to transformation in major incident management. We drew upon historical experiences with how we managed during the swine flu, AIDs pandemic, Asian and Spanish Flu. Our patient areas are now described as green, amber and red and at times it has been proven to be a logistical nightmare for senior management. Within a few weeks major changes had been made not only to patient care pathways but also to how and where specific patients were nursed depending on presentation. Triage became more crucial than ever, with senior nurses taking on navigation roles to direct patients to appropriate areas. As 2020 progressed we witnessed a drop in emergency department (EDs) attendances in Northern Ireland from April through to May. We also saw a huge effort from all specialties, including primary care to help us avoid unnecessary attendances while we prepared for the peak of the first wave. Crowding became a fear for us all. Resetting and re-designing our EDs has been integral in avoiding crowding. The Royal College of Emergency Medicine (RCEM Oct 2020) set out an 'RCEM- CARES' publication stipulating that the changes that have been implemented during the pandemic, which have proven to help reduce and prevent crowding and exit block to date, must continue post Covid-19. This publication states that in order to improve the growing levels of 'trolley waits' and crowding there must be an investment in health and social care to allow for more bed capacity and nursing staff to care for the patients.

Northern Ireland has generally performed below the targets we fight to achieve, including the time between arrival to triage, 12 hour breaches and 'trolley waits'. We constantly aim to improve these statistics by initiating improvements such as the 4 hour target initiative (2004-2005) aimed at combating crowding in ED. What must be noted is that the reasons why these targets are not achieved remain the same as the general themes discussed and explored through Gary's book. We as nurses have called for additional staff, additional beds and more funding. Instead over the past years we have watched as our acute wards reduce beds and beds that open to meet 'winter demand' are soon closed. EDs are reduced to urgent care settings, changed to walk in only or closed completely. Our nursing staff report increasing effects of burn out and work related stress and our concerns go unheard and efforts undervalued. We have a growing number of patients with increasing complexities attending EDs which do not have the space or resource to deal with the greater numbers. A recent RCEM (April 2018) publication noted that 98% of Emergency Consultants felt their EDs were in crisis.

Violence and aggression continue to plague our healthcare staff across UK and NI. A healthcare staff survey for Northern Ireland found that 14% of all staff stated they had experienced physical violence from patients, their relatives or other members of the public and of these 77% reported this. Just over 26% of nursing staff stated they had experienced physical violence from patients, their relatives or other members of the public (RCN 2018). As this survey covers quite a vast range of nursing staff from all areas we are very aware that within the emergency department and other high risk areas such as mental health, acute medicine and dementia care this percentage would be much higher and that essentially, one in four of our nurses in Northern Ireland have experienced physical violence at least once. The 2019 NHS Staff Survey showed 15% of NHS staff experienced physical violence from members of the public and patients in the past year – this rises to 34% among ambulance trust staff (DOH 2020). While it is clear that legislation is changing and penalties for these crimes are becoming harsher we have been implementing processes and campaigns within our hospitals and emergency departments to help reduce the incidence. Management of Actual or Potential Aggression (MAPA) training is mandatory for all new staff who join our emergency departments in NI and we have also implemented our 'Zero Tolerance' campaign which aims to both dissuade those at risk of becoming violent or aggressive towards staff and empower staff of their right to safety and protection in the workplace. Throughout my career I have always had the view that violence and aggression go hand in hand with the abuse of drugs and alcohol. Through my experience working within the emergency department I have witnessed and been subjected to aggression and violence from patients, all of which have been escalated due to the intoxication of drugs and or alcohol. I have never been subject to this behaviour from patients when intoxication is absent. I support and re-iterate those issues which Gary has discussed at length remain significant in emergency nursing today and continue to be one of the biggest challenges to our profession.

Professional Development (chapter 9)
Within my career there have always been Nurse Practitioners, both Advanced Clinical and Emergency Nurse Practitioners. The emergency nursing care pathway has allowed nurses the opportunity to develop and plan for their preferred career. This involves the support of educational courses available in our local universities specific to all pathways, whether clinical or management focused. The Specialist Nursing 2 year course currently available at the University of Ulster, provides the opportunity to gain specialist knowledge and skills in pathways specific to the Emergency department and the care of a vast range of minor injuries, not only that of broken bones and wounds. This course has advanced to include managing minor head injuries, eyes and ENT presentations. This then allows us to have a much more autonomous role in the care of our patients. We can request x-rays from triage, provide pain relief through either Patient Group Directives or after completing Non-Medical Prescribing courses. We can treat wounds, cannulate, obtain blood samples, perform ECGs, and prescribe fluids and nebulisers. We perform peak flow, visual acuity and many more examinations. The experience of undergoing these courses allows us to provide in-depth health assessment and history taking skills which allow us to provide advice and signposting to patients for other appropriate services and clinics. We can discharge from triage and now have the ability to refer directly to and provide appointments for services such as the maternity unit for problems relating to pregnancy, surgical assessment units

for abdominal issues, eye clinics and ENT clinics to name just a few.

All of these skills are recognised on the Emergency Nursing Level 2 of the RCN National Curriculum and Competency Framework (June 2017). The RCN Emergency Care Association (ECA) launched the National Curriculum and Competency Framework for Emergency Nursing in response to demands for clarity about the knowledge and skills nurses require to work in emergency settings at various levels. The 'good nursing practice' competencies are aligned with the Nursing & Midwifery Council code of conduct and are intended to promote professional conduct, teamwork, education, leadership and practice development.

The framework outlines professional development pathways into management, education or clinical specialist roles such as ENP previously discussed and the Advanced Clinical Practitioner (ACP). An Advanced Clinical Practitioner is an independent practitioner working within ED, assessing, treating and diagnosing all undifferentiated conditions that present to the Emergency Department covering all areas of the department – Minors, Majors and Resuscitation. The ACP programme is already well established in parts of the UK. The programme and career pathway of ACP has become increasingly coveted due to the incredible work which has been done to get emergency nurses into positions where we can utilise our incredible patient experience and skill to directly treat and assess those presenting to the emergency department. The National Major Trauma Nursing Group (NMTNG) has published competencies for trauma nurses (NMTNG 2016).

Staffing and Skill Mix (chapter 12)
It is without question that nursing has changed significantly. What will be the new normal for emergency nursing? It is extraordinary to think that in Northern Ireland we stood on picket lines in January 2020 in a bid for safe staffing and yet now we are at our worst staffing levels to date despite a huge response to the Health and Social Care workforce appeal, implemented due to Covid-19. There are many nurses across all areas of healthcare who are currently unable to work due to isolation or affected by Covid-19. We are currently under immense pressure in all areas and it remains a worrying situation. Skill mix of staff remains an issue, much the same as the stark picture Gary has stated in chapter 12. It is hoped the RCN Baseline Emergency Staffing Tool (BEST) will help in the pursuit of improved staffing. Staffing levels are at an all-time low across UK and NI due to years of under investment in funding for student nurse places at university.

Clinical Development & Professional Care (chapter 13)
Trauma
The Royal Victoria Hospital in Belfast is the regional major trauma unit for the province in Northern Ireland, with access to many specialties in major trauma management. In Northern Ireland nurses have the opportunity to partake in TNCC training and more recently have commenced in house training for trauma (TILS) as a training step before progression to TNCC candidate. TILS is an intermediate introduction to the care of a trauma patient post preceptorship and induction. These courses are extremely successful and enjoyable. They are taught by senior nurses in the emergency department, who have a foundation of knowledge and skills specific to major trauma care including the management of chest drains, arterial lines, difficult

venous access, management of massive transfusion protocols and many more. It underpins local policy and procedure and is specific to the equipment we use daily. It complements TNCC perfectly as an intermediate step.

Trauma management has come on leaps and bounds in the past few years, moving to and finally being recognised as a specialty in itself. Although England had introduced air ambulances much earlier, in July 2017 Northern Ireland's first air ambulance was available and early in 2020 a fully operational helipad opened on the Royal Victoria Hospital site. Linked with the opening of our designated trauma unit, the introduction of our local trauma triage tool and the initiation of our trauma bypass system everything was now linked.

We have been working with and contributing to the Trauma Audit and Research Network (TARN) data information. TARN is the largest European trauma registry. Data is collected from over 220 hospitals in the Republic of Ireland, Northern Ireland, England and Wales. TARN measures and monitors process of care and outcomes to demonstrate the impact of initiatives, providing local, regional & national information on trauma patient outcomes (2020). TARN has also developed its own National Major Trauma Nursing Group Educational and Competency Standards, depicting levels 1-3 for adult and paediatric trauma nurses.

Never before has our care of a trauma patient been better. The specialist pre-hospital treatment advancements include many lifesaving interventions like pre hospital blood transfusion, the speciality primary survey care by full trauma team on arrival to the emergency department and now a specific area for continued care and secondary survey. All of this has been achieved by our amazing leaders involved in improving Northern Ireland trauma care.

In Gary's first book *'It's Not All Bloods and Guts: My Amazing Life as an A&E Nurse'* on page 164 he describes how an 18year old motorcyclist died in the A&E department due to a major chest trauma and that during his experience that day he witnessed the sudden deterioration then cardio-pulmonary arrest in a previously conscious but breathless young patient. That experience of knowing there could have been a better outcome if trauma management had the advancement as it does today was difficult to read as a modern emergency nurse. Today, if that same patient presented to our regional trauma unit, our fantastic prehospital care providers have the clinical skills and equipment to assess and diagnose at the roadside, transfer via air ambulance and initiate massive blood loss protocols before the patient arrives in the emergency department. With the advancement of clinical skills and the availability of emergency consultant care pre-hospital with our helicopter emergency medical crew we have the ability to provide multiple trauma interventions such as the insertion of chest drains and effectively manage chest trauma as though the patient were already in the resuscitation room. On arrival to the emergency department, due to clear and concise pre hospital alerting, trauma patients are met by the trauma team. Within Northern Ireland and in our regional trauma hospital we have a specific set of roles, which together make the trauma team. Our trauma team is usually lead by our most senior clinician. We have roles allocated for a clinician and nurse for each of Airway, Breathing and Circulation, allowing simultaneous assessment and intervention, and oversight by both Team Lead and Scribe. I have no doubt that the advancement of trauma management has significantly reduced mortality rates and increased rehabilitation outcomes post trauma.

Resuscitation
Guidelines are underpinned in everyday practice with evidence based research. There are a number of options for airway control, plans for difficult intubation and specific airway management and sedation training for nurses. Intubation guided by video-laryngoscopes, disposable mini-tracheostomy kits and kit bags with equipment that our predecessors would swoon over. Having the option of an automated, portable CPR device or thoracotomy kits on hand if we needed them, and senior staff with advanced skills to oversee 24 hours a day in our main trauma units. Documentation includes streamlined charts, tick boxes and time lines that doctors and nurses alike have pained over in order to help carry out our duties effectively.

Advances in technology

Compared with the period covered in this book technology has advanced in leaps and bounds. In 2020 particularly through the Covid-19 Pandemic, we have taken huge strides forward. We have the ability to provide patients and families with the ability to speak to and see each other via video calls on iPads and tablets. We can communicate with each other through Vocera and call phones directly from anywhere we stand on site, this makes it easier to access specialities and our colleagues such as security or portering. Our ED computer systems and dedicated admin colleagues allow us to track and allocate patients to areas, we have access to information at our fingertips. We are able to request input from multidisciplinary teams, record notes and input decisions and updates in care. We can see when radiology interventions are complete, when investigations are reported on and what treatment is outstanding. We have initiated virtual hospital appointments for follow up review with patients and have generally improved many patient pathways. Northern Ireland has usually been somewhat behind on the advancement of medical technology compared to our mainland UK counterparts. In June 2020 the decision was made by our health minster to fund the introduction to computer based patient documentation and recordkeeping, thus promising that the days of relying heavily on paper patient records are finally coming to an end in NI. Digital transformation in Northern Ireland promises to improve patient safety and benefit healthcare staff.

Online networking and journals remain one of the best developments in emergency nursing. Online we can access training materials, communicate with and compare experiences with other emergency department's staff. We have access to podcasts, journals, reflections and so much more. Generally that 'family feel' we have among our own friends and colleagues in emergency care has expanded across the UK and Ireland.

Conclusion
There is no doubt we have a lot of work to do and a legacy to uphold in emergency nursing. We are forever grateful for the determination and fight that has been fought for us by the previous generation of emergency nurses and leaders. I'm almost afraid that now that we have been passed the baton, I'm terrified we will drop it.

Emergency care in my biased opinion will always be the best area to work, where else can you spend a 13 hour shift with friends who feel like family and perform duties that vary so much. There is so much opportunity within emergency nursing and it can help prepare you for wherever your nursing career may take you. The adrenaline and curiosity that progresses through us, we are a breed of nurse like no other and I am proud to say I am an emergency care nurse.

References

Boyle, A., 2016. *The four-hour target: what's the point?*. [online] National Health Executive. Available at: <https://www.nationalhealthexecutive.com/Comment/the-four-hour-target- whats-the-point/158287#:~:text=At%20the%20time%20it%20planned,British%20Isles%20followed%20shortly%20afterwards.> [Accessed 4 September 2020].

International Council of Nurses, 2020. *ICN confirms 1,500 nurses have died from COVID-19 in 44 countries and estimates that healthcare worker COVID-19 fatalities worldwide could be more than 20,000*. [online] Available at: <https://www.icn.ch/sites/default/files/inline-files/PR_52_1500%20Nurse%20Deaths_FINAL-3.pdf> [Accessed 13 November 2020].

National Major Trauma Nursing Group - TARN, 2016. *Levels 1 - 3 adult and paediatric emergency trauma nurse/AHP Educational and competency standards*. TARN.

NHS. 2019. *NHS publishes latest NHS staff survey results*. [online] Available at: <https://www.england.nhs.uk/2019/02/nhs-publishes-latest-nhs-staff-survey-results/> [Accessed 13 September 2020].

Nursing Standard. 2020. *Violence against nurses: government plans to double prison sentence to two years.* [online] Available at: <https://rcni.com/nursing-standard/newsroom/news/violence-against-nurses-government-plans-to-double-prison-sentence-to-two-years-165471> [Accessed 13 September 2020].

Royal College of Emergency Medicine - Northern Ireland, 2018. *What Northern Ireland's Emergency Department Consultants Really Think.* Northern Ireland: RCEM.

Royal College of Emergency Medicine. 2020. *RCEM launches new campaign to end corridor care as data shows more than 100,000 patients waiting over 12 hours in A&Es this winter.* [online] Available at: <https://www.rcem.ac.uk/RCEM/News/News_2020/RCEM_launches_new_campaign_to_end_corridor_care_.aspx> [Accessed 3 September 2020].

Royal College of Nursing- Emergency Care Association, 2017. *National Curriculum and Competency Framework Emergency Nursing (Level 2).* London: RCN.

Royal College of Nursing, 2018. *Violence and aggression in the NHS Estimating the size and the impact of the problem.* London: RCN.

Royal College of Nursing. 2019. *BEST - Baseline Emergency Staffing Tool.* [online] Available at: <https://www.rcn.org.uk/get-involved/forums/emergency-care-association/best-tool> [Accessed 13 September 2020].

TARN. 2020. *Resources-Who is TARN.* [online] Available at: <https://www.tarn.ac.uk/Content.aspx?ca=4#TRAUMA_CARE> [Accessed 4 November 2020].

INDEX

3M Health Care xii, 12, 29, 48, 136, 137, 143, 182

Accident & Emergency - A Guide to Good Practice 40-41, 197, 249
Accident prevention/Health promotion 11, 15 46, 55, 72, 133-135, 248
Advanced Trauma Nursing Course (ATNC) 54, 220
Advisory defibrillators 229
A&E Forum/Association (see RCN)
A&E (course 199) 10, 135-138, 149
Ageing population (see elderly)
Aggression (see violence)
Ambulance service 233, 253-256
Association of Emergency Medical Technicians (AEMT) xii, 18, 20, 254-255
Awards (Honours) 30, 36, 58, 68, 69, 84-85, 89, 123, 137, 159, 182, 254

Baseline Emergency Staffing Tool (BEST) 92, 203, 270
BBC programme *Casualty* 27-28
Bell Una 45, 69, 121
Bereavement Care 54, 230
Blythin Peter 17, 24-25, 32, 182
British Association for Accident and Emergency Medicine (see Royal College of Emergency Medicine)
British Association for Emergency Medicine (BAEM) (see Royal College of Emergency Medicine)
BASICS 256-257
British Orthopaedic Association (see orthopaedics)
Buckles Ethel 15, 20, 24-27, 30-31, 38-39, 103, 108, 142, 143, 219-220
    Memorial Lecture 39, 59
Butcher Kathie 39, 43-45, 59, 120, 189
By Accident or Design 51-52 95, 197

Cardiac Arrest 227-230
Castille Karen 58, 65, 74, 78, 85
Casualty Surgeons Association (CSA) (see Royal College of Emergency Medicine)
Casualty Watch 106-108, 110
Cerebral Vascular Accident (Stroke) 237
*Challenging the Boundaries (*RCN 1994*)* xiii, 50, 55, 63, 129-131, 167, 181, 261
Children 46, 55, 65, 86-88, 96, 97, 108, 134, 139, 176, 199, 224, 230, 235, 240-244

277

Clinical Specialist 148, 153, 269
Community Health Councils 77, 106-108
Components of Life model 131-132, 184
Conferences (see RCN)
Consultant Nurse xiv, 69, 88, 159-162,
Criminal Injuries Compensation Scheme 120
Crouch Robert 50, 58, 60, 61, 65, 66, 79, 84, 99, 157, 159, 160, 166, 169, 172, 186, 190
CRASH trial 223

Dependency Tool (see JDT)
Dolan Brian x-xi, 43-45, 47, 50, 68, 87, 100, 109, 110, 113, 122, 153, 155, 192, 246, 260

Elderly 64-65, 98, 107, 111, 244-249
Emergency Care Association (ECA) (See RCN)
Emergency Care Practitioner (ECP) 156, 256, 259
Emergency Nurse Practitioners xiii, 30, 33, 68, 146-159, 268
Emergency Nurses Association (ENA) 36, 38, 219
Emergency Services Collaborative 81-82, 97

Faculty of Emergency Nursing xiv, 86, 88-90, 92, 145, 166-181, 243, 259, 261-262
    Honorary Fellowship 89
    Pre-faculty specialties 175, 178
Faculty of Pre-Hospital Care (see pre-hospital care: training)
Florence Nightingale 3-4, 128, 265

GP patients/issues 6, 46, 98-100, 103, 107, 114, 119, 146
GRASP 196
Griffiths Report (Sir Ernest Roy Griffiths) 17, 31

Head Injury 222-223
Health Care Assistant (HCA) 50, 204-205
HIV/AIDS 19, 236-237
Holt Lynda 74, 77, 80, 107, 113, 122, 140, 162
Hoy Betty 10

Initial assessment (see triage)
International Collaboration of National Emergency Nursing Organisations xiv, 77
International conference (see RCN)

International Declaration of Co-operation and Friendship xiv, 76-77, 88
Interpretation of emergency (inappropriate attender) 6-7, 98-100

Joint Board of Clinical Nursing Studies (JBCNS) 10, 13, 22, 135-136
Joint Royal Colleges Ambulance Liaison Committee (JCALC) 157, 255
Jones Dependency Tool (JDT) 41, 133, 184, 199-203

King Margaret 13, 16, 42

Learning Disabilities 249, 251-252
Lee Margaret 9, 13, 148
Lomas Gabby 59, 84, 220, 223

Major Injuries 44, 52, 212, 213, 216
Major Trauma Outcome Study (MTOS) 214, 217
McEwen Yvonne 17, 18, 70
Medical Care Practitioner (MCP) 156
Mental Capacity Act 2005 251
Mental health 62, 65, 249-251
Millar report (Dr E L M Millar) 254

Milnthorp Jill 14, 15, 20, 25
Minor injury units 52, 60, 77, 79, 91, 117, 151-152, 154, 157, 256
Models of nursing 128, 131-133
Modern matrons 88, 144, 162, 251, 261
'Monitor' for A&E 35, 36, 55, 67
Moore Susan 11
Morgan Judith 75, 86, 230
Myocardial Infarction & Thrombolysis 232-233, 234

National Institute of Clinical Excellence (NICE) 107, 124, 158, 202, 223, 224, 251
National Patient Access Team (NPAT) 109, 198
National Vocational Qualification (NVQ) 50, 205
Network of Emergency Learning Facilitators (NELF) 140, 141
NHS Direct xiv, 60, 72, 78, 79, 119, 192
North Staffordshire Trauma Centre 52
Northern Ireland 119, 264-275
Nurse prescribing xiv, 67, 152, 158-159
Nurses' Registration Act 4, 5
Nursing Assessment 182-194, 265-268

Nursing Auxiliary see HCA

O'Hanlon Kate 11, 15, 20, 25, 36, 260
Order of the British Empire vii, 11, 84
Orsett Hospital 2, 17, 20, 28, 102, 104, 131, 151, 163, 182, 184, 199, 210, 212, 244-245, 256, 260-261
Orthopaedics 98, 224-225
    British Orthopaedic Association 214, 215, 217, 225
    Consultants 7, 9, 33
Overdose 234-236
Oxygen therapy 47, 221, 233-234, 254

Paediatrics (see children)
Pan Pacific Emergency Nurses Conference xiii, 35-36, 196, 246
Paramedics xii, 14, 18, 156-157, 253-256, 258, 259
Patient Group Directions 158-9, 268
Picton Claire 47, 87, 100
Platt Report (Sir Harry Platt) xii, 7
Pre-hospital care 62, 69, 173, 215, 223, 253-259

Randall Kevin 82, 89
Royal College of Nursing 4

RCN A&E Nursing Group/Forum/Association/ECA (Significant events) xii, xiii, xiv, 9, 11, 38, 83
    Conferences (special events) 11, 12, 21, 25-26, 29, 48, 68, 76-77, 88, 89
    Essex group 20
    Emergency Nurse (significant dates) 42, 45-47
RCN National Forums Committee 75
RCN Association of Nursing Practice 11, 24, 94
RCN Congress 14, 24, 34, 61, 66, 81, 122, 135, 174, 198, 230
Red Cross 253-254
Reforming emergency care 79, 80, 81, 82, 109, 110, 112
Resuscitation Council UK xii, 228, 230, 231
Royal College of Emergency Medicine xii, xiii, xiv, 12, 38, 54, 83, 263, 266
Royal College of Radiologists & College of Radiographers (see X-rays)
Royal College of Surgeons 7, 44, 103, 212, 216, 258
Sbaih Lynn 66, 69, 143
Scoping report 63, 120, 198, 216, 246-247, 250
Scotland 78, 118

Seatbelts/Rutherford study 11-12
Smith & Nephew 20, 69
Social trends 101
Staffing and Skill Mix 41, 62, 87, 195-208, 270
Stringer Jill 69, 75

The Patient's Charter xiii, 42, 49, 51, 59, 64, 66, 73, 104, 183, 184-189
Trauma 52, 209-227, 269-273
Trauma Audit and Research Network (TARN) 271
Trauma Nurse Training 38, 54, 218-221
Triage inc UK triage scale and Manchester Triage xiii, xiv, 33, 36, 37, 61, 182-194, 265
Trolley waits inc bed reduction and A&E closures 19, 34, 49, 52, 62, 85, 102-104, 107-109, 112, 114, 198, 266

Violence (aggression) 119-125, 267

Wales 82, 118
Williams Grant 86, 87, 89, 145, 158, 159, 256
Windle Jill 89, 176, 190, 192, 193, 220
Wounds 226, 268

Wright Bob 15, 17, 20, 25, 30, 35, 48,

X-rays 51, 78, 136, 147-149, 268

Printed in Great Britain
by Amazon